P9-BZO-261

SELLING Women SHORT

SELLING Women SHORT

Gender Inequality on Wall Street

Louise Marie Roth

PRINCETON UNIVERSITY PRESS
PRINCETON AND OXFORD

Published by Princeton University Press, 41 William Street, Princeton, New Jersey 08540
In the United Kingdom: Princeton University Press, 3 Market Place, Woodstock, Oxfordshire OX20 1SY

Library of Congress Cataloging-in-Publication Data

Roth, Louise Marie, 1970–
Selling women short : gender inequality on Wall Street / Louise Marie Roth.
p. cm.
Includes bibliographical references and index.
ISBN-13: 978-0-691-12643-2 (cloth : alk. paper)
ISBN-10: 0-691-12643-7 (cloth : alk. paper)
1. Women stockbrokers—New York (State)—New York. 2. Equal pay for equal work—New York (State)—New York. 3. Sex discrimination in employment—New York (State)—New York. I. Title. HG4928.5.R68 2006
332.6'2082097471—dc22 2006011999

British Library Cataloging-in-Publication Data is available

This book has been composed in Janson

Printed on acid-free paper. ∞
pup.princeton.edu

Printed in the United States of America

10 9 8 7 5 6 4 3 2 1

To the women of Wall Street,
with optimism that they can attain equity.

Contents

Preface and Acknowledgments

In early 1995, a young female investment banker attended a client dinner at a restaurant known to be a hangout of fashion models. A conversation broke out among her fellow bankers and the client about how the restaurant was chosen for its "eye candy," which evolved into a discussion of the best strip clubs across the country—a shift in topic instigated by the most senior investment banker at the table, a managing director at her firm. As the only woman at the table, the young associate felt uncomfortable but remained silent. The next day, however, she berated the young male banker who had chosen the restaurant, a man I was dating at the time. When I heard the story, I was struck by the subtle yet blatant ways that women were still excluded on Wall Street. And this was only one of many stories I heard from acquaintances on Wall Street as I started piecing together a picture of masculine bias and subtle discrimination.

This was not the extreme masculine bravado of *The Bonfire of the Vanities* and 1980s lore, but the behavior exhibited a clear pattern of hostility. Women seemed to be breaking into Wall Street firms at the entry level—an explosive change—but were barely present at senior levels, and the few women who had made it to senior levels were described in the most unflattering terms. But how could Wall Street firms maintain an environment that was inhospitable to women given the legal reforms and the publicity of discrimination suits at the time? That question formed the basis for the research that led to this book.

There are many people and organizations to thank for their help with this research. In the early stages, the National Science Foundation funded the project. Kathleen Gerson taught me how to conduct qualitative interviews and mentored me through the writing and publishing of the book. Jo Dixon generously offered her time, friendship, and moral support, and Doug Guthrie encouraged me to learn more about organizations and made them exciting. At New York University, I am grateful to Suzanne Risley, Karrie Snyder, Stephanie Byrd, Dalton Conley, Adam Green, David Greenberg, Lynne Haney, Barbara Heyns, Ruth Horowitz, Caroline Persell, Robert Max Jackson, and members of the Gender and Inequality Workshop. I would also like to thank Lisa Bernhard for careful editing and for sharing her knowledge of the securities industry, where she had worked as an investment banker. Jacqui Albano, Stephen Barnes, Robert Corre, Leah Garland, Lori Levan, Cora Marshall, Joseph E. Nemec III, and Tawnya Olsen provided encouragement and distraction during my time in New York. I owe special thanks to Adam Snyder, for his loving support during the dissertation-writing phase, and to Bill Brown, for giving me the idea in the first place.

At the University of Arizona I am grateful to Ronald Breiger, Mark Chaves, Elisabeth Clemens, Joseph Galaskiewicz, J. Miller McPherson, Linda Molm, Calvin Morill, Charles Ragin, Lynn Smith-Lovin, Sarah Soule, and Henry Walker for constructive feedback. Mark, Linda, and Ron encouraged me to write a book manuscript, and I am deeply thankful that I followed their advice. I am also indebted to the College of Social and Behavioral Sciences at the University of Arizona for a Junior Faculty Professional Research Leave that gave me the time I needed to complete the writing process.

Some of the research findings, especially in chapters 3, 4, and 5, have been published in scholarly articles in *Social Forces*, *Sociological Perspectives*, *Sociological Quarterly*, *Sociological Forum*, and *Sociological Inquiry*. I would like to thank the many anonymous reviewers for these journals as well as the anonymous reviewers for Princeton University Press for their valuable comments.

I extend special thanks to the many people who took time out of their busy lives to let me interview them. Without them, this research would not have been possible. I am also grateful to the many scholars whose important research on gender inequality in employment has provided the foundation for this work. The following researchers, in particular, contributed to the development of my ideas: Mary Blair-Loy, Paula England, Cynthia Fuchs-Epstein, Kathleen Gerson, Jerry Jacobs, Rosabeth Moss Kanter, Barbara Reskin, and Virginia Valian.

At Princeton University Press, I am deeply grateful to my editor, Tim Sullivan. He was fantastic to work with, he provided superb guidance, and his vision made the book possible. I am also grateful to Meera Vaidyanathan for coordinating the production process and to Jenn Backer for her careful copyediting.

Last, but definitely not least, I owe thanks to my family. My parents, Irene Roth, John Roth, and Anna DeVries, encouraged me to do well in school, supported me through graduate school, and expressed pride in my accomplishments in the academic world. My mother, Irene, an English teacher, deserves special thanks for making sure that I learned how to speak and write properly. The book would never have been written without the support, enthusiasm, encouragement, and love of my husband, Greg Pilling. Finally, I want to thank our son, Troy, for being a wonderful, mellow baby and sleeping through the night when he was five weeks old—without a good night's sleep, I might never have completed the book.

SELLING
Women
SHORT

INTRODUCTION

Not so long ago—as recently as the mid-1980s—Wall Street was one big men's club of smoke-filled rooms and strippers on the trading floor. Women, to the degree that they were welcome at all, were relegated to roles as secretaries and sex objects. Firms blatantly discriminated against the few women who did fight to become traders, and court cases demonstrate a long history of groping, name calling, come-ons, blocked mobility, and sexual pranks. Since then, women have made great inroads into jobs on Wall Street, and Wall Street firms have largely cleaned up their act. You would be hard-pressed to find a "boom-boom room" associated with any of the major or minor firms today.

Despite the overall improvement in the climate in these firms, since the late 1990s, three major Wall Street firms—Citigroup's Smith Barney, Merrill Lynch, and Morgan Stanley—have each paid out more than $100 million to resolve sex discrimination suits, even while denying that any systematic discrimination against women occurs within their walls. On April 19, 2004, for instance, a panel of arbitrators awarded $2.2 million to Hydie Sumner, a female stockbroker and one of 2,800 women who brought a class action suit against Merrill Lynch for sex discrimination.[1] Morgan Stanley also paid a settlement of $54 million on the eve of court proceedings in an EEOC sex discrimination case.[2] The lead plaintiff, Allison Schieffelin, received $12 million, and the settlement granted another

$2 million to diversity programs to promote the advancement of women within the firm.

Allison Schieffelin's case claimed that she and other female workers had been denied equitable pay and promotions, and had been excluded from company functions because of their gender. The EEOC investigated her charges and found evidence that less-deserving men had been promoted while Schieffelin, a high producer in international equity sales, remained in a lower-level position, and that the firm had retaliated against her when she filed complaints. Morgan Stanley's spokesperson, Ray O'Rourke, said that the firm "emphatically disagrees with the findings" and "does not practice or condone discrimination of any kind."[3]

By resolving these cases out of court while denying the allegations, Wall Street firms have avoided public scrutiny of their corporate culture and how gender inequality persists within it. And although the firms denied any wrongdoing—standard in such agreements, and therefore somewhat meaningless—the settlements serve as an indication that discrimination on Wall Street has shifted from blatant, socially unacceptable behavior to an endemic firm- and industry-wide discrimination against women and minorities. The question is, why? These firms, more than others, supposedly pay for performance by tying bonus amounts to revenue production—if you make a Wall Street firm a lot of money, you get a large bonus—so how is it that they get away with paying women less than similarly qualified men? And what can we learn from women on Wall Street about gender inequality more generally?

At a broad level, these are questions about the processes that lead to a well-known and much discussed outcome: gender inequality in the workplace. They're also questions about how paying workers based on performance evaluations affects equality when workers do not start out as equals and how systems established to level the playing field and to make companies transparent can do more harm than good. Understanding how gender inequality persists among similar men and women illuminates how inequality can persist even if men and women perform similarly. The rest of *Selling Women Short* explains just how this happens—how the road to continued gender discrimination is paved with good intentions—and offers some suggestions for breaking the mold.

This book compares men and women who worked on Wall Street during the long bull market of the 1990s, when opportunities in the securities industry were abundant. In Wall Street parlance, "securities" refers to shares, options, and derivatives that corporations issue on the public financial markets. This market environment should have provided a best-case scenario for the advancement of underrepresented groups like women. Yet men and women who obtained comparable training and entered the marketplace during the same period still found themselves separated by substantial gender inequality. Within the booming financial markets of the 1990s, they reveal how an institutionalized bonus pay system, which should have been the great equalizer, had negative effects on women. The case histories discussed in subsequent chapters can also reveal the strategies of some workers to reduce or eliminate their structural disadvantage.

Women on Wall Street

Women first entered Wall Street as professionals in the mid-1970s. At that time they faced blatant discrimination: they were excluded or ejected from meetings in all-male clubs and were often told outright that they would receive less money than men. The glass ceiling blocking their promotions was more obvious, as was their clear underpayment relative to their male peers—this despite sometimes superior performance.[4] These women had only two options: to endure compensation discrimination or to leave the profession.

This type of barefaced discrimination became less prevalent in the 1980s, largely because it clearly violated Title VII, the federal law that prohibits sex discrimination in hiring and promotion, and because the most flagrant incidences of discrimination had been attacked in court. In the early 1980s, recruiters for Goldman Sachs, for instance, asked female MBAs if they were willing to have abortions to stay on the fast track, which violated the Pregnancy Discrimination Act (PDA) of 1978 (discrimination on the basis of pregnancy is illegal sex discrimination).[5] A group of Stanford MBAs complained in 1984, producing a public outcry and leading to changes in the firm's interview questions. Views of women as reproductive time bombs did not completely disappear, but the most obvious discrimination on that basis has.

Legal challenges motivated Wall Street firms to develop internal policies and procedures to comply with equal employment opportunity guidelines and to address discrimination in hiring and promotion, sexual harassment, and maternity leave. At least on the surface, these firms made efforts to hire and retain qualified women.[6] The most obvious barriers to women's success eroded in the late 1980s, when most investment banks promoted their first female managing directors and partners. But at the same time, the sex discrimination cases of the last decade imply that discrimination and a culture of sexual harassment remained defining features of the industry.

Having won court cases to institute formal policies against discrimination, by the 1990s women on Wall Street started to fight back against the male-dominated culture of the industry, filing class action suits against major securities firms. In some cases, like the infamous "boom-boom room" case against Smith Barney, these suits focused partly on verbal and physical sexual harassment.[7] In 1995, after enduring years of put-downs, lewd remarks, sexual gestures, and practical jokes, as well as being denied promotions and access to the best accounts, three women at Smith Barney's Garden City brokerage office filed a class action suit charging the firm with sex discrimination and sexual harassment. They alleged that "the office maintained a fraternity-house culture" that was hostile and degrading to women.[8] (The "boom-boom room" was a party room in the basement of the Garden City office where male brokers held parties that excluded women or subjected women to sexual innuendo and pranks.) The suit claimed that the firm had tolerated a hostile and discriminatory work environment, and Smith Barney settled before it went to court. While the firm accepted no culpability, the settlement led to an overhaul of its sexual harassment and diversity policies.

A similar class action suit against Merrill Lynch focused primarily on patterns of economic disparity, although sexual harassment was also an issue.[9] Female brokers at Merrill entered the class action suit en masse because of discrimination in wages, promotions, account distributions, and maternity leaves. They were especially concerned about the allocation of accounts from departing brokers, walk-ins, leads, and referrals, which they claimed went disproportionately to male brokers. When a panel of arbitrators awarded Hydie Sumner $2.2 million on April 19, 2004, it was the first legal ruling to find that a Wall Street firm engaged in systematic discrimination.

In addition to these class actions, individual women also filed suits. In 1999, a former employee of J. P. Morgan sued the firm for barring her from working as a trader because of her gender.[10] Around the same time, Allison Schieffelin filed her highly publicized gender discrimination lawsuit with the EEOC after she was passed over for promotion to managing director in Morgan Stanley's international equity sales division.[11] Morgan Stanley only reluctantly, and under duress, cooperated with the investigation. The EEOC decided to pursue the case, in their first ruling against Wall Street in over a decade. The day before the case was scheduled to go to court, on July 13, 2004, Morgan Stanley settled for a total of $54 million.[12] The fact that these lawsuits have found some Wall Street firms liable for gender discrimination reveals that obstacles for women remain entrenched, even after past legislative actions have removed the most blatant displays of gender bias. The question remains, however, why such barriers exist and how they persist.

Equal employment legislation may have paved the way for women's entrance into the securities industry, but more than half of all employees in the industry are still white men (even when female-dominated positions like administrative assistants and sales assistants are included). The figure rises to over 70 percent among investment bankers, traders, and brokers, and to over 80 percent among executive managers.[13] While the number of women in professional positions has risen, and securities firms have a heightened awareness of equal employment opportunity laws, Wall Street remains a male-dominated environment. And while the most obvious forms of differential treatment have been squelched, more subtle forms of discrimination still flourish on Wall Street.

Gender Discrimination and Employment Law

Gender discrimination can take multiple forms, and employment law contains provisions for blatant and subtle forms of discrimination, sexual harassment, and pregnancy discrimination. The 1963 Equal Pay Act and Title VII of the 1964 Civil Rights Act legally protect workers from discrimination on the basis of sex in hiring, promotion, and pay.[14] Title VII prohibits *disparate treatment* of applicants or employees, defined as treating workers differently based on their membership in a protected class. For example, policies that specify that only men be hired for a job in which gender is irrelevant to performance are facially discriminatory.[15] Early female entrants to Wall Street faced differential treatment that clearly meets this definition of illegal sex discrimination. Clearly, there is no gender-specific requirement for jobs on Wall Street, and securities firms have eliminated facially discriminatory policies and managerial behavior to protect themselves from disparate treatment claims.

In most cases, though, direct evidence of discrimination is rare, and discrimination may take more subtle and insidious forms. Some subtle forms of discrimination are also recognized under Title VII. Since 1971, employment law has recognized discrimination when an employer may not be motivated by discriminatory intent, but uses a facially neutral employment practice that has an unjustified adverse impact on members of a protected class.[16] These are cases where facially neutral practices have a *disparate impact*. Examples of practices that may be subject to a disparate impact challenge include written tests, height and weight requirements, and subjective procedures like interviews. For example, entrance exams and hiring criteria on Wall Street were heavily biased in favor of white, heterosexual men until the late 1970s. A landmark decision against Merrill Lynch in 1976 eliminated entrance exams with questions such as, "When you fight with your wife, which of you usually wins?" and "When you meet a woman, what interests you the most about her?" (The correct answer was "her beauty," while the fewest points were scored for "her intelligence.") When Helen O'Bannon failed the entrance exam for its broker-trainee program in 1972, she sued for sex discrimination and won, costing the firm over $4 million.[17] Of course, disparate impact is not always as clear as in the O'Bannon case and subtle discrimination is always harder to prove than its more blatant counterpart—and therefore more common. Employers can also legally justify practices with a disparate impact on members of a protected class if the practices fulfill some "essential" or "indispensable" business necessity.

Title VII also recognizes sexual harassment as a form of illegal sex discrimination. Many of the lawsuits against Wall Street firms, most notably the boom-boom room case, involved sexual harassment claims.[18] Sexual harassment may take the form of a quid pro quo, in which submission to unwelcome sexual advances or requests for sexual favors is made a condition of an individual's employment or is used as a basis for employment decisions. It may also take the form of a hostile work environment, in which repeated put-downs and come-ons have the purpose or effect of unreasonably interfering with an individual's work performance or create an intimidating, hostile, or offensive work environment.[19] This type of hostile work environment was at the heart of the boom-boom room case against Smith Barney. But while courts have decided some high-profile sexual harassment cases in favor of plaintiffs, they decide the majority of cases in favor of employers. Sexual harassment is notoriously difficult to prove, and most workers who suffer from it never bring attention to their experiences.[20]

But here's the catch to all of these protections, the catch that rests at the heart of this book: Existing employment laws are based on principles of equal treatment and are written to be gender neutral, and these laws assume that the sexes are "similarly situated" and, therefore, that men and women should be treated the same.[21] This belies the fact that there are situations in which men and women are differently situated, pregnancy being the most obvious example.[22] When men and women are differently situated, treating them the same may have an adverse impact on women. At the same time, differential treatment in cases where men and women are differently situated is often not viewed as discrimination and not actionable. As a result, gender-neutral laws guaranteeing equal protection have failed to produce gender-equal outcomes in most employment settings. This may also be a consequence of the fact that subtle forms of discrimination are difficult to demonstrate and address through the legal system, and definitions of some types of discrimination like sexual harassment are widely variable.[23] Subtle discrimination typically occurs through unconscious preferences and prejudices that most people have, but of which they are unaware.[24] These preferences and prejudices influence how they perceive other people, their competencies, and their performance at various tasks. On Wall Street, these unconscious considerations are particularly important because pay is awarded on the basis of performance evaluations.

On Wall Street, most widespread, blatant discrimination has largely disappeared, and certainly firms have removed any official (or unofficial) sanction from such behavior. Instead, in the face of numerous lawsuits, they have instituted programs that seek to treat men and women the same—gender-neutral practices that reward employees based on performance and apparently objective measures. Given that men and women started in different positions relative to one another, these practices only contribute to the gap. And the objective measures, which often turn out to be subjective perceptions, only contribute to the ongoing problem.

The problem is surprisingly large. Few will be surprised that there was still gender inequality in pay on Wall Street in the late 1990s; that women are generally underpaid for similar work now seems a truism of employment in the United States. What is astonishing is the degree of inequality between men and women who were similar in their background and work-related characteristics, who worked in similar positions in similar organizations, and who experienced the same market conditions in the formative years of their careers. While explanations for gender differences in pay often highlight differences in education, work experience, and other productivity-related characteristics, I found that pay inequality on Wall Street was dramatic even for men and women with identical qualifications who had been in the pipeline for the same amount of time.[25] My findings reveal the mechanics of subtle forms of discrimination and how they operate through interpersonal and organizational dynamics in Wall Street firms.

The Study

To understand the dynamics of gender inequality on Wall Street, I examined the career histories of a three-year cohort of elite MBA graduates who started in top Wall Street firms in the early 1990s. Surely, if any women were going to excel and keep up with their male counterparts, they were going to be from this group. Experiences of inequality occur in particular historical, legal, organizational, and market contexts such that every cohort encounters a unique configuration of forces.[26] Men and women from the same cohort, therefore, would be subject to the same market cycles, changes in employment law, and organizational policy initiatives. Every new group in the securities industry shares certain opportunities and constraints and is influenced by the changing legal and market environment that it encounters at the dawn of its career.

The men and women I interviewed, who graduated in 1991, 1992, and 1993, were similar in their background and work-related characteristics, worked in similar positions in similar organizations, and experienced the same market conditions in the formative years of their careers. They began their careers a few years before Wall Street's longest bull market in history—the period when traders were making bucketfuls of money. I interviewed them in 1998 and early 1999, just before the market peaked in the spring of 2000, and captured their entire career histories from before the time they completed their MBAs in the early 1990s. I was able to analyze compensation outcomes and the processes leading to those outcomes.[27] I also included those who had left finance so that I could analyze their reasons for leaving Wall Street. These experiences yielded important information about the processes of gender inequality in securities firms. The career histories of this strategically placed group shed light on general processes that produce gender inequality within jobs, especially in settings where pay is based on performance evaluations. Because they faced widening opportunities in the 1990s, their experiences revealed how gender inequality within jobs can persist despite market pressures *against* discrimination.

Selling Women Short focuses on the subtle, structural discrimination that occurs through performance evaluations. It illustrates the operations of structural discrimination, which does not rest on individual acts of meanness, in which some people consciously limit the opportunities of women, but on the interpersonal and organizational dynamics that subtly and often unintentionally re-create inequality. This discrimination is embedded in the unconscious and the subjective masquerading as an objective measure of performance.

On Wall Street, these interpersonal and organizational dynamics occur through a bonus system where pay supposedly reflects performance. Despite a supposed basis in individual merit, this variable pay system not only coexists with gender inequality between workers in the same jobs, it can even help reproduce this inequality. I use my findings to delve beneath the surface of Wall Street's meritocracy to reveal how opportunity is institutionally structured, and to show the gendered and gender-neutral forces that structure—and obscure—the career paths of modern workplaces.

Chapter 1

THE PLAYING FIELD

Wall Street in the 1990s

Wall Street investment houses are the pinnacle of the securities industry, which mediates the flow of finance capital from investors to corporations, tax-exempt organizations, and other corporate entities like governments. Wall Street is supposedly "a citadel of pure economics, where pay for performance would seem to be the ruling ethic."[1] The compensation system on Wall Street is a rational incentive structure in which bonuses comprise the majority of workers' pay and are supposed to reflect the amount of revenue they generate for the firm—simple enough. Bonus structures provide incentives to invest effort, skill, and time in the pursuit of firm profits, while inequality that is not based on merit contradicts these incentives and discourages worker efficiency.

Market conditions at the end of the millennium should have encouraged greater equality. Wall Street experienced its greatest economic boom in history in the 1990s, so that securities firms had to compete for qualified employees and pay them well. Economic theories suggest that this type of competition among firms for skilled labor should eliminate inequality that is not based on merit, because discrimination is expensive if it is not relevant to performance—firms would drive away qualified workers and lose money in fulfilling an irrational impulse.[2]

Despite Wall Street's rationality and the boom market of the late

1990s, we're still confronted by systematic, if subtle, discrimination. We'll uncover how inequality can persist even under market conditions that should reduce or eliminate it and work to understand how structural discrimination may be rationalized and institutionalized.

Wall Street in the 1990s

The late 1990s were Wall Street's longest bull market. In 1995 the Dow Jones Industrial Average hit 4,000 and kept climbing. Before the year 2000 it had crossed the 11,000-point mark.[3] The firms that provided finance capital gained global power, and more and more investors entered the markets for stocks and mutual funds. Wall Street's revenues, number of employees, and professional compensation all swelled.

The securities industry is highly concentrated; the ten largest firms pulled in over half of the 1997 broker-dealer revenue from the NYSE. The top 25 firms accounted for 74 percent of the NYSE's revenue and 79 percent of its capital.[4] The financiers I interviewed worked for the biggest players on the Street: Morgan Stanley Dean Witter, Goldman Sachs, Merrill Lynch, Lehman Brothers, Salomon Brothers, Smith Barney (the latter two merged in 1997 to form Salomon Smith Barney), Credit Suisse First Boston, J. P. Morgan, Bear Stearns, and Donaldson Lufkin and Jenrette (DLJ).[5]

I asked these workers about their compensation in 1997, a year when the U.S. securities industry gross of $145 billion represented approximately 2 percent of the total U.S. GNP of $8.1 trillion and profits hit a record high of $12.5 billion. On the buy side, revenues from mutual funds and asset management also hit record highs of $10 billion and $5 billion, respectively.[6] The firms that earned the most were led by the big three in the top tier—Merrill Lynch, Goldman Sachs, and Morgan Stanley Dean Witter.[7] These firms were followed by second-tier firms of Salomon Smith Barney, DLJ,

Lehman Brothers, Credit Suisse First Boston, and J. P. Morgan in positions four through eight.

In 1996 and 1997, professional compensation on Wall Street also hit all-time record highs, and industry employment was rising.[8] By the end of 1997, employment in the U.S. securities industry reached 612,800, representing an 8.1 percent increase since the end of 1996, and a 36 percent increase over five years.[9] The hottest industry for mergers and acquisitions in 1997 was financial services, in a trend toward consolidation into megabanks.[10] The merger wave caused the share prices of publicly held financial firms to skyrocket. By all financial measures, securities firms were on an upward trajectory.

The 1990s also marked an increase in the number and proportion of women entering the securities industry, as well as the promotion to senior positions of some of the pioneers who broke gender barriers in the 1970s. Goldman Sachs named Abby Joseph Cohen a partner in 1998, in its last partnership selection before the company went public in 1999.[11] Wall Street firms are reluctant to dispense statistics on the characteristics of their workers, but many estimated that Wall Street firms hired women as approximately 15 to 20 percent of their incoming associate classes in the 1990s, an increase over earlier decades although still far from equality at the entry level—a point that has not gone unnoticed in the high-profile sex discrimination suits against the industry.[12]

While the industry as a whole was skyrocketing, securities firms (and professionals) differed in their relative success. Mergers displaced some finance professionals in 1997 and early 1998, and some force-cutting occurred.[13] J. P. Morgan announced in February 1998 that it would dismiss approximately 5 percent of its workforce, or 700 people. After the merger of Salomon Smith Barney with Citicorp to form Citigroup in 1997, the megabank announced layoff plans with the intention of cutting 6 percent of its workforce, or 10,400 jobs. Other Wall Street firms also prepared for layoffs in the late 1990s, even as the stock market continued to climb. In this context, the MBAs of the early 1990s shaped their careers in the securities industry.

Success and Failure on Wall Street

As the markets soared, many Wall Street careers were on a clear path to success and there were abundant opportunities to advance. Deal volume, underwriting and commission revenues, salaries, and the size of the workforce all skyrocketed to record highs.[14] The demand for financial services was increasing, especially in hot areas of investment banking and trading like high yield, derivatives, and mergers and acquisitions.[15] Wall Street firms also faced heightened competition from commercial banks and foreign underwriters who took chunks of traditional Wall Street business and hired away many of their talented workers by offering large guarantees and signing bonuses.[16] The fact that firms competed for skilled employees opened up workers' opportunities in the industry and contributed to escalating bonus packages.

But not everyone benefited equally from Wall Street's remarkable growth cycle in the 1990s. Even in this climate of abundance, success was a relative concept. Most men and women who stayed in a top firm and an area like corporate finance, sales and trading, or equity research were successful because compensation and rank increased over time.[17] But others were derailed from the path to success despite the favorable market conditions on Wall Street, as they encountered layoffs, downturns in particular market niches, involuntary transfers, difficult managers, or hostile work environments.[18] Thirty-nine percent of those interviewed (56 percent of the men and 27 percent of the women) were highly successful during the long bull market, exceeding the average pay for their area and cohort. But 61 percent (44 percent of the men and 73 percent of the women) were less successful despite the favorable market conditions on Wall Street. Many MBAs who entered the securities industry immediately before its longest bull market encountered unexpected opportunities for success, but others confronted obstacles to their career goals. Consider, for example, the diverse paths taken by the following four men drawn from the larger group interviewed for this study.

The Men

Roger[19] grew up in the Northeast in an upper-middle-class family. His father was a doctor and his mother was a homemaker. He had recently married another investment banker who was working on her MBA, and he had no children. Roger attended a prestigious private university where he obtained a very high GPA. He also had a high score on the GMAT. Between graduating from college and pursuing an MBA, Roger was a financial analyst in mergers and acquisitions (M&A) at a large investment bank. Financial analyst positions are typically filled by young college graduates and are the most time-consuming and lowest-ranked positions in the investment banking world. Roger entered the MBA program to take a break from the stress of being an analyst, and expected to use the opportunity to find a career in another industry. He said, "I needed to take two years off. I was burnt out after being an analyst. I needed it to release tension. Doing an MBA is really easy compared to being an analyst. Being an analyst is very stressful." At the end of his MBA program he did not find anything more appealing than finance and was in a good position to obtain Wall Street offers. Instead of returning to the large firm where he had previously worked, he accepted a job in a smaller firm.

Roger changed groups within his firm once. He was offered a position in M&A that fit with his previous experience and existing set of skills and he wanted to leave his first position, which involved a lot of business-related travel.

> I was sick of flying to South America all week and then working weekends. Then they hired a bunch of people from [a commercial bank], and I didn't want to work with an unknown quantity. So I was asked to join the M&A group that was in formation, and I [did].

He was promoted to vice president after four years as an associate, in accordance with the promotion time line of the industry. Roger strongly believed that Wall Street operated as a meritocracy and was confident that his performance was exceptional. When asked how he ranked among his peers, he said, "Within the firm, I'm in the top 1 percent. . . . Because I'm smart, I work hard, and I do a great job." In 1997, four years after graduating from business school, he earned over $600,000, and he said that he loved his job so much that he would do it for half the pay. Roger followed a linear career path, amassing experience on Wall Street before obtaining his MBA. When he reentered the industry, the positive economic climate propelled him toward even greater success and satisfaction. What he attributed to his own merits was undoubtedly the result of his skills and experience combined with favorable market conditions.

Edward differed from Roger in his experience before the MBA but also encountered growing opportunities on Wall Street. He grew up in the suburban South in an upper-middle-class family with a professional father and a homemaker mother. He attended a large public university for his bachelor's degree and graduated with a high GPA. He then worked as an accountant for four years prior to obtaining his MBA. During that time he married. He had two small children at the time of the interview (two and six years old), and his wife was a homemaker.

Edward decided to get an MBA to change careers. "I wanted a change. I had good training, but I didn't want to pursue it as a lifelong career. I was tired of being a CPA. Getting an MBA was an opportunity to change careers. It allowed me to start over." His experience as an accountant helped him understand financial analysis, but his only real Wall Street experience prior to completing the MBA degree was during the summer between his first and second years. At that time, he was a generalist in corporate finance at one of the top investment banks and discovered that he enjoyed the work.

> I liked it. I did it for the summer because I didn't understand it and thought it would be nice to leave business school with a better understanding of what happened on Wall Street. I didn't do it because I ever

> thought that I would do it full time, but I thought it would be an opportunity and I probably shouldn't waste it. After the summer I really enjoyed it. I didn't necessarily like being at the office until 3:00 in the morning but I really enjoyed the work and I thought that another two years on Wall Street would be a good thing to have behind me.

The same firm hired him when he graduated, and he expected to work there for approximately two years but not to make a long-term commitment to Wall Street.

While the job required a tremendous commitment in terms of hours and the first year was the "most stressful" of his life, he found that he fit in well with the organizational culture and continued to enjoy the work. He worked on large transactions where he had substantial exposure to client companies with huge assets. He was promoted to vice president after four years and senior vice president after three more years, as was the norm on Wall Street. He then changed firms in 1998 when a close personal friend offered him a position of greater responsibility at a smaller firm. While he was satisfied with his original position and had earned over $1 million in 1997, he was drawn toward the opportunity to be a bigger fish in a smaller pond and to work with someone with whom he had a strong personal relationship. He entered the new firm as a managing director (MD)—a higher rank than his position at his original firm. While the smaller firm did not have the same reputation and high-prestige name as his original employer, he had developed strong client relationships and was able to bring in business. Instead of working on Wall Street for two years, as he had intended, he had a very successful seven years after the MBA.

Edward was highly satisfied with his career, despite tremendous sacrifices in his personal life. When asked about work-life balance, he said,

> Initially I didn't balance it. My son was born in my first year in New York City, as a first-year associate. It was the most stressful year of my life. . . . Sacrifices in the

> first few years were huge. Time away from family was [the main sacrifice]. You miss special occasions, you miss birthdays, you miss parties, you miss, miss, miss, miss, miss.

He made these sacrifices as he followed the opportunities that presented themselves, without a conscious decision that Wall Street would be his career forever or even a full understanding of what such a career would entail. These opportunities were a product of the favorable market cycle and the resources available in his first job at a prestigious firm. He was also able to follow these opportunities in part because had the support of a homemaker wife—a fact that he acknowledged had allowed him to focus on work. He was also able to maintain a clear upward trajectory because he worked in an area and firm where he fit in well with managers, peers, and clients, and where the market was booming and deals were happening. The clear trade-off that he made was to accept a lack of involvement with his children during the first few years of their lives.

As the industry entered a bull market, Roger and Edward encountered expanding opportunities and an upward compensation trajectory. They were able to take advantage of these opportunities because they were unencumbered by other draws on their time. The combination of their talent and effort with a favorable economic climate and a good fit with their firms' cultures led to high rewards on Wall Street. But not everyone encountered the abundant and appealing opportunities that Roger and Edward did. Some men were pulled off the fast track by opportunities outside finance or by personal issues. Others were pushed out of the most lucrative jobs on Wall Street by market forces, the loss of a mentor, poor advice, or firm layoffs. In considering the next two men, contrast Edward's choice to accept limited involvement with his children with Kevin's experience.

Kevin grew up in a middle-class family in the suburban Northeast. His father worked in sales and marketing, and his mother was a homemaker. He attended an Ivy League college, where he obtained a high GPA. He subsequently worked as a two-year financial analyst in M&A at one of Wall Street's most prestigious firms before entering an MBA program. When he graduated, he returned to the same firm in corporate finance. Like Roger, he returned because he had not found anything that he preferred more. The work was interesting and he enjoyed the quality of people in the firm. Because of his previous experience, Kevin was prepared for his responsibilities, although the hours were especially grueling during his first couple of years. When asked about his expectations for hours, he said,

> I knew I would work a lot. If I had to quantify it, I thought I'd probably work maybe seventy hours a week, which is a lot. Which is a hell of a lot actually. It was worse. I don't know if that's the right number. I don't know if I actually worked more hours than that but I think I ended up working more than I thought I would have to because it was a very busy time and we were a very small associate class. It was after a bad year so they had a cutback on the amount of people they hired. And it turned out there wasn't any less work to do.

Kevin married a preschool teacher one year after completing his MBA. Their first child was born two years later, and his wife gave up her teaching position to become a homemaker. He found the hours difficult but tolerable until his first child was born, but then found that he wanted to change jobs so that he could work fewer hours and have more time with his family.

> I can't honestly say I thought about it until it happened. And then I really, really didn't want to be working as much, basically. I wanted—it sort of made you realize that you wanted to spend—at least I wanted to spend a lot more time with my family at home. My wife and my newborn child.

Kevin was also willing to accept lower pay as a trade-off. He contemplated a position in a start-up firm, but ultimately decided that it provided too little security and began to pursue other opportunities within his firm.

> I decided to stay here and look around. Around the firm in other areas but I definitely, definitely made the decision I didn't want to do investment banking anymore. It was just too much. It was too much work and I didn't have a true love for doing it so it didn't match my own priorities enough. And my wife had a very big influence. She hated it. Could have cared less about the money. She was much more concerned with [my] being around and [our] being together.

Kevin found a new position in a support role where he was promoted to vice president and senior vice president on schedule. His pay, between $350,000 and $400,000, was substantially less than he would have earned if he had stayed in corporate finance. According to a survey of executive recruiters, the median pay in investment banking in 1997 for his graduating class was $635,000, with most investment bankers receiving between $425,000 and $840,000.[20]

Kevin was unusual among men in his decision to take a less lucrative position with limited potential for growth to be more involved with his children. While the bull market provided opportunities for him to earn more money, his choices illustrate the "pull" of family life for men as well as women. A willingness to make this type of trade-off was rare, especially for men, but illustrates the desire for a balance between paid work and family.[21]

In contrast, it was not the pull of family life but the push of organizational forces that led Jacob to change both firm and function. Jacob grew up in an urban area in the Northeast in a middle-class family. His father was a medical researcher, while his mother dabbled in many different jobs. He had never been married and had no children, although he wanted to have a large family. He attended a medium-sized public university for a bachelor's degree in engineering and then worked as a hardware and software consultant for a small firm for two years. Aside from giving him some acquaintance with the people skills necessary to work with clients, this job was unrelated to his subsequent experiences on Wall Street.

Like Edward, Jacob's only Wall Street experience prior to finishing his MBA was during the summer between his first and second years. At that time, he worked as a generalist in corporate finance for a large Wall Street firm, where he gained experience in a variety of different groups and learned the jargon of the profession. When he graduated, he accepted a position at the same firm as a generalist in corporate finance. There he did two six-month rotations before he was approached to become a "relationship manager."

> I was then approached—and this is unique, there were only four of us of the fifty who were approached—to do something new. And that was to take people who are now only second-year associates and make them relationship managers, which is usually done at the managing director level. They needed more people out there talking to more clients so they gave me a list of clients that I was going to be second on. In other words, I spent the next year and a half working with three vice presidents who were calling on clients. And I served as their second, so I went to all the meetings and helped prepare all the presentations, try to formulate with them the strategy and learn what it meant to call on companies.

After one and a half years in this position, Jacob received his own clients and had to act as their primary officer.

Because his clients were concentrated in a particular region, Jacob also moved to that region after one and half years, where he worked in a satellite office. He remained in that position for slightly longer than a year after relocating and described it as the worst year of his life.

> I decided or I discovered that I'm not a good salesman and, although I may know I'm going to a client and trying to sell something to them, it is not my forte. At

> least that's what had been conveyed to me. I had been very specifically told I was too honest, too trusting, and couldn't speak confidently about things I knew nothing about. Other people can. It's not meant so cynically as just scamming but there are certain things you don't have to say. There are certain things you could guess at or say with confidence even though you don't necessarily feel that confident. Get through the moment. Look more impressive than you, I guess, perhaps are. But basically that's why you have senior people do the job, not junior people, because they know enough to appear confident and say confident things and know what everyone's talking about. . . . It was also frustrating because being in a satellite office in [this city] which [the firm] had not decided if they were going to support—how much they were going to support the [regional] office. . . . I got very little support and I spent a good year, pretty much alone, calling on clients, trying to drum up business. Whatever I thought that meant. Very frustrating. Whenever I thought I had something, no one really seemed to care. I got no support. And I was just waiting to leave.

Jacob felt isolated in the satellite office and thought that accepting the job as a relationship manager while he was still very junior had been a strategic error. But no one had warned him against taking a position as a relationship banker so early in his career—no one had taken him under his wing to guide his career decisions. He spent the year feeling frustrated and then received a disappointing bonus. His total compensation for 1997 was $275,000, which was lower than the median of $430,000 for investment bankers in his graduating class and less than his 1996 bonus of $335,000. This was the final push out of his job. Since he did not want to relocate back to New York, he decided to take a position involving quantitative financial analysis at another major firm's satellite office in his region. Jacob was optimistic about his opportunities in his new position, although at that point he was behind his graduating class.

Jacob's career trajectory illuminates how some careers on Wall Street could derail despite the upward trajectory of the industry as a whole. A lack of sound career guidance and/or strategy, organizational difficulties, the loss of a mentor, and vulnerability in particular market niches were common causes of relative failure among both men and women. As was the case for men, women could also be more or less successful in their careers on Wall Street, although some career patterns were more common among men and others among women.

The Women

Julie became a highly successful investment banker after being a financial analyst and then completing her MBA. Julie grew up in the suburban Southwest in a middle-class family. Her father was in the air force and then became a high school teacher, and her mother was a nurse. She attended a large public university for her bachelor's degree and then worked as an analyst in a major Wall Street firm for two years. Following a common path, she did an MBA degree and returned to Wall Street after investigating other industries. At the time that she returned, she was uncertain of her commitment to remaining in finance, but she had not encountered anything more appealing.

Because of her uncertainties about the longer term, Julie initially selected a different firm than the top-tier investment bank where she had been an analyst.

> My first job out of business school, I selected a firm that probably wasn't, at the time, a great investment bank. It was a great institution . . . but it wasn't a great investment bank—it was still pretty new at the investment banking business. I think the reason that I chose to go there was that, if investment banking wasn't what

> I wanted, [that firm] was known to rotate people through various areas. It is the kind of institution that has a reputation for really working with you to find an area of finance, or maybe outside of finance, maybe in human resources or something else, where you could pursue your career. In some respects I think that I made that decision, and I turned down some other Wall Street offers, because I wasn't completely convinced that it was what I wanted to do.

This firm was known to be female friendly and family friendly; the incoming group of associates was almost half women. But Julie found the environment at this firm "suffocating" and left after one and half years because of limited deal flow.

> That firm was trying to build its corporate finance and M&A experience from within. I found that very frustrating because a lot of the senior bankers did not have the level of experience that a senior banker at another firm would have because they moved commercial bankers into that role. So I didn't feel like I was learning from the people I was working for. I was constantly frustrated with that environment. I liked the people a lot, but just wasn't learning. I had friends who were associates at other firms, and could just see the kind of deals that they were working on, and I felt like I was missing something.

Julie decided to move back to the firm where she had worked as an analyst. There she was pleasantly surprised to encounter substantial internal support and client exposure. Because she knew many people in the firm from before, she received the assistance of subordinates sooner than expected. The firm where she started after the MBA had also given her solid training in M&A through their comprehensive training program, which offered her useful skills when she returned to corporate finance. These skills, combined with the resources offered to her through her network ties in the firm and the hospitable economic climate, enabled her to be more successful than she had ever imagined.

More recently, Julie had changed firms again and moved from corporate finance to the buy side of the securities industry, where she was managing investments for a large and prestigious investment bank. She said, "I view that as a career change, not a job change. I would not have left my position for a similar position." Her primary reason for changing firms was a pull toward the opportunity that was offered to her, where she was guaranteed compensation of over $700,000 in 1997. Her job change also increased her work-life balance, which she viewed as increasingly important as she moved forward. At the time of the interview, Julie was engaged to a lawyer and had no children.

Julie's opportunities were based in part on her long-term experience in corporate finance and the network ties she had developed through that experience. Favorable market conditions, combined with skills and effort, led her on an upward trajectory. She obviously benefited from others' perceptions that she was competent, suggesting that she was a high performer but also giving her opportunities to perform because she was assigned to revenue-generating work. Also, up to this point in her career, she had not had a lot of other responsibilities competing for her time. This permitted her to succeed at investment banking.

Unlike Julie, Emma entered investment banking with no experience in finance before business school and with a work background that was quite unorthodox. She grew up in an upper-middle-class family in a suburban area in the Northeast. Her father was a manager in a large company and her mother was a social worker. At the time of the interview, she was married to a bond trader whom she met in the training program at her first Wall Street firm. They had no children, although they planned to have children in the not-too-distant future.

Emma attended a prestigious liberal arts college. After she graduated, she immediately started a joint graduate program in public policy and business without gaining any work experience first. She had no experience on Wall Street before she completed her MBA, since her initial focus was on public policy and her previous internships had been in that area. Because she had not developed a passion for a particular policy area and saw the brightest and the best of her peers entering investment banking, Emma considered her options on Wall Street.

> I looked around when I got into business school and the smartest people there were going into investment banking. And a lot of people said, "If you want to go do the public service thing, go earn some money, establish a reputation, and then go off and do something in the public sector. It's much more difficult to go the other direction." So I ended up, at that time, looking at investment banking. . . . I ended up at an interview for [a major Wall Street firm]. . . . The reason that someone was attracted to me as a candidate was because I had a very high GPA. I had done well at what I'd done. But I didn't have—I was a higher-risk person because I didn't have this demonstrated background.

A major Wall Street firm decided to hire her, providing her with an opportunity to get her foot in the door. Based on the advice of women who were already on Wall Street, she chose to enter a quantitative execution function to gain some initial experience and prove her competence. She believed that working in a quantitative area would provide her with tangible indicators of performance and would increase her probability of success.

While she received good reviews in her first job, she changed firms after one and a half years. One reason she wanted to change was that at the time of her second bonus, her manager told her that she had been paid at the top of her class but she later found out that her husband received considerably more than she did She said,

> I walked into my review, got a great review, and was told that I was being paid at the top of my class. The only problem was my husband also worked for the firm

> and I knew what his bonus was. And it was substantially higher than mine. And I went back to my boss and said, "That was great. I walked out feeling good. Because you told me I was paid at the top of my class, but guess what—I wasn't paid anywhere near the top of my class." . . . That was just, to me, came down to someone trying to be a little fast and loose with the facts.

She became disappointed with her pay and disillusioned with the performance review system. Another important push factor was that the environment in her first job was decidedly hostile to women, forcing her to question her own beliefs that Wall Street was a meritocracy.

> They were downright hostile, to the point where I would do a lot of the recruiting and interviewing for our group and I was told things like, "Don't bring a woman, I wouldn't hire a woman into this group." These were more my colleagues than—you know, senior people couldn't say that. . . . When I started I was very naive. I had this image that these things that people talk about don't go on because they're so preposterous. And, if anything, I would have been the last person to say that workplaces are discriminatory. I wanted to come to Wall Street because I'm like, "This is a meritocracy. You've proven that you can do things to get here. You've gotten through these screens."

Her illusions shattered, Emma went on the job market and, with some experience under her belt, was able to land a similar position in one of Wall Street's most prestigious firms.

In her second firm, she found herself in a much more hospitable environment and she fit in well with the other members of the group. After testing her competence, a senior man took her under his wing and gave her access to the most important deals. The group was growing quickly and needed junior people to manage a large flow of deals, which gave Emma opportunities to develop skills and connections. Emma was promoted to vice president on schedule, and believed that she was ranked in the top 10 percent of her class. Her compensation in 1997 was $580,000, which was above average.[22] She anticipated leaving the industry to have children, but delayed having children because her hours became slightly better and her work became more interesting and lucrative over time. The opportunities that she encountered on Wall Street enticed her to continue working long hours.

Julie and Emma shared a number of traits. Both were uncertain of their commitment to Wall Street when they graduated but encountered unexpected opportunities that led them to become more committed over time. These opportunities were a result of the booming market and a demand for skilled labor that exceeded the availability of workers with conventional experience in the securities business. But these women's early career paths were not smooth. The assistance of others in the industry along with the abundance of deal making in their fields led them on the path to success.

While some women like Julie and Emma encountered unexpected opportunities, others confronted unexpected obstacles in their careers. Sometimes these obstacles were related to family formation, and for women these tended to involve more "push" factors than were evident in Kevin's career history. For example, Tracy's career veered off the path to success that one might have expected from a former financial analyst, and for her this occurred upon starting a family.

Tracy grew up in suburban areas in the South and Northeast in a middle-class family. Her father worked in a scientific field and her mother was a homemaker. She was married to a portfolio manager, and they had one young child and were expecting a second. She attended a large public university and attained an extremely high GPA. She then worked as a two-year analyst in M&A for one of Wall Street's most prestigious firms. When she entered business school, she planned to change careers to something that would be less demanding of her time so that she could have more time for a personal life.

> At that point in time, I thought, "Oh forget it, I don't want to be in finance anymore. I want to be a marketing major or something because [finance is] for the birds. It's too difficult and I have no life." And I like a life. So I went to business school and thought maybe I'd be a marketing major. I took my first marketing course and thought, "This is silly, they are just giving fancy names to common sense"—which isn't true about marketing but what I learned was I really have more interest in finance and decided I was going to do something M&A related or finance related. Something that was markets related. I think because it was a little faster pace, which was the other thing about M&A, which bored me to tears, was you get on a project and you could be doing it for two years. You never see the end of it.

Tracy decided to return to Wall Street in a job that would be faster paced and less time intensive than M&A. As Julie did, she selected a firm that was slightly less prestigious than the firm where she had been an analyst but that had a reputation for being more female friendly and family friendly.

The firm that hired her tried to steer her toward M&A, but she pushed hard for a markets-related job and obtained a position in capital markets. She was promoted to vice president on schedule. Two years later, she wanted to leave capital markets in order to reduce the amount of travel that her job required. At that time she was engaged to be married and knew that she would want to start a family in the not-too-distant future. Like many career-committed women, she strategically chose to become a trader so that she could continue to work on Wall Street but to work fewer hours and travel less, thus juggling childcare responsibilities with career success. She encountered some resistance from her manager in capital markets, who attempted to send her against her will to an undesirable area of investment banking with very long hours. But she managed to obtain a trading position within the firm where she would work a predictable schedule of fifty-five hours per week.[23]

One and a half years later, she gave birth to her first child. The firm offered three months of paid maternity leave, and up to six months of leave time. After her three-month leave, she returned to her trading position with regular hours, but a few months later she decided to press for a change in her work schedule.

> The thought we had, myself and my husband, was that with the first child I would continue to work and we would get a babysitter during the day and I could continue to work. And I had already put myself in a career position that I was able to have a much more reasonable lifestyle. Instead of the capital markets/swap marketing, getting in to work at 7:30 and staying to 9 or 10 and flying to the West Coast, I was getting to work early at 6:30 or 7:00 but leaving at 5:30. So I didn't make a change once I had a child. Pre-child I thought it would be no big deal. I'd do my job and come home and my child would be there and the babysitter would take care of him during the day.

But after she returned to work, Tracy tried to arrange a schedule where she would leave for a couple of afternoons a week because her field was more active in the morning. She would then work 20 percent fewer hours, with a corresponding 20 percent pay cut. She encountered substantial resistance, with managers and peers wanting to cut her salary and her bonus, while she argued that her bonus should reflect her productivity and should not have 20 percent skimmed off the top. Ultimately she was able to work out this arrangement without a reduced bonus written into the contract, but only by refusing to continue doing interviews with the press that advertised the firm as "family friendly."

The response of her managers and peers at the end of the year revealed that the firm was not so family friendly after all. They gave her poorer performance evaluations than were warranted by her profits and losses, and she received a correspondingly lower bonus. This particular firm was known to be more "touchy-feely" than most others, and had performance evaluations that were more subjective than was the norm for trading, where relatively objective measures of profits and losses are available. Contrary to stereotypes, "touchy-feely" firm policies and organizational cultures were bad for women and the most successful women steered away from them.

Because her bonus was abysmal, Tracy left Wall Street to become a homemaker. Her total compensation in 1997 was between $175,000 and $200,000, which was very low by Wall Street standards of the day. Like Kevin, she was pulled toward involvement with family, but unlike Kevin, difficulties arranging a nontraditional schedule, not receiving credit for her performance, and the low bonus were substantial pushes in her decision to leave the industry. Notably, Kevin made twice as much money as Tracy, even though he worked in human resources, a support function, while she was a revenue-generating trader.

Pregnancy discrimination, discrimination against mothers, and difficulties using "family-friendly" policies that were formally available pushed several women like Tracy off successful career paths and into smaller firms, lower-paying areas, or out of the labor force. It is important to recognize, though, that family-related obstacles were far from the only forces that derailed women on Wall Street. Usually women who left for family reasons were also dissatisfied for other reasons. Like men, women were affected by organizational and market influences but, unlike men, women frequently encountered hostile work environments, discrimination, and sexual harassment. Consider the case of Daphne, whose experience was affected by market forces and disparate treatment due to her gender and her race.[24]

Like Jacob, Daphne started on Wall Street with an unorthodox work background and was guided into a position that ultimately derailed her career. She grew up in a suburban area on the West Coast in a middle-class family. She was a third-generation Asian American and her parents were both entrepreneurs. She had never been married, had no children, and planned to remain childless. Daphne attended a prestigious private university and then worked for two years at a large blue-chip firm in sales and marketing. While she worked there, someone at a higher level encouraged her to pursue an MBA to open up her business opportunities.

When she was in business school, she decided to seek a sales position in the securities industry. Like Edward and Jacob, Daphne obtained some experience and made some connections on Wall Street by taking a summer job in an investment bank. While she was there, she attended networking functions at all of the major Wall Street firms and had an interview before she returned to business school in the fall. She attained a position in domestic sales at one of Wall Street's most prestigious firms.

Shortly after starting her job, the head of sales approached Daphne to move into sales for the Asian markets.

> Essentially, [the firm] asked me to cover the Asian product and that was in 1993 and, I don't know how much you know [about] Asian markets, but Hong Kong and Asian markets were really going to the moon in '93. That was back when they were the good markets, the glory markets. And [the firm] hadn't hired anybody to join the Asian team and they only had one person covering Southeast Asia at the time. Or I'd say non-Japan Asia. So Dan had asked me, "Would you like to change over? Emerging markets for [a big-name firm]. Gray area. Blah, blah, blah." And they sent me over to London and also to Hong Kong to meet the people and I came back and talked to Dan about it. . . . I think it's almost a direction I regret now because if I think about it, from '93 to '98, the U.S. market has had the best bull run and '93 to '98, the Asian markets have come off.

While she was a third-generation American and spoke only English, Daphne believed that the head of sales had approached her because she "looked the part." The Asian markets were booming when she accepted the position, but they crashed in the fall of 1994. All of the major investment banks cut their workforce by 15 percent in January 1995 and, because she was a junior person covering failing markets, Daphne was among those laid off. In hindsight she regretted changing her focus to Asia, because if she had not agreed to specialize in Asia, she might have been less vulnerable to cutbacks.

Through a headhunter, she found another job at a small firm that specialized in Asian markets. While the earnings potential was lower, the equity research on Asia was better at the small firm than it had been at her first firm and it had built up a reputation of being a good "boutique" research house. She said,

> The actual research was much better. It covered more companies. It had much more local knowledge of firms. [My previous firm's] research in Asia was all based out of Hong Kong so they were covering Korea from Hong Kong, Indonesia from Hong Kong, Singapore from Hong Kong, whereas [my second firm] had offices in all the local countries so they were more current and up-to-date on the talk, the rumors, the whole range. In terms of market share, if you just go with sheer client business, [my second firm] did really well in Thailand and the Philippines. . . . People in Asia had heard of it, it had built up a reputation of being a good little boutique research house so for sure it was developing almost a brand name, gaining a rep. It was a lot of fun in the beginning.

But one of her supervisors sexually harassed her, which contributed to her decision to change firms again two years later. She found a position in another small China-based firm, but she felt that "the opportunities have decreased going to a Chinese firm."

Daphne did not have an optimistic or ambitious outlook on the future. She remarked that she had substantially scaled down her expectations and ambitions since the Asian markets had crashed.

> If you look at the turnover in the Malaysian market last night, the entire market, the turnover was 12.8 million U.S. dollars. IBM trades more than that in one day. You know what I mean? If you look at the turnover of the

> Philippines last night, it was 11.8 million. So there's no way that this kind of turnover can support this industry. Proprietary losses. And we're going to go through this kind of market for six months, a year, two years, depending on who you talk to. I think it actually will take a long while for Asia to turn around. People that have a real high cost base are going to have to lay off more people. I think that the general thing that I've heard is that everybody's probably going to go through a second round of layoffs, and like I said, there are firms that have gotten out of the Asian business altogether.

Because of this turn of the Asian markets, Daphne's current ambition was only to have a job at the end of the year. Her compensation in 1997 was between $100,000 and $125,000, which was much lower than the average for her graduating class and below average for equity research.

Each of these career histories reveals links between individuals' careers and personal, organizational, and market forces. Although these are only eight cases, as a group they illustrate the general paths to relative success or failure on Wall Street during the 1990s and some of the gender differences in these paths. While both men and women can be found on each path, the paths were not gender neutral—women encountered more obstacles to success. Informal processes like mentoring and formal practices like account allocation procedures and the bonus review process also contributed to an unequal distribution of men and women across these paths and led to gender inequality in the industry as a whole.

The reward system played an important role in creating successes and in derailing some Wall Street workers. Wall Street claims to pay for performance—by evaluating performance and awarding bonuses on that basis—but the bonus review process was not really neutral and merit based. People described how reviews could be manipulated so that the reviews reflected the bonus rather than the bonus reflecting the reviews. Performance evaluations were also subjective, especially in areas of the industry where individual contributions were hard to measure. Subjectivity could benefit workers and provide them with opportunities if their managers and coworkers favored them. But these influences could also reproduce inequality because more advantages went to white men.

At the same time, Wall Street maintains a myth of meritocracy, whereby a majority of workers view the bonus system as fair even though it produces systematic inequalities. This context provides an opportunity to evaluate the impact of seemingly rational incentive structures on the gender gap in pay. If women perform as well as men when they share the same productivity-related characteristics, work in the same organizations, and work the same number of hours, then why are there gender differences in compensation on Wall Street? What affects the evaluations of managers, peers, and subordinates? Is there more or less gender inequality on Wall Street in comparison to other industries? Are some areas of Wall Street better for women? Why? One must examine the institutionalized practices of Wall Street to understand the patterns of gender inequality that persisted in this cohort of professionals. Chapter 2 begins to provide an understanding of these institutionalized practices by exploring the bonus pay system and the division of labor on Wall Street.

Chapter 2

PAY FOR PERFORMANCE

Wall Street's Bonus System

An important feature of Wall Street is a bonus system that pays workers on the basis of performance evaluations. Unlike occupations that pay hourly wages or annual salaries, this is a variable compensation system. Most Wall Street professionals receive a fixed salary of $80,000–100,000 per year, but the majority of their pay takes the form of a bonus that is based on performance reviews. Wall Street's bonus system allowed workers in the 1990s to reap the benefits of booming financial markets. Among workers who received a bonus in 1997, the median total pay was $410,000, suggesting that the average bonus for vice presidents with five to seven years in the business was approximately $300,000–$325,000. Variable bonuses provide incentives for employees to work hard, to put in long hours, to work on the biggest and most important deals, and to work with the most important clients.[1]

This compensation system implies that pay is distributed rationally on the basis of individual merit. Fourteen percent of the men and women I interviewed *explicitly* described the compensation system as a meritocracy, expressing a common belief that Wall Street pays workers based on the profits they produce, and not on their gender, race, or other accidental characteristics. In the late 1980s, Patricia Douglas of Shearson Lehman Hutton said, "The bottom line is the only thing that counts anymore. If you can make money for the firm, no one cares if you're female or black or anything else. You could be *blue*, and the only question anybody would ask would be, 'How much business are you bringing in?' "[2] Echoing this sentiment a decade later, Penny said, "You could be green and a Martian. If you produce revenue, they just don't care, which is one of the charms of the firm." Penny worked as a trader and made about $750,000 in 1997.

Pay for performance implies that performance can be measured, and Wall Street firms measure performance through an elaborate evaluation system. Each employee is evaluated by his or her manager(s), peers, and subordinates in what many referred to as a "360-degree review." Leslie said,

> The whole firm takes it so seriously. There are these huge packages, everything is automated on the computer, so you fill in many pages' worth of questions and you have to get reviews from people at your same level, below you, and above you. Minimum of six. All the people in the firm that you work with. And people can ask you, too. Some people will be asked by twenty or thirty people to do their reviews. It's just a massive process. It's very impressive, I think, that they take the time to think about it and do it this way and that they put so much emphasis on it and that it is so important. And I think that your rewards are directly related to these reviews. They have a lot of weight.

Managers compile these reviews and use them to rank each employee relative to his or her same-level peers. Compensation amounts are then based on these rankings, and many Wall Street workers viewed their reviews as directly related to their pay.

This compensation system heightened the equation of money with the value of work and of workers, so that Wall Street workers were driven by compensation as a measure of their success and professional worth. If this was not their initial motivation, they learned over time to equate their value with their bonus. Danielle remarked,

> I still say the money never meant that much to me but it does. But it does. Where you're ranked in your class, what they think of you, what your future is there, *it's a reflection of a lot of things other than the money*. I guess I hadn't realized that so much either. So, going in, I knew it was very well paying and I knew whatever I was making would be fine for us to live on, but it wasn't until I got there that I understood the competitive aspect of it.

As Danielle suggested, success and career satisfaction were tightly linked to relative pay and to the belief that pay accurately reflected ability and effort. So bonuses took on a symbolic importance in addition to having a straightforward pecuniary value. Bonus pay was more than just money—it was the marker of personal and organizational success.

But Wall Street workers often did not have accurate information about others' pay, making it difficult for them to ascertain whether or not they were paid fairly. Wall Street firms are deliberately secretive about the distribution of bonuses, giving managers much discretion over them and preventing employees from knowing whether they are underpaid relative to their peers and by how much. This secrecy makes it difficult for workers to establish whether or not pay really reflects performance.

The relationship between pay and performance was also questionable because there were several nonmerit influences that clearly affected bonuses. Several people referred to firm revenues as a "pie" where the year-end bonus was based on at least three things: (1) total firm revenues for the year (how big a pie there is to divide); (2) the revenue production of the group and its contribution to the firm's profits (how large a slice of the pie is allocated to the group); and (3) the performance of individual employees relative to their peers, as evaluated by others within the work group (how large a bite each employee within the group deserves). Given this pie metaphor, more than individual performance is involved in computing the year-end bonus.

At the firm level, the profits and losses of the firm affect the amount of money that is available to distribute, setting natural upper limits on the amount of money that was available to pay out regardless of how hard employees worked or how talented they were. Barbara remarked,

> You know, when you talk about bonus pools, every firm is going to have something that impacted their bonuses that's different. [One firm], for example, always has other substantial impact from proprietary donor losses that wouldn't affect . . . other Wall Street firms.

The profits and losses of the firm influenced the money available for bonuses in ways that were unrelated to the performance of individuals.

All employees receive higher bonuses when the firm has a lucrative year, and all Wall Street firms pay larger bonuses in a bull market. Stan, who worked in sales, described the effects of the market on his pay.

> I think we've been—everyone in this industry has been a huge beneficiary of a huge bull market. If you were to ask me when I got out of school if I'd be making what I'm making this year, I would have fainted probably. It has been much higher than my expectations.

The long bull market meant that there were plenty of deals to work on and high profits for Wall Street firms, generating ever larger pies to be distributed as bonuses to revenue-producing employees. Freshly minted MBAs who landed in groups where deals were flowing were well poised for success.

On the other hand, proprietary losses in the firm's portfolio of investments and economic downturns also lead to lower bonuses regardless of individual effort and ability. Tracy, a trader, observed that the reviews could reflect the firm profits more than they reflected workers' performance.

> The funny thing is they always get swayed in terms of how much the firm is paying out. If the firm is having a

> sucky year, and they're not going to pay, suddenly you have all these areas of development that you need to work on that you were doing just fine with last review or even six months earlier when you have your midyear review. You're doing fine but . . . this year the firm did not do well and they did not pay well and everybody got these ridiculous reviews saying, "You're not doing well in this, that, and the other thing." Whereas, literally, your six-month reviews were late by three months so three months ago we were all doing fine. . . . Because they can't say, "Oh, you did phenomenal. You met your P&L [profit and loss] expectations. You used your balance sheet effectively. Your peers thought you were great. And we're decreasing your pay by 66 percent because we had a bad year." I guess they think it's a lawsuit waiting to happen or something. So they kind of give you a less-than-raving review. It doesn't happen every year but, in turn, when they think they're paying you well, they'll give you good reviews, too.

In her view, firms tailored their reviews to reflect their ability to pay, and reviews could be manipulated to justify the bonus rather than used as a basis for it. George also described how he had received a low bonus one year because his firm had proprietary losses, leading him to swiftly change firms.

> They had a very, very bad year. Enormous proprietary losses. They fired 20 percent of their personnel. They were almost down to their knees and the atmosphere was extremely bad. When you fire 20 percent of your people and you never know if it's you, it's not fun. . . . After compensation, which was very bad, I told my boss that I would just leave the firm and I left the firm after about five weeks . . . for an increase in total compensation of around 250 percent vis-à-vis my low. This was just more proof that there are very strange things happening in this industry. If you can, by finding

> another job, increase your salary by a factor of two and a half, that means obviously my compensation was too low.

He viewed his low bonus as a consequence of firm-level effects and not his performance. As in this case, proprietary losses and mergers could lead to low bonuses and to layoffs with no connection to junior workers' skills or efforts. Clearly, then, performance was not the sole or perhaps even the primary determinant of pay.

Just as firm profits set upper limits on bonuses and could affect performance evaluations, the work group also entered the equation. People who worked in groups where their firms had solid expertise and good reputations were more likely to be successful. Chris described how his second firm's reputation increased his revenue-producing ability in sales.

> It's a much more trading-oriented firm . . . there is almost a trader worship. The options traders always made a lot of money, compared to everyone else, for the firm. But the reason for that is even though they were kind of stumped and they would not show good prices, believe it or not, people will deal with [my firm] outside the bid-ask spread. Which is amazing! Outside the bid-ask spread for products. If the market offers at say 10, people will deal with [my firm] at 12. They will pay more just because it's [my firm] and we can provide the services that others can't. It's amazing! These guys were living on it. They were doing things that no one else would do, and there were fat, huge spreads.

Chris was in a position where his opportunities to succeed were amplified by the firm's prestige and reputation in his area. Each Wall Street firm had areas of strength, and workers in those areas encountered a constant stream of transactions and abundant opportunities to prove themselves.

By the same token, working in groups that had a poor flow of business could negatively affect careers and compensation despite the overall boom in the market and regardless of individual merit. Eleven percent of workers (14 percent of the women and 6 percent of the men) changed jobs because of limited deal flow. When securities firms reduced their workforces, workers in areas that had poor earnings were the first to go even though they were not responsible for generating deals or new accounts as junior employees. It was not their own performance that sealed their fate.

On the other hand, their own performance supposedly affected differences in bonuses among professionals performing exactly the same job. These individual differences were based on performance reviews, and could be very large. But while these differences were defined as merit based, performance evaluations may be affected by subjective influences, including gender biases, especially in areas where individual performance is more difficult to measure.[3] Given the importance of manager and peer evaluations, it would be difficult or impossible for merit to be the only criterion for bonus allocations. Approximately two-thirds (64 percent) of the men and women I interviewed pointed to criteria affecting bonus allocations that were unrelated to merit; job performance was never the only contributor to actual compensation.

For example, political alliances could produce more positive evaluations and higher pay. Grant, who left investment banking to work for a former client's start-up company, viewed alliances with managers as more important influences on bonuses than reviews or job performance.

> The manager [will] have to basically say, "All right, out of my ten people, for which two am I going to absolutely scream and yell to get my way? And once I do that I'm out of ammunition. I don't have enough political capital to get the rest of the people on the list paid the top. So I'll fight for these two, and these six will get the middle and whatever." So it really came down to how you were fitting in with that manager.

Managers ranked employees based on their perceptions of their employees' competence, effort, and relative contributions, as well as on feedback about the perceptions of coworkers and clients. But these perceptions could also be swayed by managers' affinities for particular workers that were only tangentially related to actual skills or abilities.

The Division of Labor on Wall Street

It is clear that some influences on bonuses are unrelated to the skill and effort of individual workers. One important influence on pay that deserves additional attention is the division of labor on Wall Street. The various areas of securities firms had different relations to revenues and different procedures for evaluating performance, so that the financial functions in which professionals specialized affected their careers and their pay. Major securities firms contain several interlocking functions, including three broad areas on the "sell side": investment banking, sales and trading, and equity research. These sell-side functions analyze corporations' financial condition, underwrite debt and equity to be issued on the public market, and sell debt and equity issues. These functions are usually further subdivided into "groups," which specialize in particular industries or financial products. They have been the traditional domain of investment banks since the 1933 Glass-Steagall Act, which prohibited institutions that underwrite securities from offering advice to investors on purchases of securities. Because Glass-Steagall was dismantled in the 1980s, most major contemporary securities firms also have merchant banking, proprietary trading, and/or asset management divisions, which manage portfolios on the buy side. These divisions purchase debt and equity interests as investments for institutional or personal investors and manage portfolios of investment securities.

Within the five main functions, specialized "groups" focus on specific industries, geographic regions, or financial products like asset-backed securities, high-yield securities, or foreign exchange options. The work group's revenues for the year affect the pool of money available to distribute as year-end bonuses within the group,

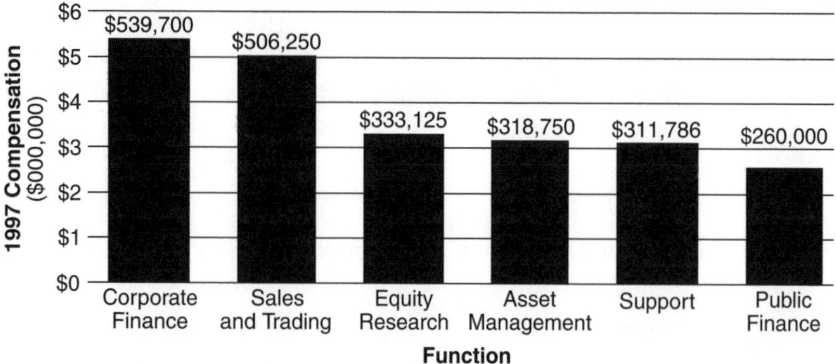

Fig. 2.1. Average compensation by function

leading compensation to differ by area of the industry. The various areas also had different relations to firm revenues and different algorithms for calculating bonus pay, leading some areas to be more lucrative than others. Figure 2.1 illustrates average pay by area for the men and women I interviewed, revealing that average income was highest in corporate finance ($539,700) and then sales and trading ($506,250).[4] The lowest average pay was $260,000 for public finance, and equity research was in the middle. In the sections that follow, I highlight what workers in different areas do and how performance is evaluated in each area of the industry.

Investment Banking

Investment banking functions are divided into corporate finance and public finance. In corporate finance, investment bankers analyze corporations' financial condition and profitability. They use their analyses to underwrite new stock issues, assisting private companies in taking their shares onto the public stock market for the first time in initial public offerings (IPOs) or using already publicly held firms' equity growth to issue additional shares on the public market to raise capital. Some investment bankers use assets or mortgages to structure new securities using mathematical models of projected returns on investment. Others help corporations negotiate M&A, analyzing the prospective profits and the value of each party's shares.

In public finance, investment bankers underwrite loans and securities for tax-exempt and government institutions. Public finance differs from corporate finance in terms of the type of clients and also in the fact that corporate finance underwrites both debt and equity, while public finance underwrites only debt.

Investment bankers typically work long and unpredictable hours. Senior bankers pitch business to prospective client organizations and develop relationships with clients who require ongoing financial services, while teams of more junior employees evaluate the clients' financial condition, develop presentations, and structure deals using mathematical models. Junior associates work long hours because they are assigned to multiple deals with strict deadlines for analyses and presentations. In the first four to seven years in the business, workers are not required to bring in business but sometimes work literally around-the-clock. As an investment banker's career progresses, the hours usually decline and generating client relationships becomes more important.

Investment bankers work on deals with teams of other bankers, and their fees reflect the collective enterprise of the team. Relative contributions to the team effort are evaluated by other team members, and clients' impressions are also considered. As a result, individuals' bonuses are partly dependent on the performance of others in the group and the perceptions of their managers, coworkers, and subordinates. The opinions of managers are especially important since they are on the compensation committee. These managers have to tease out the individual contributions of multiple team members in order to rank individuals. Because this task is not accomplished easily or accurately, managers have some discretion as to how to rank subordinates.

Since the elimination of fixed commissions in 1975 and the gradual erosion of commissions for selling securities, fees for investment banking have become an increasing share of firm revenues.[5] Client companies pay investment bankers fees for "deals" that issue stock or securities, or that arrange mergers and acquisitions. These fees affect the amount of money available for bonuses in each investment banking group, so that the number and size of the group's deals influence individuals' compensation by affecting the pool of money to be distributed among workers. Rosalind, who worked in mergers and acquisitions before starting a small securities business with a more senior banker, remarked,

> I think it was important that I worked on deals because there were people who worked on a lot of things that didn't close. For example, consumer products are a good example. There were a lot of people [in that group] who would work on a lot of different things throughout the year but nothing really got done and no fees came in. You were told that you weren't, as a junior person, held accountable for that but I never really believed that, which is why I really wanted to find a place where deals were happening and get it done. On a basic level I think it was important that you worked on deals and brought fees in.

In the early years of Wall Street careers, workers were not expected to bring in clients, but their group's flow of revenue-producing work was important for their bonus pay as well as their longevity in the industry.

In large securities firms, investment banking areas often specialize into groups by industry (e.g., metals and mining, technology), region (e.g., Asia, Latin America), or financial product (e.g., mergers and acquisitions, high-yield, asset-backed securities). These specializations define the pool of client organizations, which affects bankers' pay because some types of clients engage in deals with larger fees. For example, automotive, oil and gas, and large industrial companies generate more corporate finance revenue than do retail industries. Differences in specializations could produce gender inequality because men were more likely to work with clients from higher-revenue industries like natural resources, technology, or financial institutions while women were more likely to specialize in lower-revenue areas like emerging markets. Emerging markets groups serve countries with relatively small GDPs, so their clients pay smaller fees even though their deals involve a similar amount and type of work. Olivia, who worked in emerging markets with developing countries in Latin America, said,

> I cover little countries. I cover Colombia, Venezuela, Peru, Panama, and Central America. Those countries issue little—the governments issue little securities. They're on a different scale. If I do a $200 million transaction, my boss says, "Oh. Okay." But if Argentina does a billion-dollar deal, that's great. Now, it's great because it's big. Because it gives them a big lead table so [the firm] is number one. But ultimately the effort that you put into a $200 million deal, for a country where that $200 million is a lot, doesn't count only because they want the revenue generated. It's not big enough.

In other words, her group's revenues were limited by its clients' GDPs, not by the skill required or the effort expended on the deals. Interestingly, white men started to abandon emerging markets before the 1990s and were largely replaced with white women, immigrants, and nonwhites.

Public finance also pays less than corporate finance because it has nonprofit institutions and municipalities as clients. Women were more likely to work in public finance and none of the men I interviewed worked in public finance. Fisher notes that men fled the public finance side of the business in the late 1970s when "eager young fast-trackers in august investment-banking firms dodged public finance in favor of corporate deal-making."[6] Because clients in public finance generally pay smaller fees, bonuses are also lower than in corporate finance, even though the hours and travel are often equally difficult. Regarding her bonus, Caitlin explained,

> I am in the top for my level in my department. [My current firm] is cheap. The same job at [another major investment bank] would pay me more money. The

> same job anywhere in corporate finance versus public finance would pay me a lot more money. So, for my department, I'm doing great! If you look at comparables outside, and mind you I don't get to keep all of that bonus—10 percent is restricted stock—at the end of the day I am not raking in the big bucks. And I have this pretty rough lifestyle.

Caitlin described in detail the personal sacrifices required by high travel demands and long hours in her job, even while it did not provide as much pay as corporate finance positions. Tamara also worked in public finance and noted that it pays much less: "The profits are a lot lower because you're working for nonprofit organizations." So clients' ability to pay was at least as important as investment bankers' efforts or skills. In general, corporate finance is a high-paying area of the industry, with some variation by industry or regional specialization, and public finance is relatively lower paying (even though it pays very well by the standards of the labor force as a whole).

Few compensation figures were available from the industry, but a survey of executive recruiters who worked with major securities firms provided some figures for corporate finance that corresponded closely with the average figures for the men and women in this study.[7] The survey summarized average pay in corporate finance in 1997 for different MBA cohorts, indicating that "low"-range Wall Street professionals who had graduated in 1993 earned $300,000 in 1997. Most of them were approximately thirty years old at the time. This amount is more than twice the $128,521 cutoff for the ninety-fifth percentile of household income in the United States for the same year.[8] Table 2.1 compares the survey data, published in *Investment Dealers' Digest*, with the medians for corporate finance employees in the study.[9] The earnings of these men and women are similar to industry estimates for corporate finance, representing 92.5 percent of industry estimates for 1991 graduates, 97.2 percent for 1992 graduates, and 107 percent for

TABLE 2.1
Average Annual Pay Ranges for Investment Bankers, 1997

MBA *Class*	*Low*	*High*	*Median*	*Median in This Study*
1991	$425,000	$840,000	$635,000	$587,500
1992	$390,000	$740,000	$540,000	$525,000
1993	$300,000	$600,000	$430,000	$460,000

Note: Based on the table, "Money Still Talks: Average Annual Pay Ranges for Investment Bankers, 1997," in *Investment Dealers' Digest* 1998b, compiled from executive recruiters who work with Bear Stearns, Chase Manhattan, Credit Suisse First Boston, DLJ, Goldman Sachs, Lehman Brothers, Merrill Lynch, J. P. Morgan, Morgan Stanley Dean Witter, and Salomon Smith Barney. Only one of these firms, Chase Manhattan, was not included in the present study. The final column of the table includes only the respondents whose area in 1997 was corporate finance. Statistical tests comparing measures of central tendency could not be computed.

1993 MBAs. Unfortunately, no industry data were available for public finance.

Sales and Trading

Sales and trading functions buy and sell securities on the public stock exchange. Prior to 1975, the NYSE was a unique cartel with unlimited power to establish commission rates, and it maintained a policy of fixed commissions for member firms and prohibited discounts for large orders. Institutional trading and mutual funds that involved high-volume trades increased in the 1950s and 1960s. Facing pressure from the SEC, in 1968 the NYSE instituted a volume discount on transactions over 1,000 shares. The SEC finally eliminated fixed commissions on May 1, 1975, leading the relative importance of commissions to decline after that time.[10] This decline generated diversification and innovation in financial services in order to expand sales and trading revenues.[11] For example, derivatives were created so that firms could structure fees into the securities themselves.

Despite the decline in commission rates since fixed commissions were eliminated, sales and trading is still known to be one of the better-paying areas on Wall Street. These areas involve substantial direct client contact, especially over the phone. Sales and trading are driven by market conditions and tend to be very stressful during market hours. Like investment banking, sales and trading are often divided into groups or "desks" based on industry, region, or product. But unlike investment bankers, salespeople and traders tend not to work long hours after the market has closed unless they are entertaining clients. Unfortunately, no industry figures are available for pay in sales and trading, but the median income among the salespeople and traders I interviewed was $450,000.

Individual performance can be monitored more accurately in sales and trading than in investment banking because of P&L records. Justin, who earned $650,000 in 1997, described his compensation in sales as based directly on revenues.

> We, out of this department, aren't really on a bonus structure. It's more of a commission structure. Institutional sales, you know. It can be considered as a bonus but it really isn't. It's more a percentage of what you bring in. Well, what happens is, many times they will get a bonus; the bonus is more or less within a percentage range of what they are bringing in, in terms of revenue during the year.

Some salespeople and traders receive a commission, rather than a bonus, while others receive a bonus that is at least partly based on their profits and losses.

Of course, the distribution of accounts could be equitable or inequitable, and inequality in account distribution might contribute to a gender gap in pay in sales and trading. Barbara, who worked in sales, noted that the account allocation was unfairly biased toward people who were verbally demanding—who tended to be men—rather than toward those who were more effective at selling.

> I don't think the account process is fair. . . . I think people who are more aggressive and go in and ask for more accounts, get the accounts. I don't do that. It's probably my own fault. Sometimes I do, but not as much as a lot of people here—a lot of men. I find men . . . go in there and say, "I want an account. I deserve it. I've been working my butt off. I did x, y, and z with this account." . . . I think the people who don't produce with certain accounts go in and say, "That account, I didn't get anywhere without account. I need another account." And then they keep that account, and get another account. Then he'll say to me, "You know, Barbara, you have lots of sales credits. You have nothing to complain about." Yes, because I'm producing with the accounts I have! I also see cases where other people do get an account and produce with it and are not necessarily rewarded—like being given a bigger account, a more challenging account, or an account that . . . people should be rewarded by getting bigger accounts. Showing that they can get a 100 percent out of what's there. They should get a bigger account.

From her perspective, sales accounts were not distributed on the basis of merit, and the allocation of departing brokers' accounts favored men who were poor performers because they tended to be pushy.[12] So while most Wall Street firms used profit and loss criteria for rewarding sales and trading employees, opportunities to perform in the form of good accounts could be unequal. This type of discrimination in the allocation of accounts is exactly what female brokers at Merrill Lynch alleged in their class action suit.

Equity Research

Equity research departments advise sales and trading, investment banking, and asset management with in-depth analyses of companies and market trends. Financial professionals in these areas are called "analysts." Research analysts tend to work more predictable hours than do investment bankers, and their amount and extent of client contact vary widely. Some analysts juggle multiple roles of tracking stocks, scouting for merger ideas, seeking lucrative underwriting business for their firms, and/or generating sales commissions. They usually specialize by industry and write reports analyzing the health and profitability of companies in their industry. *Institutional Investor* (*II*) magazine ranks equity research analysts in all major industries every October. These rankings are based on a survey of investors who use analysts' advice to select investments. *II* rankings are a vote of confidence and a lure for prospective investment banking clients, leading these ranks to dramatically increase an analyst's pay.

Analysts' reports recommend that salespeople and traders buy, sell, or hold stocks and bonds in their industry. These analysts also advise investment bankers of companies in their industry that would make good prospective clients for underwriting or M&A business, and provide information on companies that are already clients. The expertise of an analyst can make or break an investment banking deal, and some client companies work with particular investment banks because of the reputations of their analysts. Since the erosion of sales commissions, working with investment banking has become increasingly important for research analysts because investment banking fees represent an ever larger share of firm revenues.

In equity research, evaluations depend on whether or not an analyst has an *II* ranking and the degree to which salespeople, traders, and investment bankers trust or follow his or her advice. Evaluations from sales and trading and investment banking are necessarily somewhat subjective, and there is some evidence that Wall Street firms deliberately maintain ambiguity about how analyst pay is related to investment banking. Andy Kessler, who was a highly ranked technology analyst, described how working on investment banking deals affected his pay in equity research.

> Analysts didn't get paid directly for deals at Morgan Stanley. One year, they actually put in a formula to do

> just that, but someone in management wised up and put a halt to it. They didn't want a paper trail back to the formula, so banking compensation remained a loose concept. A good or bad word from bankers could add or subtract 25 percent of my pay in a heartbeat.[13]

This insider's quote suggests that Wall Street firms prefer to maintain some discretion over bonuses when they can—and they can for equity research.

Still, because of their increasing role in investment banking deals and their rising visibility among industry clients, analyst pay rose dramatically in the 1990s, and equity analysts with high *II* rankings were sought after and paid exceptionally well. *Investment Dealers' Digest* estimated that most top-ranked analysts earned $600,000 to $900,000 while senior analysts without *II* rankings earned in the range of $200,000 to $350,000 in 1997.[14] Among the men and women in equity research I interviewed, only two had top *II* rankings, and their compensation was $650,000 and over $1 million, respectively. Compensation ranged between $162,500 and $375,000 for other equity analysts who remained in top firms, with a median of $280,000.[15] These averages are very similar to the published industry figures for the same year, suggesting that the people I interviewed were quite representative of the research analysts on Wall Street at the time.

Asset Management

Employees in asset management areas manage portfolios of investments and earn commissions when they buy and sell stocks and mutual funds. They rely on research analysts' advice in choosing securities. Asset management usually involves similar hours to those of trading. But because it depends on commissions and the growth of investments over time, asset management is usually less lucrative than conventional sell-side areas. Evaluations in asset management often involve direct calculations similar to sales and trading, such that portfolio managers and proprietary traders are paid based on the value of assets they manage or the profits on securities they purchase and sell for the firm. No industry data were available for asset management, but the median income in asset management in the sample was $300,000.

Support Functions

Securities firms also require a corporate infrastructure in the form of internal divisions involved in risk management, corporate strategy, operations, information technology, public relations, and human resources. For example, employees in risk management analyze the actions of salespeople and traders to ensure that they do not compromise the economic stability of the firm, monitoring the volume of trades to ensure that no trader or salesperson is gambling too heavily with the firm's capital.[16] To illustrate, in 1994 Nick Leeson, a trader in Hong Kong, lost over a billion dollars and bankrupted Baring's, the British investment bank. Risk management employees are the "back office" that oversees traders to reduce the likelihood of this type of fiasco. In Leeson's case, he was given risk management guidelines but no back office to make sure that he followed them. Trusting Leeson to be his own back office was the firm's biggest and most devastating mistake.

Workers in support areas work regular business hours or a little bit longer. Bonuses in these areas tend to be lower than in other areas because they are not directly involved in the production of revenues, even though they provide valuable indirect support for front-line areas. Their bonuses are based on evaluations of other workers, both within their function and in direct-revenue areas with which they have contact. Because there is no direct evidence of profits generated for the firm, these evaluations are necessarily somewhat subjective.

In most areas of Wall Street firms, promotions for the first six years are "lockstep," occurring at regular intervals for employees who persevere. In this regard, the progression of this career path resembles other professional schedules, like academic tenure clocks or legal partnership timetables. Sarah said, "It's a fairly predictable path unless there's something definitely wrong. Unless you're having some problems, I should say. But in general, it's a fairly predictable path." At the entry level, professionals in sell-side functions have the title of associate. Those who remain in the industry for four years are promoted to vice president.[17] Promotion to senior vice president[18] occurs after another two years, while promotion to the highest level, managing director, is less certain and often depends on one's active development of client relationships and ability to bring in business. As securities professionals move beyond the level of vice president, their hours often become shorter, their pay increases, and they describe the work as more interesting. Many Wall Street professionals view the first four years as both a learning experience and an endurance test. Those who are unable to hang on to these high-paying, stressful jobs through this period never regain access to the profession's fast track.

Two things should be clear about this division of labor. First, if women disproportionately work in the lower-paying specializations, then this may explain some gender inequality in pay on Wall Street. It is well-known that sex segregation of men and women into different jobs is responsible for a substantial proportion of the gender gap in pay in the labor force.[19] Internal segregation of women into lower-paying areas of the securities industry may similarly explain a substantial amount of gender inequality in pay. Second, performance evaluations always have nonmerit influences but they are also more subjective in some areas than others. Performance and pay may be more loosely coupled in those areas. Subjectivity has the potential to overreward workers who are liked by their senior managers relative to their performance and to underreward those who step outside the mold. This could be detrimental to women who try to break into the most male-dominated areas of the industry.

Conclusion

This chapter has provided background on the securities industry, its compensation system, and influences on individual bonuses. This background suggests that although Wall Street defines its pay system as a meritocracy, this is really a myth. There are a variety of influences on bonuses that are unrelated to individual merit, so that pay based on performance evaluations is not purely merit based. Some of the influences on bonuses are gender neutral, like the total firm revenues. But as the remaining chapters will illustrate, Wall Street's distribution of rewards also has a disparate impact by gender and leads to structural gender inequality in two ways. First, performance itself is a consequence of opportunities offered (or denied), and decisions about how to distribute these opportunities to perform are subjective. Women workers—and remember, by objective standards, these women matched their male counterparts—described how managers did not assign them to the most important accounts or deals: managers promoted those who closely resembled themselves and/or their clients. By the same logic, managers deliberately assigned their female employees to work on accounts with female clients, but those accounts tended to be less lucrative. Senior male managers also sometimes took men under their wing because they shared common backgrounds and interests, and they gave them better access to lucrative accounts and deals. In these ways, opportunities to perform were distributed unequally by gender.

Second, while the compensation system on Wall Street seems rational and efficient, performance is hard to measure. The harder it is to measure, the more subjectivity affects evaluations. Both the men and women I interviewed talked about the subjectivity of the performance review process, and women often pointed to gender double standards and discrimination in their evaluations. When criteria for performance are unclear, performance evaluations allow subjective biases to operate unchecked. In a male-dominated industry and culture, these subjective biases encourage gender inequality.

This background on the securities industry is important for understanding how gender inequality might occur *even if there are no gender differences in performance*. The distribution of men and women across areas within the industry is one possible contributor, if women disproportionately work in lower-paying areas. The infiltration of subjective perceptions also potentially leads to gender differences that are not performance based. In fact, because of this subjectivity, the bonus system permitted very subtle and unconscious discrimination against women to operate with impunity. But before analyzing the specific subtle mechanics of inequality, it is important to know how much gender inequality there was on Wall Street in the late 1990s, both in absolute terms and net of other influences. The next chapter explores these differences.

Chapter 3

A WOMAN'S WORTH

Gender Differences in Compensation

Few will be surprised that there is still gender inequality in a male-dominated environment like Wall Street. Despite laws forbidding gender discrimination in employment since 1964, continued gender inequality in the U.S. labor force has been well documented. Inequality in average pay has declined since the 1960s, when female full-time, year-round workers earned an average of 60 percent as much as their male counterparts. By the late 1990s, women were earning an average of 75 percent as much as men, partly due to increases in women's wages and partly due to declines in men's. But this falls short of equality, and there is still a substantial gap in earnings even for men and women with similar backgrounds, education, and work hours. This chapter will reveal the size of the pay gap between full-time professional men and women on Wall Street and analyze some possible explanations for the inequality.

The Gender Gap on Wall Street

Among the men and women who still worked on Wall Street in 1997,[1] total compensation ranged from $100,000 to over $1,000,000 with a median of $410,000. There were substantial gender differences within this range: women's median earnings were $325,000, while men's were $525,000. While both men and women on Wall

Street had tremendously high earnings by national standards, people tend to view differences in relative terms. This led to perceptions of pay that might seem warped outside of this industry. For example, Penny, a highly paid trader, said with a straight face, "You know, there are people on Wall Street who don't make *a lot* of money. There are plenty of people making *only* $300,000 a year."

In this context, women's mean earnings were 60.5 percent as much as their male peers from business school a mere four to seven years after graduating. This falls short of women's 75 percent relative earnings in the U.S. labor force for the same year.[2] The raw numbers revealed the magnitude of gender inequality even more powerfully. The gender *difference* in average pay among financial professionals was an astounding $223,368.

What might explain this large gender difference in pay? Some economists have argued that gender differences in "human capital," defined as the investments that workers make in their skills and productivity through education, training, and work experience, cause the gender gap in pay.[3] In their view, women invest less in their human capital because a majority of women prioritize family over career.[4] The expectation that they will take primary responsibility for caregiving in their families then reduces women's commitment to paid work. In other words, women choose different types of jobs from men because they expect to interrupt their labor force participation in order to bear and rear children. More specifically, women are likely to prefer jobs with fewer penalties for interruptions and with fewer or more flexible hours. In contrast, men prefer to maximize their earnings because they expect a lifelong commitment to paid work. This leads them to invest more in their education, training, and job-related skills, which translates into higher productivity and higher pay.

But previous research has also demonstrated that human capital accounts for only 30–50 percent of the existing gender gap in pay, while a gender gap remains even between men and women with identical job preferences and investments in human capital.[5] Also remember that the men and women I interviewed were highly similar in their work-related characteristics, or "human capital," and yet

Table 3.1
Background Characteristics

	Men	*Women*	*Total*
Married	69%	55%	61%
Parent	53%	34%	42%
White	97%	86%	91%
Economics major	47%	61%	55%
Math major	28%	16%	21%
Undergraduate GPA (average)	3.46	3.41	3.44
GMAT score (average)	655	673	665
Experience as an analyst	28%	23%	25%
Experience as a summer associate	50%	46%	47%
Total	32 (42%)	44 (58%)	76 (100%)

Note: None of the differences between men and women in this table is statistically significant.

exhibited very large gender differences in pay. Because of the way in which I selected respondents, they shared the same educational credentials, had similarly technical backgrounds, and entered the industry at roughly the same time. Table 3.1 summarizes the percentages of men and women with various background and human capital characteristics, illustrating that gender differences were relatively small in background characteristics like marital status, parental status, and race. Men and women were also extremely similar in specific human capital characteristics, such as having a relevant major in their bachelor's degrees, undergraduate GPA, score on the GMAT, and the likelihood of having work experience on Wall Street as a two-year financial analyst or summer associate prior to completing their MBA.

Of course, it is possible that some of the gender gap could have been a result of unaccounted for differences in men's and women's backgrounds, education, experience, or work effort. I used a statistical model to analyze gender differences in compensation while accounting for the characteristics that workers brought to their jobs.[6] The results of this model reveal significant earnings penalties for women net of differences in the characteristics that workers brought to their jobs on Wall Street and the hours that they worked (see table B.2). Together, gender, marital status, parental status, undergraduate major, and hours per week explained approximately 41 percent of differences in total compensation. As one would expect, weekly hours had important effects on earnings so that working more hours led to higher pay. Each additional hour increased annual compensation by approximately 5.3 percent.[7] At the same time, men and women estimated that they worked a similar number of hours per week and had unequal compensation even when they worked the same hours. Women earned 39 percent less than men with the same background, marital and family status, undergraduate major, experience in the industry, and hours per week.

Given the similarities between these men and women in their backgrounds, qualifications, and hours of work, how can we understand this large gender gap in pay? One possibility is that men and women do not hold the same positions in Wall Street firms. They might hold different ranks, although all of these men and women should have been promoted to the level of vice president or higher if they remained in the industry in 1997. Some of the gender difference could also have been caused by women moving into lower-tier firms more often than men. While most men and women continued to work for one of the original top nine firms, some moved into other financial firms that compete with traditional investment banks. Those who had moved out of the top firms typically went to smaller firms or commercial banks, where they did "the same thing" as they had before. But while these firms sometimes wooed employees with guarantees of high initial compensation, working for one of the top firms was associated with a better long-term earnings trajectory. If men were more likely to remain in a top firm, then this might explain the gender difference in earnings.

Men and women might also work in different divisions of Wall Street firms, leading to pay differences. As chapter 2 illustrated, some areas of the industry were more lucrative than others. Studies have overwhelmingly found that men and women tend to work in different occupations, establishments, and jobs, and that women's jobs pay less than those dominated by men.[8] Women tend to work in lower-paying occupations, to be employed by lower-paying establishments, and to occupy lower ranks or have lower-paying job titles within organizations.[9] Many scholars argue that men and women have differential access to occupations and establishments because of discrimination by employers in hiring and promotion.[10] While such deliberate actions by employers may play a role, others have also suggested that subtle cognitive processes such as co-worker, manager, and client preferences to associate with others like themselves, or expectations that men will be more competent, lead to obstacles for women and discourage them from competing in male-dominated environments.[11] Regardless of why men and women end up in different jobs, previous research has estimated that differences in pay between the jobs that men and women do explains between 35 percent and 89 percent of gender inequality in pay.[12] In other words, a substantial amount of the pay gap is a result of differences in wages *between jobs* held by men and those held by women.

What might explain large pay differences between jobs held by men and those held by women? Between-job pay differences could be based on skill level, productivity, or market effects. In other words, jobs with more women may require less skill, be less time intensive, or have lower demand for workers relative to the number of workers interested in the job. Women may provide a glut of available workers for jobs that have flexible scheduling, shorter hours, or schedules that coincide with school hours and accommodate child rearing. But studies have shown that predominantly female jobs pay less than male-dominated jobs with similar skill levels and do not offer better starting salaries, benefits, or scheduling flexibility. In fact, predominantly female jobs tend to have less flexibility and autonomy and more rigid scheduling than male-dominated jobs, suggesting that they do not accommodate mothers' family-related needs.[13] These facts have led many to argue that women's jobs suffer from the cultural devaluation of all things associated with women or with femininity.[14]

But how does this devaluation of predominantly female jobs occur in rational bureaucratic organizations? Research on organizations has illustrated that their strategies for determining the pay rates of different jobs are partially based on custom and other criteria that are not productivity related.[15] Nelson and Bridges argue that many organizations determine pay rates by comparing jobs within the organization to similar jobs in other organizations. By doing so, they can attempt to establish market rates and also appeal to the logic of the free market—a logic that the courts and the public generally endorse. The importance of nonmarket mechanisms for setting pay rates is then overlooked and rationalized using market logic. But the definition of jobs as "similar" to use as benchmarks involves subjectivity and sometimes uses gender composition as a criterion. In other words, female-dominated jobs are often compared to other female-dominated jobs rather than to male-dominated jobs that may be functionally equivalent. This has led many scholars to conclude that women's jobs pay less at least partly because women do them.[16]

Regardless of the reasons that jobs with more women tend to pay less, internal sex segregation of Wall Street firms could explain some or most of the gender gap in pay. As chapter 2 suggested, there are pay differences by area of the securities industry that could produce gender inequality if men and women did not work in identical divisions. Table 3.2 summarizes the percentage of men and women in this study who were at each rank, in each area, and remained in top Wall Street firms at the end of 1997. This table illustrates that men and women were equally likely to continue to work for a top firm, but that women were more likely to rank below vice president while men were more likely to rank above vice president.[17] It also shows us that women were more likely to work in equity research or public finance while men were more likely to work in corporate finance.

Also, despite the fact that table 3.2 shows no difference, industry data suggest that fewer women work in sales and trading in the securities industry. In 1998, 2,100 (15.6 percent) of Merrill Lynch's 13,400 brokers were female, and at Salomon Smith Barney women

TABLE 3.2
Gender Differences in Job-Related Characteristics

Job-related Characteristic	*Men*	*Women*	*All Cases*
Hours/week (mean)	64.22	60.23	61.93
Corporate finance (%)*	53	30	39
Sales and trading (%)	13	16	14
Equity research (%)*	6	25	17
Public finance (%)*	0	9	5
Asset management (%)	19	11	14
Support function (%)	9	9	9
Less than VP (%)*	16	36	28
VP (%)	56	59	58
Above VP (%)*	28	5	14
Top firm 1997 (%)	90	80	84
Total 1997[a] (mean)**	$566,111	$342,743	$431,434
Total	32	44	76

Note: Some of the differences between men and women presented in this table are statistically significant.

[a] For compensation, the total number of cases included in the analysis includes only 68 cases (27 men and 41 women) because five refused to disclose their income and three had left Wall Street prior to receiving a 1997 bonus.

Two-tailed significance: $*p < .05$ $**p < .001$

represented 15 percent of the 9,900 brokers, or a total of 1,485.[18] It is also well-known that women have traditionally been most successful in equity research, and the women I spoke to confirmed this. Mia, who had been a research analyst, said, "There are quite a few females in equity research. A high ratio compared to other fields."[19]

There was also some evidence that women were more likely to work in the lower-paying support areas over time, often moving to support functions from revenue-producing jobs. Jessica, who worked in corporate finance, described the attrition of her female colleagues at her first firm.

> At my other firm, there were only [women] in administrative positions. If they liked you they managed to

> move you out of a producing role but you got to stay. I kid you not. Two of my best friends, one of them worked in corporate finance and one of them worked in real estate. Both of them were moved to administrative roles . . . one of them has been there for three and a half years and one has been [there] for two and a half years. So they both still work there and both are still well compensated and everybody loves them. They're not producers.

Confirming that women were more likely to work in support functions, Kevin observed that his department, human resources, was one of the most female-dominated departments in the bank. "There might even be more women than men. I'm pretty sure HR has the highest percentage of female workers of any division." Of course, this disproportionately female area is a support function that manages people, has traditionally been women's domain, does not directly produce revenue, and is among the first to be cut in an economic downturn.

While women seem to often work in different jobs than men, a question that remains is whether or not men and women earned the same amount when they worked in the same areas of the same firms. In other words, how much *within-job* gender inequality was there on Wall Street? To address this question, I statistically accounted for rank, area, and whether or not someone continued to work in a top firm using a multiple regression model (see table B.3).[20] Accounting for these job characteristics as well as workers' characteristics explains about 54 percent of the variance in total compensation, which is 13 percent more than the model with background and human capital characteristics.

As expected, area of the industry was an important influence, although accounting for it did not eliminate the gender gap. Those who worked in corporate finance earned 173 percent as much as otherwise similar peers in support functions, and salespeople and traders earned 210 percent as much as similar others in support functions. These areas were also the most male dominated. But, net of all other influences, women still earned 29 percent less than comparable male peers in similar organizations, at the same rank, and in the same areas.

Interestingly, weekly hours no longer affected pay once these effects were taken into account. This suggests that workers do not trade off higher pay for the opportunity to work fewer hours. It also contradicts claims that women choose lower-paying positions because they provide them with more time to devote to their families.[21] In fact, the areas with higher concentrations of women, like public finance and equity research, were not the areas with the fewest weekly hours. Sales and trading offered the most reasonable and predictable hours as well as very high pay but was among the most male-dominated areas of Wall Street.

I used the statistical model to compute annual pay by weekly hours for the "average man" and "average woman" on Wall Street, using the mean for all other characteristics in the model. The equations for men and women produced the graph in figure 3.1.[22] This figure illustrates the gender gap in total compensation after accounting for all other influences. It reveals that women earned less for each hour they worked, in comparison with men who brought identical characteristics to the job and who worked in the same areas and organizations at the same rank. In other words, there were substantial gender differences in pay among otherwise similar recent entrants to Wall Street that cannot be fully explained in terms of the characteristics that workers brought to their jobs or the characteristics of the jobs that workers held. The concentration of women in lower-paying jobs within the industry was not the whole story, and work effort in terms of hours devoted to the job could not explain the gender gap. In fact, hours dropped out of the second equation. So why did women earn less than otherwise similar men even when they worked the same number of hours in the same areas of the same firms in a single industry?

Settings like Wall Street may be particularly likely to produce this type of within-job gender inequality in pay. Nelson and Bridges found that within-job gender pay differences are especially common

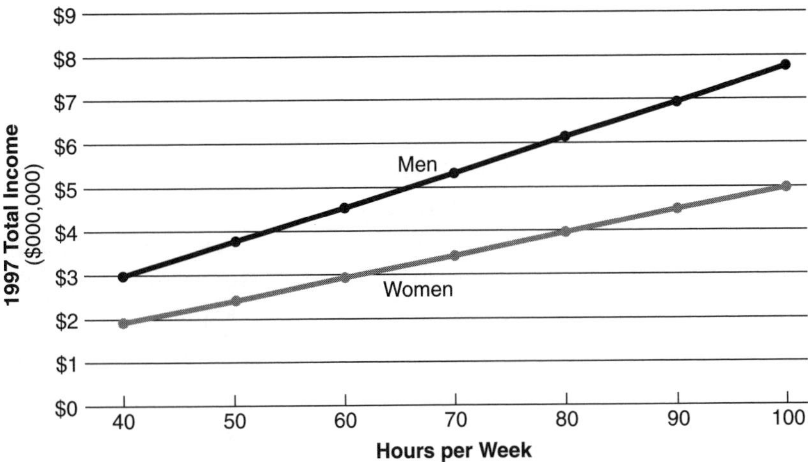

Fig. 3.1. Gender differences by hours worked

in higher-paying jobs and jobs at higher organizational levels. They claimed that this may be because managers have more discretion to determine pay levels in these jobs.[23] In Wall Street's compensation system, pay differences across individuals in the same job were institutionalized and justified as merit based. But managers also had substantial discretion over the relative pay of their subordinates. So it makes sense that workers in the same job might receive different pay. But why would this variable pay produce systematic gender inequality?

It is, of course, possible that men outperformed women. While I do not have performance data, this seems unlikely given all of the productivity-related and job characteristics that were accounted for in the statistical models (see appendix B). Of course, aside from differences in ability, performance could be affected by differences in opportunities to perform (access to accounts or deals) caused by different network ties within the firm, with mentors, and with clients. But many Wall Street workers also believed that subjective biases permeated the bonus system and produced discrimination over and above any actual differences in performance. In fact, it is clear that gender differences could be produced in a setting like Wall Street through subtle, or even unconscious, discrimination that infiltrated the performance review process.

Managers' and coworkers' assessments of performance are likely to be influenced by a cultural division of labor outside the industry that rewards men with higher earnings in the labor force, allocates primary responsibility for childcare to women, and reproduces assumptions about the competence and the preferences of men and women. This division of labor forms a taken-for-granted building block of labor market institutions and cognitive assumptions that are shared by organizational members.[24] For example, definitions of ideal workers as those who are completely dedicated to their work, without career interruptions or outside responsibilities, privilege male workers. Even in cases where women act like ideal workers, cultural assumptions about women's roles, priorities, personality characteristics, and work commitment can produce suspicion about their long-term trajectories or their competence. This can encourage managers and coworkers who fill out performance evaluations to view women with extra scrutiny, which puts them at a disadvantage vis-à-vis men in the same position or with the same performance. Because gender relations in the larger culture influence organizational culture and practices, gender inequality is embedded in Wall Street's performance evaluation and bonus system. This produces inequality even when men and women have similar qualifications and skills and work the same hours.

Wall Street workers often suggested that this type of bias in the bonus system was the source of gender inequities, implying that bonuses were not entirely based on merit. In fact, because a variety of nonmerit influences affected bonuses, subtle forms of discrimination could routinely produce lower earnings for women and a gender gap in average pay. Thirty-two percent of the women described subtle discrimination in the compensation system as a cause of lower-than-expected earnings. Heather remarked,

> I do think [my firm] has a big issue with subtle forms of discrimination. Apart from racial discrimination, which I really have not witnessed, but certainly in terms of

> women and women getting promoted. Maybe we haven't reached the point in time where enough women have been in the workforce long enough to be at very senior levels. But I do tend to think that men are given the benefit of the doubt in this organization, and I think it is just easier for men. I mean, I never thought this coming out of undergrad. I thought that the world was a pretty fair place. All you had to do was work hard and success would follow. As time goes by, it becomes really obvious that women are not on the same playing field.

The "subtle" forms of discrimination that women described largely involved double standards, stereotyping, the stigmatization of women who were "too masculine," the rewarding of stereotypically masculine behavior among men (even when it reduced job effectiveness), and underallocation of accounts to female workers.

Many women on Wall Street described roadblocks to success that were related to the gender division of labor in the family, or they anticipated that they would encounter difficulties when they started families. They also encountered higher standards for competence by their managers, peers, and subordinates. When they adopted the masculine work styles that were typical of the industry, they were sanctioned for violating expectations of femininity. They had greater difficulty gaining access to accounts and deals, and developing solid relationships with managers, coworkers, and clients. The pay-for-performance system meant lower pay as a result of these obstacles, even when women worked as many hours as men and had similar skills.

Conclusion

Because unconscious and invisible assumptions about gender are at the foundation of work organizations, men and women may receive unequal rewards even if compensation and promotion practices or market pressures encourage greater equality. Pay practices can seem gender neutral while having a disparate impact on male and female workers. Wall Street in the late 1990s is an excellent case in point. While the bull market should have encouraged greater equality among skilled professionals because of the high demand for securities workers, women on Wall Street earned 40 percent less than their male counterparts from business school. Even accounting for differences in background, area of the industry, rank, and firm prestige, women earned 29 percent less than similarly employed men. This gender gap occurred irrespective of hours of work and despite seemingly gender-neutral pay practices based on performance evaluations.

While it is not possible to ascertain true performance measures with my data, subtle discrimination seems as likely to produce systematic gender inequality as actual differences in performance given the similarities between these men and women and the variety of nonmerit influences on pay. Subtle discrimination could be based on assumptions about gendered family roles and could occur among clients as well as managers and coworkers. As the next chapter will explore, preferences among managers for junior employees who resemble themselves or who have higher social status could affect access to opportunity, pay, and promotion. Those who promote their own careers may also receive more than those who wait for others to notice their contributions, and men are more likely to promote themselves while women tend to have less of a sense of entitlement.[25]

Chapter 4

MAKING THE TEAM

Managers, Peers, and Subordinates

As we have seen, there was a large unexplained gender gap in pay on Wall Street in the late 1990s. Given that the bull market should have discouraged systematic inequality that was unrelated to productivity, what stalled progress toward gender equality? An important source of subtle discrimination involved relationships with managers and coworkers, which shaped the opportunity context for individuals' careers.[1] Anyone who has ever held a job knows that office politics always matter. Even when salaries are fixed, relationships with managers and coworkers influence the likelihood of receiving a promotion or being laid off. But Wall Street's performance review system heightened the direct impact of managers', coworkers', and subordinates' opinions by allowing them to affect annual pay. Personal likes, dislikes, and prejudices could influence the evaluations that are used to determine bonuses.

For associates and vice presidents in investment banking, managers' and coworkers' perceptions were especially critical since they did not usually originate their own deals. They worked on deals as part of a team, and their managers and coworkers evaluated how well they performed. When asked how the deals he had worked on had affected his bonus in investment banking, Neil said,

> It's really more of a focus on the review process here, in terms of what others say about you and basically it's

> just the review process [that] dictates how well you do. So it's really a little bit irrespective of the actual deal. It's the team and their perceptions and the client's perception of you and your performance.

If managers', coworkers', and clients' perceptions of performance contributed significantly to relative rankings, then good relationships with them could help at bonus time. These relationships particularly affected assessments of performance in investment banking, equity research, and support functions, and they could affect account allocations in all areas. Given the importance of manager and coworker relationships, discrimination by managers and coworkers could derail Wall Street careers. This affected men's careers as surely as women's, but women more often experienced this negatively. Gendered contradictions also arose more for women because Wall Street has a masculine culture that conflicts with cultural constructions of femininity.

Wall Street's Culture of Machismo

When people think of discrimination, they usually think of it as something deliberate. Wall Street has been associated with blatant discrimination, especially since the infamous boom-boom room suit against Smith Barney, and 32 percent of the women I interviewed experienced clear instances of discrimination. Blatant discrimination continued to flourish in the 1990s because Wall Street's informal culture involved a lot of machismo and some outright hostility toward women, especially in the most male-dominated areas. As previous research has found, organizational settings like the securities industry contain deeply rooted gender norms and ideologies.[2] These understandings of gender affected hiring decisions on Wall Street and the climate faced by women after they were hired. Illustrating this climate, Barbara described the environment in trading at her first firm as hostile and filled with bravado.

> People yelling, screaming, throwing things. "Fuck you." "No. Fuck you." People were just really different. Again,

> your experiences are exclusive to the group you worked in in each firm. Here, I would say, that if there's an off-color joke, people tend to tell it quietly. They know it's inappropriate. They sort of look around. Whereas at [my first firm], it wasn't like that at all. They would practically go over the top. It was massive. At [my first firm], we had strippers come to the floor. They would not be allowed to strip, but they hired women who would come in for people's birthdays and things. . . . When I was on the trading floor, someone did actually sort of sexually harass me. I was working on the equity floor. . . . I was sitting in a chair, and when I got up he bent down and smelled my chair. And then he made this joke about how he wanted to—I don't remember, but I remember hearing him say something really crude.

Brenda also started on the trading floor before she moved into equity research and then asset management. When asked if she fit in at her first job, she said, "[My first firm] was a harsh trading environment and it just wasn't pleasant. Did I fit in as they passed along the *Hustler* magazines down the aisle? No." Barbara's and Brenda's experiences were hardly isolated incidents, since a third of the women described a hostile work environment at some point in their careers on Wall Street. They were also more likely to encounter this if they worked in the highest-paying and most male-dominated areas of the industry. Both of these women changed firms and areas of the industry partly because of this discrimination.

The culture of machismo and fraternity-like environment is the stuff of Wall Street lore and bred lawsuits like the infamous boom-boom room case and Allison Schieffelin's complaint against Morgan Stanley. It also led to comprehensive sexual harassment policies and grievance procedures within Wall Street firms, as well as a variety of diversity initiatives in hiring, promotion, and retention. But despite the frequency of obvious discrimination against women, most inequality occurred without a conscious intention to discriminate and was subtle enough that it was difficult for firm policies to address. Subtle forms of discrimination, although they were less visible than their blatant counterparts, produced advantages for white men.[3]

Outsiders in Wall Street Firms

Many instances of discrimination, both blatant and subtle, occurred through relationships within Wall Street firms. Consider, for example, the case of Sabrina, the only African American I interviewed, who worked as a research analyst on Wall Street.

Sabrina had a bachelor's degree in accounting and had worked as an accountant before getting her MBA. Like many others, she pursued a Wall Street position in order to pay back her student loans. She landed a position as a research analyst in a major Wall Street firm that was actively seeking minority applicants. There she was one of two women in her ten-person group, and the only African American.[4] Sabrina's background in accounting gave her some skills that were useful for the job, but she did not have direct experience in the securities industry prior to completing her MBA. The firm that hired her provided no training and she had no support from her peers or the senior analyst who was assigned to be her mentor. Sabrina found herself rapidly falling behind the curve. When she expressed concerns to the head of her department, he told her that she would have to succeed somehow but offered no tangible support.

> I went to him with my concerns and he said, "That's not good. That's not good." That's all he said. . . . The only thing he told me was he wanted to see me do it. He didn't care how I did it. Just do it. Terrible to do that to someone, I think. He might as well not have given me the job instead of trying to make himself feel good and say, "Oh, we integrated the department." There's no way with my background in accounting that you could expect me to be in fixed-income research

> with primary coverage on industries when I have no training in that. I'm not saying that other people have not come into that industry without experience doing fixed-income research and made it work. Some have. Some way. I just think they weren't dealing with the pressures that I was. Maybe my personality wasn't set out for it. I don't know. I just know it could have been a lot less painful if I had been given some support.

In her account, the firm tried to meet equal employment opportunity demands at the point of hiring but had no apparatus for encouraging the success of nontraditional employees. Their affirmative action and diversity policies seemed to stop at the front door, at which point it was up to individual managers to help junior employees succeed. Some managers were committed to providing support to nontraditional junior employees; some women had powerful male mentors. But this was the exception rather than the rule, and these firms did not require this of senior workers. So workers like Sabrina were typically at a disadvantage in gaining support through relationships with managers and coworkers.

Sabrina was very unhappy on Wall Street and encountered some blatant discrimination from coworkers. She said,

> When you walk up on your secretary and she's telling "nigger nigger" jokes in your face, to your coworkers, how do you deal with that? What do you say? "I'm going to give up all of this money because my feelings are hurt." Because I know the secretaries always put my work at the bottom of the pile because they know I don't have any power here. . . . In the firm that I was at, it was against women as well. It was not friendly to women at all. Not friendly to minorities. Some firms have more of a reputation for being more friendly to women. This was not one of them.

After three years, she left to join a client firm on the buy side of finance. At the time, she was afraid that she would be laid off by her first firm because every other nonwhite in her firm had left or been fired. When she interviewed with the client firm, they contacted her manager and informed him that she was interviewing. Once he knew that she was looking for another position, she felt even more unwelcome than ever and decided that she had no choice but to take the job. Her second firm was a friendlier environment and more gender mixed, but offered lower pay than the investment bank where she initially worked. Sabrina was not ultimately successful or happy in her second position either and she was disappointed with her compensation. She verified with management that her bonus was at the very bottom of the range and at that point she left the industry. Her total compensation for 1997, before she left, was between $100,000 and $125,000, which was considerably lower than the average for Wall Street research analysts.[5]

After leaving finance, Sabrina entered a master's program in a technology-related field. She planned to work as a technology consultant to financial services firms in a capacity where her skills and expertise would be more important than relationships with and evaluations of peers. She believed that discriminatory stereotypes of her as a black woman had undermined her credibility and limited her success in the securities industry. When asked if she had experienced discrimination, she said,

> I don't want to believe that it's true. I really don't. But sometimes I think there are subtle things going on. I still don't want to believe that it was intentional but sometimes I just think that if your perception of someone is that they're not as smart or they are an exception, it can't help but color how you feel about them—especially if something is as subjective as research and investment opinions.

From her perspective, discrimination on Wall Street was subtle and insidious. It occurred because managers and peers scrutinized outsiders like her more highly and did not give her the benefit of the doubt. Because of Wall Street's bonus system, the lack of support from managers and coworkers translated directly into lower pay that Sabrina believed did not reflect true differences in merit. As a result, she decided to pursue a career with more objective criteria for evaluation, although it was unlikely that her new career would be as lucrative.

Sabrina's career history reveals the difficulties encountered by outsiders in this institutional environment. Wall Street firms were not especially diverse and Wall Street's culture was often inhospitable to nontraditional employees. Most men and women described their work groups as mostly or all male and as mostly or all white, especially if they worked in high-paying areas of the industry.[6] Two universal cognitive processes produced subtle forms of discrimination in relationships with managers, peers, and subordinates that Sabrina and others encountered: the tendency for people to prefer others who are like themselves and cultural beliefs that men are more competent than women, even when their actual performance is similar.[7] On Wall Street, these cognitive biases profoundly affected opportunities to perform, evaluations of performance, and pay. Their effects were also more visible to those who were at a disadvantage than for those they privileged, as is often the case with this type of favoritism.[8]

Birds of a Feather Flock Together

Managers, peers, and subordinates on Wall Street exhibited a common tendency to prefer to associate with others who were like themselves. Experimental research has found that individuals have "homophily" preferences, which means that they automatically and unconsciously prefer to associate with others who are similar to themselves.[9] Similarity or difference may be established in many ways, but traits like gender and race are immediately visible and often affect friendships, trust, and sponsorship of others.[10] In other words, people tend to feel more comfortable in same-sex and same-race friendships and to favor junior colleagues of the same gender and race.[11]

At least four men and women explicitly described this type of preference for similar others as "natural." Daphne, the Asian American research analyst whose career history was outlined in chapter 1, remarked,

> People pull from within their own. So you'll have a whole taxi company of Indians or Pakistanis or whatever it is. To the extent that I think that Wall Street is kind of an "old boys' network," you don't find too many men that want to pull in that many women. . . . I think that's the whole idea behind—if you want to say prejudice or anything. In general, people are more comfortable with someone who is like them. They understand how they think, so I think it does work into the way we interact with people. Just off the bat, I might have something more in common with an Asian American.

This "natural leaning" often improved white men's opportunities, pay, and career trajectories on Wall Street because white men dominated the business. It also contributed to higher rates of attrition, migration into lower-paying areas, and lower compensation for white women and nonwhites.

Given that most people favor others who are like themselves, workers who resembled their coworkers and managers had advantages. White men on Wall Street sometimes implied that similarity to others in their group had offered them advantages and made the work environment more fun. When asked about the social environment in his corporate finance job, Ken said,

> That's one of the reasons I joined the group. Great social environment. There's a fair amount of people from [my home state] in this group, so we have this kind of common bond and we go out a lot in this group. . . . There's a lot of camaraderie in this group. We'll go out probably once a quarter for a big dinner somewhere and get drunk and stuff. We have a golf year-end planning

> thing in the summer, which the whole group goes to. It's at Evan's Country Club. And year-end at Christmas time we have a big group party and planning conference, which is a big blowout. Every night there's a group dinner basically here, where somebody will order the dinner for the whole group and at that point it's just the analysts and associates pretty much and VPs that are here. So there's a lot of interaction and we all get along really well.

Similarities could be established on a variety of bases—Ken stated that many of his peers were from the same state—but gender and race similarity was usually at least implied, as it was in this case. When asked more explicitly about diversity in his group of thirty people, Ken said, "One woman. At most there's only one to three women max. We've had a couple of Canadians. Every now and then we have some Canadians and some Brits." So the camaraderie in Ken's group emerged in a context without much real diversity.

While it was implicit in Ken's account, the use of gender as a dividing line for similarity and difference was also sometimes explicit. Chris, the only man who worked in a female-dominated group in sales, said, "I fit in much better with the traders than with the salespeople. Maybe because most of the salespeople are women, and men hang out with men. I'm the only guy on my side of the desk. It's me and four women." Similarly, Stan said that he fit in with his group "because it is a bunch of men, a lot of whom have played sports. It's a bunch of guys that like to hang out and talk about that kind of stuff and do that kind of stuff." These two men were both highly successful, earning well above the average for their area and graduating class. In fact, the success of men with strong peer relationships highlights how preferences among men to associate with other men helped junior male workers on Wall Street form useful alliances with coworkers and managers. This enhanced their access to lucrative accounts and deals and to informal networks of information. It also improved their performance evaluations because of their managers' and coworkers' positive opinions of them.

By the same token, these preferences often led women on Wall Street to feel excluded from inner networks because of their dissimilarity with their peer group. About her former work group on Wall Street Rosalind said,

> As we all know, it's rarely an overt and obvious thing. It comes more in the form of the fact that I think it's human nature that people like to work with people like themselves. People that they like and get along with and are comfortable with. So sometimes that means that you have what some people might call "a boys' club." And we certainly had that . . . in the group I was part of.

For junior women in male-dominated areas, preferences for similar others made it more difficult to establish solid relationships with coworkers and managers. This, in turn, limited their mentorship opportunities and network ties, thus reducing their opportunities and affecting their evaluations.

Of course, the same preferences operated among women who worked primarily with same-sex peers. A few areas of Wall Street had female managers and were female dominated, and women who worked in these groups talked about the value of social support from other women. Tamara said,

> I'm very fortunate in my job. There are a lot of working mothers. My boss is a working mother. That's really important. Because without that support I don't know if I would be able to continue working. You're always in self-doubt, did you make the right choice? . . . In the whole firm there are a lot of women. And lunch time is usually . . . there's a back room and we all sit in the back room and we talk about the trials and tribulations of being a working mom. And we laugh. You really need to laugh it off. You compare stories. "Is your

> kid doing this?" "Did your kid tell you he hated you today?" Because you've got to laugh it off.

But while her managers and coworkers were similar to her and provided her with social support, Tamara worked for a small regional public finance firm with very low relative compensation. In fact, women were most likely to find themselves among other women in lower-paying niches within the securities industry.

Danielle had also worked with many other women in similar family situations before she moved into a small investment firm. After she left her Wall Street firm, she missed the support that she had received from other women in the workplace.

> It felt like a lot to give up. A lot of it was the social side of work. I guess what I was going to would be intellectually still as satisfying but I was going to an environment that was so different. And it was painted by my experience. . . . You [don't have other working mothers around who are valuable] resources to call upon.

For Danielle and Tamara, preferences among women to associate with other women, especially when they shared similar family-related concerns, made them feel at ease and socially supported when they were at work. Their experiences were similar to men's experiences in male-dominated groups. But this offered men more advantages than women because most areas were male dominated. Also, women's advantages in female-dominated work groups took the form of social support but not higher pay, since the groups with more women paid less. So preferences to work with similar others offered women support in areas where they would earn less.

Informal support networks had another side as well because they set boundaries around network insiders that dissimilar peers found hard to penetrate. Workers who were in the minority became isolated through the same process that offered comfort and support to those in the majority. Sabrina, the African American research analyst, experienced acute isolation in an all-white and male-dominated environment on Wall Street.

> It's like when you get to the point where when you see another brown face, it's like, "Hi! What are you doing here?!! How did you get in?" It's that kind of feeling because you're so isolated from everyone until you leave and go home. You never really do that in a meeting but it's kind of like you walk into a room and there's twenty males or maybe eighteen and two women. . . . It happens fifty times and on the fifty-first time there's someone else in there that looks like you and you go to the bathroom and it's "God, how are you? Who are you? How long have you been doing this?" If I was sitting on the other side of the table and all I ever saw was people who looked like me and talked like me in my work, all the time, and always had been bombarded with negative images of someone that was not like me and then all of a sudden someone is there, I'm sure I'd probably react in the same way. Always weighing what that person said or judging it to see, "Can I trust this person?" And I think whereas someone else might be allowed to make a mistake or mistakes, when you're one of the Other, I don't think you're given that time or leeway or room.

Like Sabrina, who felt isolated because of her gender and especially her race, 23 percent of the women described being isolated or excluded in male-dominated work groups. They observed that their male managers' preferences for junior workers who resembled them led them to hire, mentor, and assign the most advantageous job opportunities to younger men. Melissa, who worked in public finance, said,

> I don't know that women have been given equal opportunities to get to the positions that males have in the last ten years or so. . . . I mean, my boss is someone

> I could go hang out with just fine, and he can go hang out with guys just fine. But the boss above him—I get the sense that he would much rather hang out with the guys than with women. And a lot of these men have wives who stay home and don't have careers. It's just what they're used to.

She believed that her opportunities were limited by senior managers' preferences for those who resembled them, even in public finance where there were more women than in other areas.

Such preferences could contribute directly, if unconsciously, to decisions about bonus allocations. In fact, some workers believed that being liked by senior managers was more important for junior employees than working on important deals. Grant, who left corporate finance to work for a former client's start-up company, remarked that having a powerful mentor had more impact on one's bonus than actual job performance.

> I think it was other factors that go into the bonus calculation, that have nothing to do, in my judgment, with which deals you worked on. Even the level of talent wasn't necessarily an indicator of the bonus. What you tended to see happen was the person who would dole out the bonuses within the group would develop favorites and that might be someone who worked with that person for five or six years and sort of had that mentor/mentee relationship that was unbroken. . . . If you were their sidekick for years and years, they would fight to get you the top of the range throughout your entire career. And you saw all the time, people who were great analysts and say they were [at the] top of their analyst class. They were very highly skilled and they'd stick with the person they worked for then, and they were an average associate, and let's say they were a lousy vice president. They were paid the top of the range the whole way, even though they were getting progressively lousier.

In this account, bonuses had much less to do with merit than they did with manager preferences. These preferences could produce systematic gender differences in pay that were not related to performance because most managers, especially in the highest-paying areas, were men. Their affinities for those who resembled them could easily put women at a disadvantage in account allocations, performance evaluations, and relative compensation.

One way that managers' preferences for junior employees who resembled them disadvantaged women was by reducing their access to accounts and deals. At least 24 percent of the women and 9 percent of the men said that their managers' preferences for coworkers who resembled them had limited their access to accounts and deals. For example, Amanda started in corporate finance, but her firm had a limited flow of deals in her specialized area. She found the pay to be disappointing relative to her expectations and to the very long hours that she had to work. She also believed that she was paid less than her male peers, because her managers assigned women to detail-oriented work for prospective clients while the men were assigned to work on the group's small number of live deals. Amanda described her expectations for pay in corporate finance.

> I did expect the pay to be fairly good but I realized it wasn't as good as [that of] some of my peers. . . . I think in some respects it was because I wasn't working on deals, because there were so few deals and the deals that they had were given to the guys. . . . Maybe because they did more politicking than myself. That was the primary reason. And it was run by guys and guys like to work with guys.

Her initial perception was that success in the job required hard work, long hours, and quantitative skills. But alliances with more senior employees offered men in her group better access to clients and accounts for reasons unrelated to effort or ability to execute transactions. This led her to transfer into equity research, where there were more women, and then to move to a buy-side firm where her earnings were lower. At the time of the interview,

Amanda earned between $150,000 and $175,000, which was substantially less than the $430,000 average for her peers who stayed in corporate finance.[12]

Favoritism among managers also maintained inequality through selective mentorship. Sixteen percent of women and one man felt that their access to mentors had been limited because they differed from their managers in their gender and/or race. This put them at a disadvantage vis-à-vis others with more support, since thirty-five of the more successful Wall Street workers (43 percent of the women and 50 percent of the men) pointed to mentors as instrumental to their success. While women were not significantly less likely to have a mentor, they were significantly more likely to need one because they had less access to coworker networks. Especially in cases where workers were in the minority within their work group, the inability to find a mentor could produce a disadvantage in competition for resources and access to deals. Jessica described mentorship and peer network processes in M&A at her first firm.

> Sunday night was basketball night where everybody in the department goes and plays basketball. I don't play basketball. (Laughter.) So there was a big social network there that revolved around men's sports and men's activities, and to be on the outside of that really impacted my ability to develop relationships with people. And at the end of the day, if you don't have people who are looking out for you, you don't have a strong relationship with them, it doesn't work. And there were a lot of instances where some of the senior guys would take some of the junior guys under their wing. How did they do that? "Well, I'm moving on Saturday, come help me move my furniture." Well, nobody was ever going to call me and say, "Move my furniture." I have better things to do with my Saturday. But just by definition of what the activities were, I was not a part of it.

While Jessica was highly successful in corporate finance, she had a hard time breaking into the social networks in her first Wall Street job. Luckily she moved into a somewhat more hospitable corporate finance environment, although even there her manager had a bad reputation for gender discrimination (which she said he deserved). While this had not derailed her at the time of the interview, she was contemplating a career change. And the types of difficulties breaking into intrafirm social networks that Jessica described did derail the careers of eight other women (18 percent).

Of course, many women did have mentors. When asked if they had a mentor, 70 percent of women said that they did, and 65 percent of their mentors were men.[13] In fact, some senior men on Wall Street seemed to be highly committed to encouraging women to succeed. Emma described her mentor in corporate finance as someone who took a lot of time teaching her what was important in her job, but also as someone who made an effort and took an interest in working with women.

> He's really into this working with a woman thing. So he's very funny. All the Deborah Tannen, Mars/Venus stuff. Like I pose something and [a man thinks he's] supposed to solve it—he's very aware of that stuff. He's really into it. So it is kind of funny because we have these conversations where I'll be, "I was just alerting you to an issue. I don't want you to solve it. I just wanted you to be aware of it. It doesn't have to be a big conversation." So it's interesting because he's very aware of those types of things.

Emma's mentor, whom she found in her second firm after leaving a hostile environment in her first job, was very supportive of her career and helped her gain access to the most important deals in her group.

Most mentoring relationships, like Emma's, were informal; senior workers took on the responsibility of grooming junior ones without being prompted by firm policies or senior management. Sometimes Wall Street firms did assign mentors to junior workers but without making them accountable for helping their protégés succeed. For example, when asked if she had a mentor, Sabrina, the African American woman who worked in equity research, said,

> They gave me someone who they said would serve in that role but he had no vested interest in seeing me succeed and basically did nothing to help me. He wanted to use me as his assistant to help him and so I quickly fell behind the curve that they thought I should be on. But they told me there wouldn't be any training so it was kind of like, "We let you in here but we're not going to do anything to help you. No one gets help." That's their thing. But it's not true . . . but it's not official help. It's if you're lucky enough to have someone befriend you, you'll have a career on Wall Street. . . . White males helped white males. White females helped white females. You'll even have a white male helping a white female but then there was that . . . what I call the FQ: "Fuckability Quotient." The more fuckable you are in their eyes, the more they will help you.

Sabrina believed that dissimilarity with others in the group had prevented her from obtaining real support from a mentor—either from the one the firm assigned to her or from someone else in her group. Given her nonfinance background, this could have provided her with important support that would have helped her succeed. But many Wall Street workers remarked that the most effective mentoring relationships arose informally due to affinities between junior and senior employees. In these relationships, senior professionals tended to take similar others under their wing, leaving people like Sabrina to sink or swim on their own.

In addition to assistance from mentors, informal networks of coworkers were also helpful resources for those who were similar to their peers. These networks provided good sources of informal information and strategies for success. But exclusion from these workplace networks was common among women in corporate finance and sales and trading, where their peers were predominantly male. Tracy, the trader we met in chapter 1, was among the 41 percent of women who felt excluded in her job.

> Me and this other woman were total outcasts. . . . There were, on our immediate desk . . . six of us. The rest of the group would play golf every weekend. They'd go out to dinners and whatnot. We were never invited once. It was pathetic. To tell you the truth, because of that we had absolutely no desire to do anything social with them, but they were like a boys' club and we were just the two chicks who didn't fit in. It wasn't fun. They certainly didn't sit and talk to us on the desk and they ignored us at work, but socially they completely ignored us. And it was obviously a little harder to fit in when somebody spends the whole weekend with the other three of them, playing golf and going on vacations together. Going to strip clubs together and stuff like that. It's kind of hard to fit in.

In this case, men in the group engaged in male-bonding activities and excluded their female colleagues. By doing so, they built valuable relationships with each other that improved their satisfaction at work and their informal network resources. They also successfully excluded women, thus maintaining more such resources within their own clique.[14]

The tendency of managers and peers to offer resources to similar others assisted many white men and reduced the success of women on Wall Street. Social psychologists have found that the tendency to prefer similar people occurs in all settings—a tendency that can produce gender inequality in male-dominated jobs. This had two consequences for women on Wall Street. First, over time women increasingly left the highest-paying and most male-dominated jobs for lower-paying destinations because of their exclusion from mentoring and coworker relationships. This contributed to increasing sex segregation over time as exclusion from inner networks and lack of access to accounts and deals pushed 43 percent of the women out of male-dominated areas. Because the highest-paying areas also tended to be the most male dominated, this contributed to gender inequality in pay. Second, workers who were able to mobilize support from their peers and managers, who were mostly white men, received more favorable evaluations and this translated directly into higher bonuses.

Of course, preferences to work with similar others cannot explain all barriers to success for women on Wall Street. The few men in mixed-sex or female-dominated work groups still received pay advantages over women. This is unsurprising given that research on male tokens in female professions has found that men rise further and faster than their female colleagues despite being in the minority.[15] In fact, men seem to receive advantages in pay and promotion regardless of the gender composition of their groups because they are men. This can be partly attributed to unconscious cultural assumptions that men are more competent and work committed than women.

A Woman Has to Be Twice as Good as a Man

Another important source of subtle discrimination was a tendency to view men on Wall Street as more competent than women and to hold women to higher standards. This tendency is common in contemporary Western culture, where men are awarded higher social status than women. In experimental research, social psychologists have consistently found that men are viewed as more competent, are given more opportunities to demonstrate their competence, and are given the benefit of the doubt more often than are women.[16] This is especially true when the task being performed is a stereotypically male one, as was the case with all Wall Street jobs. Performance and evaluation bias are expected under these circumstances, but research has shown that women are viewed as less competent even for female-typed or neutral tasks. Race has produced similar findings with respect to whites. These findings are largely attributed to cultural hierarchies in which men are granted higher status than women. In simple terms, people tend to evaluate women's performance more harshly than men's, even when it is equal or superior.[17] Remember that Ginger Rogers did everything

Fred Astaire did, backward and in high heels, for less credit and half the pay.

A gender bias in assessments of performance was apparent on Wall Street. Seventy-three percent of the women believed that their opportunities to perform were limited by assumptions that women are not competent in securities jobs. Because Wall Street is traditionally a male domain, managers, coworkers, and clients often assumed that men had natural abilities in finance. In contrast, 23 percent of the women felt that their managers and coworkers assumed that they were incompetent. The industry culture's emphasis on displays of masculinity as an indicator of competence heightened this problem. Maureen described performance expectations and evaluations for women in corporate finance.

> First of all, clients always assume that I'm a junior person on the team. Always. Even clients who know me, if there's a new analyst,[18] a male analyst, they will assume he is senior to me. Always. People here automatically assume that women are dumb. Dumber than men [and] not as insightful, which is very often not true. Very often. I see it all the time and a lot of it comes from the behavior. Junior men will jump in and make a point, even though they're absolutely wrong. I see it all the time. They are so 100 percent wrong and one will sit there and—I did it this morning—watch a junior person go through all this stuff and finally, rather than tell him, "You're absolutely wrong. You don't know how to do arithmetic. You don't understand a basic model," which is the real issue, I said, "Why don't you walk me through the math." And the associate starts to explain it to me and I know what he's trying to do and I said, "Walk me through your arithmetic." And the second number he said was an absolutely wrong number. He couldn't explain it but approached it very differently. And I think women are discounted very heavily because

> of that. . . . I think the work women do is far superior in terms of the attention to detail and level of concern that it be right. I find that an absolutely 100 percent true corollary in the junior women, and men are very sloppy and make mistakes all the time. [They also don't think] through stuff a lot of times. They just sort of jump.

She believed that men in her work environment consistently had lower expectations of women and evaluated them as less competent. But while she viewed women's performance as generally superior in quality and accuracy, she found that women constantly needed to prove themselves because of double standards and the valorization of masculinity in this industry.

Assumptions that women were less competent meant that women had to actively demonstrate superior competence. Thirty-four percent of the women specifically pointed to double standards or undue harshness in evaluations in comparison to their male peers. Karen, whose firm had asked her to move from M&A into a much lower-paying administrative position, noted that men in investment banking provided each other with valuable assistance and informal mentoring, while women were held to higher standards for competence.

> When was the last time I got a stock tip? I've never gotten a stock tip from a guy. But they are always giving each other stock tips. It's that kind of thing. It's just the hanging out in somebody's office and bullshitting with them and getting invited to play golf with them. . . . Around here, at least, if you're liked, you don't have to be a star performer to get ahead as a guy, whereas women, I think that category doesn't exist. It doesn't matter whether they like you or not, they base it more on your performance. But for guys, it can be a very mediocre white male, but because he's liked and he's congenial, he gets through the ranks. And it just

> doesn't happen for women at all. You really have to prove yourself. There are so many examples of that here. It makes my stomach turn sometimes.

Karen believed that men gave other men the benefit of the doubt, holding them to lower standards for performance and giving them advantages in their performance reviews. She also believed that her lack of success in M&A was at least partly a consequence of additional scrutiny of her as a woman.

Further illustrating the additional pressures caused by gender stereotypes, Emma described how her manager and peers had tested her because they assumed that she was quantitatively inept.

> When I started work, the person who ended up being my mentor came to me and said, "Can you amortize a loan?" Which is the most insulting question in my business. Can I amortize a loan? I should have been able to amortize a loan when I came out of high school. So he did this little test. I went and I amortized my little loan for him and everything and then he was fine. I thought that was insulting that they would have done that. I was once at a dinner when we were all in our training program and I was talking to someone and it was so insulting because this guy was in corporate finance so he was going to be some general relationship manager and I said, "I'm in asset backs." And he said to me, "Oh, are you comfortable with numbers?" My friend who was with me from the [university where I did my MBA] was like, "What a jerk!" I graduated from the most—I wanted to go to [that MBA program] because it was all finance. I graduated at the top of my class at this place. I get a job at the most quantitative product on Wall Street and this jerk in corporate finance asks, "Are you comfortable with numbers?"

Because she worked in a quantitative job and women are supposedly not good at math, she was tested in multiple ways and was assumed to be incompetent until she proved otherwise. As a result, she faced performance pressures that a man would not. For example, even though she later found the support of a powerful mentor, she left her first firm because of a work environment that was blatantly hostile to women.

Gender stereotyping produced subtle discrimination in bonus allocations because assumptions about differences in competence biased evaluations of performance, permitting nonmerit criteria to enter into bonus allocation decisions. In other words, the bonus system allowed subtle structural discrimination to occur because stereotyped assumptions unconsciously influenced evaluations by managers, peers, and subordinates. Thirty-two percent of the women and one man described discrimination in performance evaluations. For example, Karen said that she was harshly evaluated and not given credit for her performance in her previous job in mergers and acquisitions.

> I just feel I wasn't getting credit in the review process. I wasn't getting credit for such things as really good client relationships, whereas guys who were kind of inept on client relationships would get rewarded more. And I think part of it was that the men just thought, "Oh she's really cute. Of course the clients like her." Versus the fact that I gave the clients what they wanted. I was very service oriented and performed well. I never was given credit for really strong client relationships and they turned it—they always accused me of more the social aspects of it rather than the fact that if I had been a guy it would have been that I was good at my relationships.

She believed that her managers and peers had failed to credit her for her strengths because of their stereotypes of her as a young woman, and that these stereotypes had limited her success and reduced her pay. She believed that she would have received more credit for the same performance if she had been a man.

Stereotypes about competence and appropriate roles in the hierarchy also affected the way subordinates viewed more senior women on Wall Street, so that women who had proven themselves and attained positions of power were often especially negatively regarded. These women faced expectations that they would behave in appropriately feminine ways, even though cultural constructions of femininity clashed with definitions of managerial competence in Wall Street's male-dominated culture. As other research has found, people have a difficult time accepting aggressive and dominant behavior from women, like speaking with a stern facial expression, making a lot of eye contact while speaking, or making verbal or nonverbal threats.[19] At the same time, women on Wall Street had to exhibit these types of "masculine" personality traits and contradict expectations of femininity to prove their competence within Wall Street's culture of machismo. This created a double standard for their actions, made it difficult for them to wield authority in the workplace, and led to more negative evaluations of women in high positions. Three men and four women made derogatory remarks about senior women on Wall Street. Dave said,

> A lot of the senior women tend to have, the few that we have, many of them tend, on average, to have harsher personalities than the men that are senior. Now granted, there's a lot more men. But there's some trend [that] in order to make it as a woman you have to be a little harsher to get ahead.

While the women who made it to senior levels developed reputations as "psycho bitches" and "bitter career babes," impressions of them may also have been colored by the fact that they were in positions that men were supposed to hold. They also probably had to work even harder than men to obtain those senior positions in the first place.

Women who had to manage subordinates encountered double standards for their behavior firsthand. They faced assumptions that they should be feminine and nice, on one hand, and that competent managers exhibited supposedly masculine characteristics of firmness and authority, on the other. Fourteen percent of the women had difficulties managing subordinates because of these contradictions. Karen remarked,

> A great example—and this has happened to me many times—I'll talk firmly to an analyst and say, "I need these numbers by this time. And you better proof it. And I want it right and formatted." That will come back to me that I was being a "bitch." I'll get a call from the staffer that says, "You can't talk like that." Whereas a guy, my officemate, would say to some guy—same guy—"You know, you're such an asshole. How can you be so stupid? Don't you know this is how you do this? And don't come back into my office until it's right." And that doesn't warrant a phone call. It's a guy talking to a guy versus a woman talking to a guy. And that happened time and time again. Jean sat right next to Paul, and Paul is notorious for screaming and yelling at people in front of other people. Not behind closed doors. And he's infamous because he threw a stapler at an analyst or associate one time. At a woman. So he is famous for these sorts of things, but he's not viewed in the same way as Jean was viewed. Jean was viewed as a "bitch" whereas Paul was viewed just as really tough. And [there was] almost breed loyalty. Paul, you wanted to do well for him, whereas Jean you almost wanted to screw her or something because she was a bitch. And they sat right next to each other. You knew that they competed day to day to move up the ladder for resources and good deals and stuff.

As Karen's quote illustrates, women were perceived very differently as managers than were their male peers, even when their behavior was similar. In fact, as in this example, men could get away with far more outrageous behavior without losing loyalty and support from their subordinates. Also, as Karen noted, differences in perceptions that are based on gender stereotypes influenced access to resources and opportunities in the industry.

As a result, women in managerial roles on Wall Street faced clear double standards for their behavior. Sometimes they worked hard to avoid being pushovers, and then received negative evaluations from their subordinates that they believed would not have been given to their male peers. Emma was very surprised when her evaluations suggested that she needed to be nicer when managing subordinates.

> The review comments that I had that were negative are that I'm perceived as being pretty demanding and I come off as being somewhat tough, and I thought that was so ironic. My biggest thing in my review was that I should be softer, which I thought was a riot, coming from this perspective that you're a woman. Here I am always afraid that I'm going to be the one that's the pushover and I'm going to be the one that comes off as too nice and too soft and everything, whereas the perception is that, if anything, that people want more handholding and more of that. . . . That was the thing that killed me. I'm like, "Oh my gosh! Be softer!" Of all the things I would have thought they would say, that would probably have been the last thing. But I think that—if you're a man that's the way you should be, but [as a woman] you're supposed to be nicer.

While Emma encountered the message that she should be more feminine and nice, other women who were nice found that their subordinates did not respect their authority or take them seriously. When asked about her managerial style when she first started managing analysts, Renee said,

> I think that I saw them as my equals. In this business, that is a bit of a mistake when you are junior because then they lack respect. If they even sense a little bit of hesitancy or weakness, if you don't have that underlying confidence, you are dead meat. So that backfired on

> me. I just didn't feel confident being cocky, because I didn't really have the confidence that I knew what I was doing. My style now is very different.

In other words, when women were softer and more considerate, as might be appropriately "feminine," they were viewed as ineffective managers. This meant that women who managed subordinates had to walk a tightrope between being too harsh and being too much of a pushover. Subordinates also sometimes defied their authority. Allison said,

> I remember when I started working with analysts, I had this guy who had been a Marine in Desert Storm and then came back to be an analyst, so he was my age. He had a huge chip on his shoulder. He was there for just two years to make time, before you could go to business school. I had the worst time with this guy because he was basically an asshole to me.

It is important to remember that, in addition to making their lives more difficult and negatively affecting their ability to perform, problems with subordinates could directly affect workers' bonuses because subordinates filled out performance evaluations. Meanwhile, no men described contradictions between expectations of them as managers and cultural expectations of them as men. This was one of the ways that women found themselves subject to different standards in a male-dominated industry that subtly reinforced structural discrimination.

Conclusion

In sum, women on Wall Street faced subtle discrimination in relationships within their work groups. Since most work groups, especially in areas that paid the most, were dominated by men, women stood out from their peers. This led to their exclusion from mentoring relationships and peer networks in the highest-paying areas of Wall Street, unless their managers were especially conscientious about promoting and encouraging them. But in most cases, subtle gender discrimination on Wall Street occurred because men in the highest-paying areas of the industry offered assistance and resources to other men, and because of cultural assumptions that men are more competent. While preferences for similar others and a cognitive bias in favor of higher-status groups may be universal, they have egregious effects in a male-dominated context like Wall Street. This subtle discrimination was further aggravated by a culture of machismo in which women faced contradictory expectations of them as feminine, because they were women, and as masculine, because of their position. These contradictions were especially pronounced when women had authority over men. The mechanisms of subtle discrimination did not impose a "glass ceiling" in the sense that no women were able to succeed, implying that a single success story would shatter the barrier. Rather they made women's climb up the ladder of success more arduous at every step of the way. In fact, these mechanisms probably further thinned out the numbers of successful women as they moved up the ranks and encountered less favorable business cycles at the turn of the millennium.

Pay structures on Wall Street also seem to have amplified the effects of subtle forms of discrimination on pay inequality because subjective evaluations of performance affected bonuses. While Wall Street trumpeted its pay system as a meritocracy, unconscious preferences for similar others and cultural beliefs that men are more competent meant that the bonus system produced larger-than-average gender differences in pay and put women at a greater disadvantage than they would have been if fixed pay scales had been used. These processes were largely unconscious, but they affected the opportunity context of Wall Street, expanding white men's opportunities while limiting those of most women. These subtle cognitive mechanisms structure career paths in modern workplaces, reinforcing and reproducing gender inequality without being recognized by those who benefit from them. It is important to note that these same mechanisms also influenced relationships with clients. The next chapter explores how the client nature of the business and presumed client preferences subtly influenced gender inequality in pay.

Chapter 5

BRINGING CLIENTS BACK IN

The Impact of Client Relationships

The last chapter suggested that managers' and coworkers' preferences—for others like themselves and more generally for men—often reduced women's opportunities to perform, influenced evaluations of women's performance, and reduced women's pay in ways that were unrelated to performance. But what about clients? Did clients share these preferences? And how did client relationships affect the jobs held by women, their opportunities, and their pay? In this chapter, I look at how Wall Street workers perceived client relationships, and how these perceptions sifted men and women into different areas and influenced their opportunities and pay. Managers also acted on assumptions about client preferences in ways that reinforced gender inequality on Wall Street. Given the client orientation of Wall Street firms, acting on presumed client preferences made rational business sense even if it was unrelated to financial skill or qualifications. But this also reinforced gender inequality on Wall Street.

Client Relationships

Some areas, like administrative support and proprietary trading, had no external clients. Others, like equity research, served both internal and external clients.[1] But contact with external clients in research was usually driven by investment bankers or salespeople, and equity analysts were less responsible for wining and dining clients. On the other hand, investment banking, sales, and trading involved direct and intensive client relationships. In these areas, being liked by clients affected performance, evaluations, and bonuses.[2] As with managers and coworkers, an important aspect of client relationships involved social compatibility and network ties. Dave remarked that there were several ways to obtain clients, and most of them involved being an insider in a client's network.

> There's a couple of ways to get clients. The easiest way is some senior guy basically dies and transitions his client to you. Not necessarily dies, essentially he leaves the firm. The client feels that it fit in with the firm, and perhaps there's a transition period where you kind of step up and you take over the client. . . . You inherit the client. That's the easiest way. The second way to do it is to work on a transaction with a client and over time they develop an affinity for you because they kind of like you working on their projects. And that can happen at a junior level, too. Then when you switch firms you can call on them as a more senior person, and maybe trade off the fact that you don't work at this firm anymore but that they liked you. You also can . . . work on an account, and then the guy you know leaves and goes to work for another company. You can then market to him and you can have that company as a client. I guess another way you can do it is, sometimes you have friends who are in the industry . . . who work at GM, and Xerox, and IBM and wherever. If you are a banker then you can call on your buddies who may have moved up the ranks and, if you're some senior guy, then they're some senior guy. Call them up and say, "Hey!" Whatever. Those are some of the ways. I guess the only other way you can get clients is to be an expert in

> something, whether it be a product or an industry. Sort of start selling yourself as an expert.

All of the methods for obtaining clients that Dave mentioned, with the possible exception of the last, involved network ties. He implied that clients and prospective clients have connections with and affinities for particular Wall Street workers. Even at the junior level, strong client relationships could increase access to accounts and lead to better performance evaluations. The strength of these network ties could be a consequence of skill or ability, but not necessarily. But Wall Street firms naturally rewarded strong client relationships because they increased repeat business and referrals. This reduced the amount of time and effort that these firms had to expend on direct marketing and allowed them to sell their services at full price.[3]

As associates and vice presidents, investment bankers were rarely expected to originate client business themselves. They primarily worked on deals with the clients of senior bankers in their work groups, focusing on execution. As Grant noted, this was something that changed after the first five to seven years in the business.

> One of the big frustrations of being a banker at a firm like that is you grow up executing deals because it's an apprenticeship, essentially. At a certain point they expect you to go and pitch business and bring in business as opposed to executing. But at the same time they really don't have training programs designed to help you make that transition. And bringing in business is really salesmanship. It's selling. You're just selling financial products. Executing business is different. It's being smart about financing. What should the balance sheet look like? Being very good with numbers. And client skills because you want to keep the client happy throughout the process.

As Grant noted, junior workers were not generally responsible for bringing in business, but client relationships still affected their assignment to accounts and deals, as well as their long-term trajectories. These workers were beginning to build the relationships with clients that would lead to successful deal origination later on (assuming that they were able to successfully make this transition).

So strong client relationships were very important, but women were less able to develop these relationships because of the preferences for similar others that were discussed in the last chapter.[4] Communication is easier and similar interests are more common among people who are socially similar, making trust easier to establish. Trust is very important to clients that use Wall Street firms to oversee large transactions because of the high stakes involved. As a result, clients preferred bankers, salespeople, and traders who resembled their own management—when they had a choice. In a sense, this was performance related because Wall Street is a client-oriented business and relationships with clients are a critical part of performance. Having poor client relationships or being a difficult person for clients to deal with would certainly have a negative impact on evaluations. But even agreeable Wall Street workers who did not resemble their client base were at a disadvantage vis-à-vis similarly or even less-skilled workers who looked more like their clients. Women who specialized in male-dominated industries claimed that strong relationships with clients were hard to establish, especially compared to their male peers. On the other hand, in some sectors, growing numbers of client organizations were run by women or had commitments to diversity.[5] Women had advantages with these clients but they represented less lucrative accounts, so that these so-called advantages reinforced inequality in the industry as a whole.

Client–Service Provider Similarity

As with managers and coworkers, clients seemed to prefer Wall Street workers who were similar to them. This increased the ability of workers who resembled their clients to relate to them. Jorge, who worked in Latin American emerging markets, discussed the advantages of interpersonal similarities in client relationships.

> One of the clients said, "Let's hold the Venezuelan to discuss the issue." And he explicitly wanted a Venezuelan. I don't think a Mexican would work or a Peruvian would work in that discussion. It was this very specific thing which would make everybody be more comfortable and talk in the same wavelength and it could happen. . . . That's an advantage because that makes the work flow, and the decisions and everything work a lot smoother, quicker. . . . The way you talk, the way you mention things, the subtleness, makes you a lot quicker and efficient.

In his view, similarity improved his communication with his clients and increased the efficiency of transactions. He viewed this as an advantage in his area of emerging markets.

These same processes could hinder the client relationships of workers who were very different from their clients. Danielle commented on her disadvantage in corporate finance.

> At the end I did a lot of work with oil and gas clients and I definitely felt like a freak when I was with them. The New York woman, Jewish, is not . . . they were going hunting for their outings. Actually, when I was seven or eight months pregnant, I was so happy because I had two hunting trips that I was invited to and I was able to say, "I can't go hunting, I'm eight months pregnant." So the client base reflected the bankers, to a large extent.

Danielle specialized in a financial product rather than an industry so that relationships were less important than expertise, but she still found it hard to find common ground with some of her clients. This common ground was very important for the development of long-term relationships that were essential in the most lucrative investment banking areas, especially as workers became more senior.

Clients with primarily white male management, like large automotive, transportation, natural resource, or industrial companies, seemed to prefer white male bankers. Women often moved out of jobs serving these types of clients because they believed that it was harder for them to develop solid client relationships than it was for their male peers. Allison described the client relationships in her first corporate finance group, which served industrial Fortune 500 companies.

> My clients knew that I did good work for them and stuff, but you knew that—and this happens even though you're thirty years old—they think of you as their daughter. Their attitude is kind of like, "Isn't she cute? She's the hard-working associate." It just used to be so hard to get across, "I am the account officer." It was the client. It was all of these copper-mining companies, companies that make bottles and things, where . . . the client base was very middle-aged, white, and male. No one ever treated me poorly or anything like that, but I think that over time they'd rather hang out with their banker who is a guy. . . . I think that I'm at least as capable as most of the guys in my group, but it's just more natural, and in the end this business is not how smart you are, or anything like that, it's relationships. I just think that you're never going to have a relationship with Chrysler as a woman—and there are exceptions—I used to fight the tide, but I don't want to do it anymore.

As a vice president, she had reached a point where client relationships were increasingly important. Disadvantages compared to men in her position led her to move into a more diverse group. But she admitted that her long-term earnings would be lower.

> I think that I'm in an area now that is more . . . I think it's an area that's better for women. It's a very gender- and ethnically diverse part of the business. But I will tell you, I think that over time, I will earn less. It's a less sexy part of the business, quite frankly. I think that over

> time my earnings trajectory will not be what it would have been in the other group.

Women often had difficulty establishing solid client relationships in the highest-paying areas of corporate finance or sales and trading, and this contributed to their migration into lower-paying areas.

Of course, a few women who worked in client-intensive and male-dominated areas managed to earn average or better pay in spite of having greater difficulty establishing rapport with clients. Often they worked hard to find or develop common interests outside of business to strengthen their relationships. Maureen, whose $425,000 compensation was average for her graduating class in corporate finance, talked about the importance of having some topic with which to bond with clients.

> Everyone has their topic that they bond with clients on. Most people it's sports. Some people, it's golf. Some it's fishing. Fly fishing is actually a big one for some. Professional sports is a big one, so it's either football, hockey, or baseball. Kids is a huge one! People always talk about their kids. . . . I have none of those. I travel and—it's interesting—it's the thing I have that I can actually talk about. Because inevitably people will find out that I travel or somehow we have a conversation and other people travel also so that's actually the topic of conversation I can socialize with clients with.

The majority of client-bonding topics that Maureen and others in corporate finance mentioned involved stereotypically masculine interests.[6] Maureen rejected these options and forged her own path, although she was dissatisfied with her pay and felt that there was discrimination against women by coworkers and clients. Other women deliberately took up stereotypically masculine interests instead in an effort to enhance their client relationships.

Golf was the most common pursuit that women learned in order to cement their client relationships. Of course, technically, golf should have been unrelated to performance or merit in the securities industry, but it was an important bonding activity for many bankers and their clients. Six women described learning to play golf so that they would be better able to relate to clients and, to some extent, coworkers. Caroline, a very successful investment banker, said,

> I finally decided that I had to learn to do it if I ever want to attend closing weekends. I fought it for a long time because I thought it was a very boring sport, and I would much rather be on a sailboat any day than be on the golf course. But there is no question that golf happens to be a very centering thing, or rallying thing, for people in this industry. It's very easy to schedule a golf outing. It's not so easy to schedule, say, a sailing outing. So from a practical perspective, if you want to be a part of those events, you need to take it up.

Three women also described other women they knew who had learned to play golf for that purpose, and five lamented that they had not been willing to learn to play golf even though it might have helped their careers. Larissa, an Asian American woman who worked in sales, said, "I don't play golf so I think I'm left out when they play golf, but I have to learn to play."

While some women believed that taking up this type of sport would help their careers, they also sometimes observed that efforts to adopt stereotypically male pursuits were not necessarily effective. Allison described this in relation to knowledge about sports.

> I think it's just harder. You're at an added disadvantage in getting the whole relationship going like some of the men can much more easily. You know, it's frustrating sometimes because I'm not an idiot about sports. But a lot of them know that you're just as smart as the guy associates and they trust you, but if you said, "Who do you want to sit next to on a plane going from New York to L.A.?" Even if they have a great time talking to you, in the end, they're just more comfortable with the guy.

Like Allison, many women were at a disadvantage even if they tried to take up interests like golf. Of course, this disadvantage was independent of their actual financial skills, although clearly it affected their opportunities, perceptions of their performance, and their pay.

Sometimes women who recognized that client relationships could derail them developed strategies to avoid areas that worked with clients that were inhospitable to women. Elise started out specializing in oil and gas companies but did not perceive high long-term potential there because of the client base.

> I think I worked hard to fit in and I think I did fit in but it didn't come naturally. It is oil and gas. Need I say more? I don't work there anymore. I don't go elk hunting on the weekends and these guys do. . . . You realize the more senior you got, the more important the client side was and the clients in the oil and gas side of the business, in my own perspective, they didn't discriminate against me or anything, but they didn't understand me and I didn't feel they were as comfortable around me as they were other guys that were more like them, where they could kind of go to girlie bars at night or go hunting. It's fine with me. I'm not here to pass moral judgment but I wasn't going to be successful there.

She was very successful in another area of corporate finance, where she specialized in a financial product instead of an industry. She changed jobs deliberately because she believed that her professional success would be less dependent on friendships with clients in her second group.

As Elise described, client-entertaining activities in corporate finance, sales, and trading often consisted of recreational activities that fit stereotypes about the clients, which could exclude women. This included activities like outings to strip joints that reinforced gender boundaries in Wall Street firms. Including female bankers in these events might have made them less effective at building relationships, because they involved activities that build solidarity among men in all-male settings.[7] Some men might also have preferred to avoid this type of activity, even if it meant monetary trade-offs. But even if this did not represent an ideal choice for many men, for them it was a choice that women usually did not have because assumptions about gender and sexuality infused Wall Street organizations.[8] As the last chapter illustrated, the masculine culture in this industry did not valorize masculinity under all circumstances—only when it was enacted by men. When women behaved in masculine ways, it violated assumptions about them *as women*. As a result, women on Wall Street could not attend topless bars or participate in cigar smoking and hunting for sport without stepping over the boundary of appropriate heterosexual femininity.

On the other hand, some jobs were more hospitable to women. Women were more likely to work in jobs that did not directly serve external clients, so that client preferences could not affect their performance or their bonuses. This might explain why women were more likely to work in lower-paying areas with little or no direct contact with external clients. In other jobs, like most equity research positions, client contact tended to focus on analysis of companies' profitability and often originated in other divisions. In fact, it may be that women have traditionally been most successful in equity research because research analysts work relatively independently and have less-extensive and more task-oriented relationships with clients.

Wall Street workers also believed that some clients had preferences for diversity and were more hospitable to white women and nonwhites. Clients with executives who were women or with strong organizational commitments to diversity seemed to prefer bankers who reinforced their own worldview. Occasionally there were clients like this that paid large fees, but clients with preferences for diversity tended to have less money and were more common in areas like public finance. Among those I interviewed, only women worked in public finance, and this was at least partly because managers in public finance departments believed that their clients preferred to see diversity among the bankers. Women in public finance explicitly noted that their departments recruited a greater diversity of workers because of beliefs about their clients' preferences. Melissa explained,

> In public finance, often when you are dealing with these public entities they like to see a diverse group. For public finance, you'll often see much more diversity within the group than in corporate finance. . . . I think sometimes being a woman in this side of the business is helpful. But it's sort of funny. It's a little bit like playing the game. If we know that we are going to visit an African American client, we will think, "Who is African American who can come with us to visit that client?" Or if we know that we are visiting a female client, we definitely would want to bring a female banker. So it's not that we are trying to be diverse ourselves, it's that we are trying to appease the client base so that we can get deals.

Similarly, Tamara remarked, "Public finance tends to attract more minorities. Sometimes we can't get hired for a deal unless there's a minority banker on the deal." Securities firms deliberately displayed diversity in public finance to cater to these perceived demands among nonprofit and government clients. These clients had more internal diversity, were subject to stricter affirmative action regulations, and were more committed to principles of equal opportunity than were many corporate clients. But they also paid lower fees, so that women were most wanted in areas that paid less. Public finance had the lowest average pay.[9]

While some clients seemed to prefer diversity among their bankers, there were also clients that were indifferent as long as they obtained the necessary financial expertise. Women could succeed in these areas, where client relationships were based on product delivery rather than camaraderie. Danielle said,

> The world was divided into relationship and product. And I was a product person. So I only worked with

> clients when there was a specific transaction and I would market our product alongside a relationship banker. And then once we got the mandate the work really geared toward the product people and the banker was just there as lead-in. So it was initially through marketing but really the relationships developed through the transactions. And I had, I guess, four or five clients that I did multiple transactions for—that were very, very difficult ones—and I got to be very close with them through that.

As in this case, client relationships in investment banking could be solidified through the actual execution of financial expertise. Caitlin described how technical expertise cemented client relationships in her public finance position.

> Relationship management is huge but it is a technical sell that we have. We have a client that we have been getting nowhere with the last two years, and they are technically a client but they haven't given us any business in the last two years. We advised them on an M&A deal two years ago, but they did two bond deals with other firms since then. Finally we got hired on this little deal, which is now going to hopefully turn into a huge deal, and at the last two meetings, including one we did yesterday, we did very technical analysis. We had two analysts working on it all night. Now that we finished those meetings, they think, "These guys are great!" So that is part of the client relationship, delivering good product. The two sort of go hand in hand, but you have to know what your client wants to be able to create the product that they want.

So some workers, like Caitlin and Danielle, worked in areas where client relationships stood or fell on the basis of technical expertise, in contrast to others who described client relationships as dependent on close relationships with industry CEOs.

At this point it is worth noting that presumed client preferences could be important, but there were also limits to clients' power to demand Wall Street workers with particular characteristics. Reskin and Roos offer a queuing metaphor that is useful for understanding the conditions under which client preferences matter.[10] They argue that hiring preferences form a rank-ordered *labor queue* in which employers favor certain types of workers—particularly white men.[11] Because employers give them first dibs on Wall Street jobs, white men get their pick of the jobs that they find most desirable. For the jobs that remain when white men are no longer available, employers are forced to hire their second choice—white women and nonwhite men. As a result, areas that were less interesting to men were the areas where women could be most successful. Regarding the gender composition of her second job, Nicole remarked,

> I would say internally it's still not 50/50 anywhere, however, in [my second area] it may well be 50/50 only because it's one of the less well-paid parts of the bank. But in a funny way for the same reason it's a place where women have sometimes been able to get ahead faster.

As in this case, women were able to advance in some lower-paying areas that were unappealing to men.

Following the queuing metaphor, white men fled the public finance side of the securities industry in the late 1970s and abandoned emerging markets in the 1980s. White women and nonwhites replaced them. Clients' preferences for white men may not have changed, but their preferences alone cannot ensure that firms will be able to hire and retain white men in the areas that provide services to them. A female informant who had worked in emerging markets with clients from highly male-dominated countries in Africa, Asia, and the Middle East said that clients' needs for finance capital superseded their preferences for white men.[12] These clients never objected to working with female bankers, even if they might have preferred to conduct business with men—they needed finance capital more than they needed white men to provide that capital. In other words, clients will adjust to obtain the services they need. The customer may always be right, but clients also had to settle for their second choices if their first were not available.

But in high-revenue areas of Wall Street that remained desirable to white men, the perception that clients preferred to be entertained by and to develop buddy relationships with white male bankers reinforced inequality. As long as there was competition among workers for jobs that served these industries, those who resembled the client were privileged. High-paying, male-dominated industries presumably preferred men, and men wanted to maintain jobs serving these industries because of their high pay. Since the revenue potential of the client base directly affected the pay of these groups, perceptions that clients prefer service providers who are similar to themselves contributed to inequality in pay. Also, because workers who resemble their clients may have an easier time developing solid client relationships, Wall Street firms may act rationally when they try to appease the presumed preferences of their clients.

Managers, Client Preferences, and "Rational Discrimination"

Not only was client rapport harder to come by for women who worked with male-dominated industries, but managers also assigned workers to accounts based on the assumption that clients preferred to work with bankers like themselves. Managers tried to anticipate the preferences of their clients without necessarily being conscious that this produced de facto discrimination. Given a large pool of workers, Wall Street firms could select bankers, traders, and research analysts who resembled the clients to work on accounts or deals. In doing so, these firms simply acted rationally on the assumption that this was what their clients preferred.[13] In this way, Wall Street firms used clients' real or expected preferences to "rationally discriminate" in the assignment of accounts. This limited the opportunities of workers who did not resemble their clients, and it pushed workers to enter areas where they would resemble their clients. For example, Latin American and Asian workers said that managers channeled them into emerging markets. Emmanuel, a Latin American investment banker, described being moved from a domestic corporate finance group.

> I was not happy about that because I thought the Brazil office here was a mess. And I didn't like the people who worked there. I didn't want to go. . . . I went there dragged, kicking and screaming and very unhappy.

Emmanuel was essentially forced to move into a group that he did not want. In contrast, Daphne, the third-generation Asian American described in chapter 1, was encouraged to move from domestic to Asian sales.

> Is there a reason why they asked me if I wanted to cover Asia? I think I was the only Asian American in the training program. You know what I mean. The chances of them asking some white guy who doesn't know much about Asia would be lower, so subconsciously they would say, "She might not speak the language but she at least looks the part." But I hadn't mentioned anything to [the firm] saying, "Gee, can I do the Asian product?" But I'm sure that came into their thinking when they asked me. . . . And it doesn't matter that I'm third-generation American. I think people will always see me as Asian. How many times do I get asked, "Do you speak Chinese?" But if I was white and the same number of generations, no one would ask, "Do you speak Dutch?"

Daphne's manager encouraged her to specialize in Asian sales, even though she had no special knowledge about Asia. She attributed this invitation to her manager's assumption that Asians prefer to work with other Asians, even if they speak different languages and come from different cultures.[14] Daphne took the opportunity because the Asian markets were booming, but a subsequent crash and volatility in the Asian markets led the firm to lay her off soon afterward.

A similar "rational bias" sometimes increased women's access to female-run clients. This could have been an advantage, except that it highlighted their difference from their male peers while giving them privileged access to clients that were small in number and that tended to pay lower fees. Rosalind worked in corporate finance with large and predominantly male-dominated companies.

> I remember once someone came to me and said, "We have this project that just came in. A real estate project. It's got a woman CEO and we really want to put a woman on the project." And I was a little offended by that. I have really mixed feelings. On the one hand I wish I had the opportunity to work with more senior women, so the bottom line is it probably would have been a good experience. On the other hand I felt sort of tokenish. I'm sure a black person would be offended if they said, "We have a black client and we want a black person working on it." It's very strange.

Managers in decision-making positions may have felt that the assignment of women to this account was rational, but the same tendency led them to assign more men to the larger number of deals involving clients with male management. This reproduced gender inequality in pay because the clients that pay the highest underwriting fees are dominated by white men. Female- and minority-owned organizations have less capital, replicating inequalities in the larger economy. While this might change as more businesses are run by women, it points to some of the reasons why women were more likely to work in areas with little or no client contact (equity research, administrative support), where clients preferred diversity among their bankers, or where men had lost interest (public finance, emerging markets). These clients tended to pay less, increasing women's worth in areas where they would earn the least.

Conclusion

Contrary to stereotypes that women are better at relationships than men, relationship-intensive jobs were often detrimental for women and women fared best in jobs where they did not have to manage client relationships or where those relationships were based on their expertise rather than social ties. In client-contact jobs, client relationships were integral to performance but not necessarily in ways that were related to ability or skill. Of course, client satisfaction affected the ease of transactions and the likelihood of repeat business and referrals, so it was rational for Wall Street firms to cater to clients and to reward employees for strong client relationships. Since clients appeared to prefer Wall Street workers who resembled their own executives, this privileged white men in the highest-paying client-contact jobs even if their qualifications and skills were similar to or worse than those of women. As a result, client relationships contributed to gender inequality in performance, evaluations, and pay.

Wall Street firms acted on these assumptions about client preferences and channeled women into jobs without client contact or onto accounts with clients that paid lower fees. Firms had the ability to assign women to work with higher-paying clients, increase their exposure to client accounts, and encourage greater integration. But these measures were not part of their equal employment opportunity initiatives, which largely affected hiring but not account allocation. In fact, encouraging relationships between male-dominated clients and female bankers might seem contrary to these firms' actual interests given presumed client preferences. On the other hand, assumptions about client preferences could be wrong. The evidence about responses to the influx of women into emerging markets suggests that clients may actually be quite flexible. As long as this is an empirical question, it is an area that equal opportunity efforts could target and where beliefs about gender preferences could be dispelled.

The perception that clients preferred to work with financial professionals who resembled them affected the behavior of women professionals and their managers. Some women on Wall Street developed strategies to avoid jobs involving clients where they were at a disadvantage. Sometimes women strategically (or serendipitously) chose areas with high revenue and pay potential where their performance was dependent on product delivery rather than being CEOs' confidantes. But often difficulties with client relationships encouraged women to move away from specializations in male-dominated industries over time and to enter positions with limited client contact. Along with manager and coworker relationships, this contributed to the funneling of women into lower-paying areas. Another reason for this funnel was work-family conflict, although this appeared to be less about preferences for the "mommy track" than many ordinarily think. I explore the Wall Street work culture, Wall Street workers' typical family arrangements, and their contributions to work-family conflict in the next chapter.

Chapter 6

HAVING IT ALL?

Workplace Culture and Work-Family Conflict

The last two chapters illustrated how Wall Street's compensation system permitted subtle gender discrimination in relationships with managers, coworkers, and clients to influence gender inequality in pay. Work-family issues also contributed to the gender gap in pay because a workaholic organizational culture clashed with the broader cultural assignment of child-rearing responsibilities to women. Workplace time norms equated time on the job with commitment to the job and demanded all-encompassing career devotion. These norms converged with the gender division of family work and gender discrimination to create a set of institutionalized obstacles to women's equality. In this chapter, I examine how a culture of long hours, gender norms from the broader culture, and childcare arrangements among Wall Street workers interacted to produce inequality.

The Gender-Parenthood Wage Gap

It is well known from other settings that mothers earn less and fathers more than their childless counterparts.[1] In this respect, Wall Street was no exception. Figure 6.1 illustrates differences in pay for childless women, childless men, mothers, and fathers, while

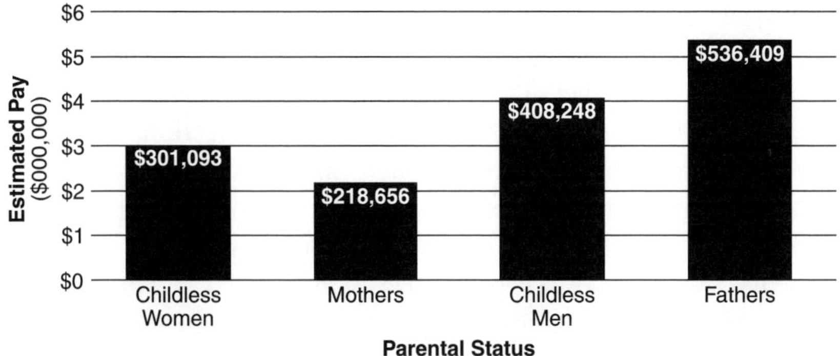

Fig. 6.1. Estimated pay by parental status

accounting for differences in undergraduate major, Wall Street experience prior to business school, weekly hours, rank, and firm prestige.[2] This figure clearly shows that mothers earned substantially less than their childless female peers while fathers received a large earnings bonus.

But why do men's earnings increase and women's decrease when they have children? The common wisdom is that women become less committed to their careers when they have children, and make the choice to stay home or to reduce their work commitment to care for their children. At the same time, as primary breadwinners, fathers become more career committed as they acquire more financial dependents. While reality is more complicated than this "commonsense" assumption implies, it suggests that fathers will and mothers will not maintain the devotion required to succeed on Wall Street.

Around-the-Clock Devotion

Most Wall Street jobs required long hours and offered little flexibility. As a result, the ideal worker on Wall Street was a workaholic who was willing to work very long hours and had no external obligations. Workers without outside lives had better access to accounts and deals and were evaluated as better performers. Of course, a workaholic culture is not unique to Wall Street. Some scholars have argued that all workers increasingly work longer hours, sometimes by choice.[3] Others assert that managers and professionals work an increasing number of hours although many would prefer to work less, while many other workers are underemployed.[4] But all agree that inflexibility, in the form of long hours, face-time, and rigid schedules, is especially entrenched in high-paying jobs where workers demonstrate career commitment by centering their life on their work.[5]

Within this segment of the labor force, financial service professionals have experienced particularly large increases in work hours in the last few decades because consolidation, globalization, and new technologies have inflated competitive pressures. As a result, many Wall Street jobs require a willingness to work around-the-clock, especially in the career-building years. Caroline, a highly paid and highly satisfied investment banker, said,

> This is a job where you have to be prepared to subordinate everything else in your life to the job. It's very rare that you can say that you're going to take the weekend off and not have anything be there waiting for you, [and very common to] feel that you are somehow compromising something that you are working on because you didn't devote some time to it. There's always more than you could possibly handle in terms of things you need to do. Everything is always time sensitive, so a lot of things on a personal level have to take a back seat.

Junior workers in particular had to put up with having social plans and vacations canceled at the last minute. Many Wall Street workers, like Caroline, accepted this as part of the job, but others became more resistant to the workaholic nature of the business as time wore on. For example, Allison was a single woman who had recently changed jobs to improve her control over her personal life. But she still found the time demands of her job unreasonable.

> The fact [is] that up until recently, I could have a weekend planned and something could come up [such] that . . . I would have to be in the office all weekend and I would have to cancel everything. . . . Even now, I can make plans to meet somebody at nine o'clock at night—nine o'clock at night—and I can't tell you how many times I have to cancel. That's ridiculous! That's nine o'clock at night!

As Allison suggested, most securities jobs, especially those in investment banking, required long and often unpredictable hours.

The bull market of the 1990s escalated the pressures for continuous work. Dave described the revolving door of business deals, remarking that client firms might do one important deal every decade or two, but that investment bankers worked on one after another. "The downside of course is that you work a lot of hours and there's not a lot of rest because when the company does an IPO they take the summer off, but you're on the next idea or the next transaction." So while the client firm might have a break after completing a large transaction, the investment bankers who orchestrated it would already be working on their next IPO, merger, or acquisition.

The demands for long hours were partly fueled by managers' need to continually pitch new business in order to compete with other firms. Senior bankers kept their subordinates busy even though they did not always need everything they asked for. Allison described how they worked junior employees to the bone because they could.

> You basically work because of managing directors, and these managing directors have targets. They need to make the firm X millions of dollars, and there's basically a bunch of people below them, and there's really no checks and balances. If I were one of those people, who had to make that target, and there were bunch of people below me, I would probably have them doing all this stuff all night, too. Why not? Chances are, the

> more people you have working for you the more hours a week, the better chance that you'll have to hit something. There's no one there to say, "You can't keep having them stay up all night." Because, frankly, for everyone like me who says that I don't want to stay here all night anymore, there are five other people who are willing to stay all night for the money.

Managers did not need to have an efficient strategy for deploying their subordinates, leading them to demand extremely long hours from junior bankers. Because Wall Street careers were so lucrative, young workers were willing to sacrifice sleep and their personal life to meet these demands.

Most investment bankers thought that the job simply required someone who could maintain work as his or her *primary* priority and that anyone with different priorities could be replaced. Forbes blamed this on clients rather than managers, but the punch line was the same. When asked about family-friendly policies, he said that they simply were not feasible in investment banking because of the kind of service that clients expect.

> You can't sue the client if they hire a guy from [another firm] who is working ninety hours a week. So that's who you're competing against doing business. And if that's who your competition is, you either do what he does or you get out of the business. . . . And some people try to wrestle with that and try to legislate against the firm or try to argue for some position but clients dictate. It's only the clients who force us to work ninety hours a week. It's not that we choose to. . . . It's just—clients pay us ridiculous sums of money. They expect continuous work for that.

Clients expected Wall Street firms to deliver on their deadlines, and these firms promised more than their existing staff could produce without working very long hours.

As a result, the workers with the greatest opportunities to succeed were those who could offer unlimited devotion to work and unrestricted access to their personal time. When asked if his firm offered any flexible work arrangements to accommodate workers' family responsibilities, Emmanuel said,

> Honestly in this job it doesn't matter because it wouldn't work. The fact is that if you're not doing it with enormous energy and dedication, somebody else is doing it. . . . Whoever is wanting to be a star will be willing to sacrifice their personal lives a lot more and, to the extent that you're equally talented, they will have an advantage career wise. You cannot be a rising star in M&A, working fourteen hours a day and traveling half the week, which is what it requires, and be at home all the time with children. It just doesn't happen. Either one or the other.

From workers' perspective, competition required very long hours and skewed the work-life balance in favor of work. Competition among firms for clients and among workers for pay reinforced this workaholic culture on Wall Street. This was not a reflection of workers' preferences to work long hours, but was shaped by explicit management strategies. Wall Street firms convinced workers to meet intense demands by offering large financial incentives through the bonus system.

Embedded within Wall Street's workaholic culture is an assumption that the ideal worker has no responsibilities outside of work. Family scholars have often observed that the definition of an ideal worker in advanced capitalist societies assumes a support person to take care of all nonwork aspects of life and is based on a breadwinner-homemaker division of labor in the family.[6] This is what most sociologists call an "institutionalized" assumption, or one that involves habitual and legitimized patterns of action that span organizations and are resistant to change.[7] Modern organizations have institutionalized employment practices that treat workers as though they have no family responsibilities, implicitly assuming that most families have a breadwinner-homemaker division of labor even though this is no longer the statistical norm.[8]

Illuminating how these assumptions about family structure affect workplace options, Clarkberg and Moen compared workers' preferred work hours with their actual work hours. They found that workers often had to choose between not working at all and working forty or more hours per week, leaving those with preferences for part-time work unable to realize their preferences.[9] They concluded that organizational policies and employer expectations "have largely remained structured along the all-or-nothing breadwinner/homemaker cultural template."[10] Blair-Loy and Wharton found a similar cultural assumption in a large financial services firm, where the workplace culture is most influenced by senior and highly paid workers. These workers, who seemed to enjoy spending long hours at work, were also the most likely to have a homemaker wife and thus to have family situations that did not compete with their "devotion to work."[11] Their influence on the professional demands on their subordinates meant that their unfettered career devotion structured expectations that were applied to others.

In some ways, these time demands may seem gender neutral, because both men and women who were willing to work very long hours could succeed, but they had a disparate impact on women because gender profoundly shapes the structures of work and family life. Assumptions about the gender division of labor in the family inform the organization of work and the treatment of workers as men and as women, putting women at a disadvantage in the workplace because employers, workers, men with families, and even women themselves define care work as women's responsibility. In a broader culture that assigns all responsibility for childcare to women and demands that women's devotion to family trump all other commitments, family formation is guaranteed to have differential effects on male and female workers.[12]

This assignment of care work to women is clearly structured and collective, but workers often individualized it, describing it as a matter of personal choice.[13] Regarding women who returned after a maternity leave, Jeremy said,

> I do know some people that came back and never really . . . they sort of lost that eye of the tiger. Women that no longer had the intensity for the job and would go on the mommy track, do part-time work, or less time-critical work. But that's just a personal thing.

In an industry that demands around-the-clock devotion, most men and women viewed career reductions for family reasons as "just a personal thing." But the desire to work fewer than sixty hours per week is relevant only because of the way that Wall Street organizes work, which is hardly about "personal choice." In defining it as a choice, most workers did not challenge the underlying assumption that workers had no family responsibilities and, ideally, had stay-at-home spouses to manage all nonwork concerns. This posed problems for workers with childcare responsibilities.

The Allocation of Childcare

Given that most securities jobs conflicted with involvement in family life, how did parents who worked on Wall Street manage childcare? And how did their childcare arrangements fit with the workaholic culture of the industry? To address these questions, I asked workers with children how they expected becoming a parent to affect their careers before they had children, how being a parent had affected their careers, and how they managed childcare. I asked childless men and women if they hoped or planned to have children in the future and, if so, how they expected becoming a parent to affect their careers and how they expected to manage childcare. These workers envisioned only two options for managing childcare: a breadwinner-homemaker family in which the wife/mother is the primary caregiver, or hiring full-time childcare. Both men and women on Wall Street made enough to support a homemaker or to pay for full-time,

Table 6.1
Childcare Arrangements

Childcare Arrangement[a]	*Mothers*	*Fathers*	*Total*
Paid childcare	12 (80.0%)	3 (17.6%)	15 (46.9%)
Breadwinner-homemaker	3 (20.0%)	14 (82.4%)	17 (53.1%)
Total	15	17	32

[a] This reflects the childcare arrangement that the respondent used at the time of the interview. Some changed from one approach to another: in three cases, they switched from paid care to a breadwinner-homemaker division of labor.

high-quality childcare. But differential childcare arrangements by gender had a disparate impact on men's and women's careers because women took on responsibility for childcare in all cases, either doing all of it or arranging for another woman to do it.

Table 6.1 illustrates the approaches that parents took to childcare. Over four-fifths of the fathers had breadwinner-homemaker families, and 80 percent of the mothers hired caregivers. In fact, while breadwinner-homemaker families have become less common in the general population, they remained the norm for men on Wall Street and this norm was embedded in Wall Street culture. Maureen remarked on the uniformity of Wall Street men's family trajectories.

> I think that in this environment, there is very much a standard of men at a certain age being married and, with few exceptions, whose wives don't work. Certainly, they don't work after they have children and everybody has had their first child at a certain step—when the men turn thirty—when they are about a third-year associate.

As Maureen indicated, the breadwinner-homemaker family pattern was an informally institutionalized norm for men on Wall Street. The support of stay-at-home wives meant that these men were able to devote most of their energy to their career and were perceived as more committed and stable when they married and had children.

Fathers with traditional wives were able to dedicate themselves to their career and were assumed to perform better because they had almost no family responsibilities aside from work. When asked how he and his wife managed childcare, Jorge said,

> For the first three years it was pretty much her by herself with help once a week or something like that. [Now] have somebody who comes four times a week and on the weekend for babysitting on Saturday night. But I really don't do anything at home. I would say we have more of a standard, old-fashioned [arrangement]. . . . I go to work and she takes care of everything in the house.

Like many male Wall Street professionals, Jorge had a full-time homemaking wife in addition to some paid domestic assistance, taking no responsibilities for caregiving himself.

Because of this, men with traditional wives had career advantages because they could put extremely long hours into their career that many other workers could not. Nick described a particularly strong devotion to his career, wearing a pager and checking his voice mail every hour over the weekend. But with three small children, he could only sustain this with the support of a stay-at-home wife. When asked if anything detracted from his satisfaction with his job, he said,

> No. Maybe time for my family, but that is also self-inflicted. I want to spend time working. . . . I don't have dinner with my kids during the week. I'm not the dad who reads them a story or gives them a bath. I also see less of my wife during the week. But I love it. She's supportive. She's independent and acknowledges how important it is for me.

In many ways, Nick was the ideal Wall Street worker because he put work ahead of other priorities.[14] Fifty-three percent of the fathers were able to focus on their careers with this intense level of devotion because they had traditional wives.[15] The large number of these men in this industry meant that the definition of the ideal worker did not have to shift to accommodate different family realities.[16]

This ideal worker notion disadvantaged workers who did not have stay-at-home wives. Caitlin, a single woman, said,

> Most of the vice presidents I work with are married, and they go home where they have a stay-at-home wife who has picked up their dry cleaning and maybe hired a maid, made their weekend plans. And sometimes it's tough because it's not that I want to have a wife at home, but there are advantages to that.

The norm of a stay-at-home spouse for men on Wall Street put women who were single or whose spouses worked in equally demanding careers at a relative disadvantage in living up to the demands of the workaholic culture.

How did this ideal worker notion affect women's family decisions? Given that the broader culture assigned time-consuming child-rearing responsibilities to women, some women deliberately avoided or delayed childbearing. These women, whose average age was thirty-three, were in their prime years for family formation as well as career building. They were more likely to be childless than other women in their age group–66 percent did not have children, compared to 28 percent of women aged 30–34 in the U.S. population.[17]

Nine percent of women said that they preferred to remain childless while 57 percent were childless but hoped or planned to have children eventually. Those who were childless by choice all cited personal reasons but also acknowledged that this decision fit well with their careers. Caroline, a highly successful married investment banker, said that she was unsure that she had the patience required for parenting, but she remarked,

> It really doesn't have much to do with the job. My own personal feeling is that I'm not sure that I want to have

> children . . . [but] I can't say that you can separate the two things entirely. I know that I could not do what I am currently doing and have children. . . . My current situation would be absolutely impossible if I had children.

Like Caroline, 52 percent of the women who did not have children said that they would have to change jobs if they had children.

Women who wanted children sometimes struggled with the career trade-offs that they would have to make. Melissa worked in public finance and was engaged to be married, and had only recently decided that she wanted to have children.

> For a very long time I didn't think that I did want children. . . . I think that part of it also is that career is important. I see how much time it takes and how little time I have for myself, and I look at my friends who have children, and I see how much time that takes. I don't envy their lives. I look at my friends who are having kids, and I don't envy what they have to go through having little kids. . . . Right now my career involves travel, and sometimes it involves travel at the last minute. It involves hours that are very inflexible. I am often here late, and I usually don't know how late I'm going to have to stay until I actually leave. I think that that part of it would be very hard—to be in this job and have a family, unless I had a full-time, live-in nanny or something.

Like Melissa, who worked in an area with more women and still believed that it was impossible to effectively combine her job with parenting, women on Wall Street generally viewed motherhood as incompatible with their careers.

As a result, 9 percent of the women were specifically delaying childbearing because they encountered expanding career opportunities. Emma, a highly successful investment banker, said,

> I have two choices here in investment banking. Either I have a nanny raise my children or I don't work. This

> isn't a part-time kind of thing. Not because the firm is bad about it, but because this is an eighty-hour-week kind of job. So, if I wanted to do the nanny thing that would be fine or I would just stop working. . . . At this point my husband and I are so focused on career, the nanny thing doesn't really seem that appealing and as a result we just keep delaying having children.

These women delayed childbearing because they were reluctant to hire surrogate childcare providers. They had husbands who also worked on Wall Street and earned even more money than they did. But within their own jobs, the lure of more money, more interesting work, and better hours over time encouraged them to remain childless.

Childless women's stories reveal that while combining career and family has become increasingly common among contemporary middle-class and affluent women, most women on Wall Street still viewed career and family as an either/or choice.[18] This was partly because Wall Street's workaholic culture made it difficult for parents without a stay-at-home spouse to attain career success. Of course, with average earnings of over $300,000, women on Wall Street also earned enough to support a homemaker. But the cultural institution of gender affected them here as well, since women's partner choices and parenting ideologies tended to assign them more childcare duties as well as offer them less career support.[19] No women had partners who were or expected to become homemakers, and no women described this type of arrangement as even a possibility. In fact, 42 percent of the women with partners, including one-third of the most successful women, said that their partners earned significantly more money than they did.[20] Most of their partners were other financial professionals, doctors, or lawyers. So where most men found women who were willing to leave the labor force, women did not pair up with men who were likely to become homemakers, either because of the men who were available to them, because of their preferences for men of at least equal career status, or both.[21]

Since they lacked the support of a homemaker, mothers who continued to work on Wall Street hired full-time childcare. Eighty percent of mothers and 18 percent of fathers hired childcare providers for their children so that both parents could have full-time careers. But women in these families took on more responsibility than men for arranging childcare and for caregiving when they were not at work, so that their career opportunities were still restricted in ways that men's were not.

Men whose families hired childcare had wives who wanted to remain employed. They all earned substantially more than their wives and considered themselves to be the primary breadwinner. Hugh's wife worked in real estate and they had a full-time nanny. His remark about family-friendly policies at his firm revealed his distance from the actual care of his two very young children. "I always see a lot of memos on that topic but since it doesn't apply to me I don't pay much attention to them." The three fathers whose families hired childcare were all uninvolved with caregiving and arranging childcare. But while there were no obvious personal or professional costs to hiring caregivers for these men, they also did not reap the benefits of a traditional wife who took care of everything outside of work and supported their careers. The advantages of the breadwinner-homemaker arrangement are clear when comparing the average income of men with stay-at-home wives to the few with employed wives. Fathers with employed wives had average incomes similar to those of childless men ($375,000), rather than the higher average income of sole breadwinners ($628,846), suggesting that traditional wives dramatically improved men's opportunities, evaluations, and pay.

For women, hiring childcare was the only child-rearing solution that allowed them to continue their careers. Seventy-five percent of the mothers who hired childcare providers said that they were equal or primary breadwinners. But they were married to men with similarly demanding careers or to men with less demanding careers but who nonetheless worked full time. And because of broader cultural assumptions, mothers were responsible for childcare when paid caregivers were not present and did more childcare even when their husbands had less demanding and lower-paying jobs. Danielle said,

> We have a full-time nanny who is here every day from 8:00–6:00. You're only speaking to me so you're only hearing my point of view. During the week when she's not here I'm the one who is really responsible. Both in terms of just physically being here but also things I'm noticing—who needs diapers, who needs socks, who needs to go to the doctor—which isn't just a question of physically being around when the nanny leaves. That's been my responsibility.

Childcare concerns that extended beyond the purview of the paid care provider typically fell upon the mother's shoulders, regardless of how demanding her career was. As other research has found, mothers felt responsible for spending time with and caring for their children in ways that fathers did not. Ultimately both men and women allocated responsibility for childcare to women.[22]

This responsibility could negatively affect women's careers. For example, Barbara discovered that unforeseen changes in her family life forced her to seek new childcare arrangements and made it impossible to balance work and family.

> I would say, in the beginning, it worked fine. Also, my husband, at the time, was in a fixed-income research job, and he had very similar hours to me, if not better. I worked basically from 7:30 to 5:30, and he worked 8:00 to 5:00. Or, that's when he had to work. He could do work on the computer at home. We had a nanny who came during the days to our apartment, so we were able to basically share relieving the nanny. This changed the same month I became pregnant with my second child. My husband was recruited by [another Wall Street firm]. . . . Then he no longer had the same amount of free time as he had before. . . . More of the childcare

> responsibilities fall on me now that my husband has a much more demanding job. Really I think that that's what makes working hard. If you share all of the responsibilities equally, then you can do it. But if you both have the same type of demanding job, it's hard when you have to carry more of the responsibilities.

Barbara was considering taking a leave of absence so that she could devote the necessary energy to finding a new nanny. Because mothers take on more responsibility for arranging childcare and for filling the gaps when paid care providers are not on duty, even when their jobs are as demanding as those of their partners, surrogate caregivers did not support women's careers the way that stay-at-home wives supported men's careers.

Parenthood and Work Hours

Given childcare arrangements on Wall Street, it is clear that men and women were differently situated with respect to work-family conflict and that women had greater difficulty exhibiting the requisite career devotion. But whether or not men and women really differed in their commitment and productivity after having children is still an empirical question. While commitment and work effort are difficult to measure accurately and hours are not a perfect measure of productivity, one would expect women's family responsibilities to lead to reductions in hours and that compensation differences would roughly correspond to differences in hours. Figure 6.2 compares fathers, mothers, and childless workers by average hours per week, revealing that mothers do not work substantially less than childless women or fathers and that fathers work fewer hours than childless workers.

As this figure illustrates, women with children worked the fewest average hours, although not by much. But mothers' earnings penalty could not be attributed to differences in their hours, since

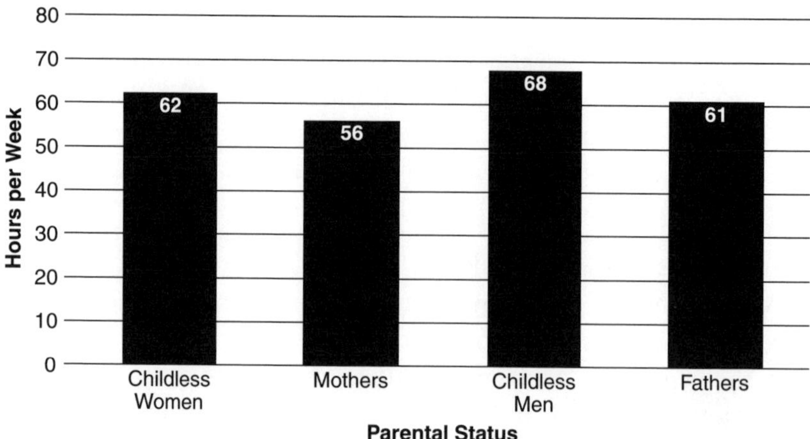

Fig. 6.2. Average weekly hours by gender and parental status

fathers worked less than childless men or women and they made the most money. Mothers received an average of 53 percent as much money as fathers while working 92 percent as many hours.[23] Of course, some workers are more productive than others within the same amount of time, but mothers were much more likely to say that they had become more efficient at work so that they could work fewer hours while still performing as well. Meanwhile, fathers worked 90 percent as many hours as childless men, but received 122 percent as much money.[24] Table 6.2 illustrates differences in average pay, average hours, and average pay per hour, revealing that mothers received the least pay per hour and were less well compensated for their work effort.[25] So how was it that women suffered an earnings penalty over and above their change in hours?

A Matter of Perception

While mothers did not substantially reduce their hours, coworkers' and managers' perceptions of women were influenced by gendered assumptions about work and family roles that spilled over into the

Table 6.2
Hours and Pay by Gender and Parental Status

	Average Pay (Raw Mean)	*Average Hours/Week*	*Average Annual Pay/Weekly Hour*
Childless women	$356,944	62	$5757.16
Childless men	$482,857	68	$7100.84
Mothers	$314,357	56	$5613.52
Fathers	$590,625	61	$9682.38
Total sample	$431,434	62	$6966.48

workplace. Gutek first framed the term "sex-role" spillover to refer to the way that assumptions about gender permeate definitions of occupations.[26] She argued that predominantly female jobs like flight attendant or secretary take on stereotyped feminine characteristics, such as nurturing or being attractive to others, which then become part of the job description. Similarly, male-typed jobs like construction worker or litigator take on stereotypically masculine traits like aggressiveness, competitiveness, and predatory behavior.[27] Family-role spillover, the assumed gender division of labor in the family, is a specific form of sex-role spillover that leads coworkers and managers to presume that mothers are more committed to children's hands-on care while fathers are economic providers. This form of sex-role spillover is one way that organizations are invisibly gendered, with differential impact on men's and women's careers that is cloaked in the rhetoric of "personal choice."[28]

To illustrate how gender-differentiated family roles biased perceptions of workers, consider Ken and Jacqueline's very different remarks about the effect of marriage on assessments of their career commitment. Ken had recently married and noted that wearing a wedding ring led others to see him as more stable and serious.

> It seems to give you more credibility. When you go in and you've got a wedding ring on or something I think people tend to have an impression that you're more

> mature or whatever. The same thing goes for gray hair and balding and stuff. You can just command more.

Marriage improved men's image as stable and mature workers but had the opposite effect for women. In fact, women's image could be tarnished by the knowledge that they were married because they then seemed closer to becoming mothers and therefore less committed.

Jacqueline was warned by career counselors to avoid disclosing her marital status in job interviews. After she landed an equity research position, she found out that her manager would not have hired her if she had known that she was married.

> At [business school] . . . you're told that being married is a disadvantage when you're interviewing for a job. Because if you go in with a wedding band, they sort of view you as a temporary employee and it's a negative because they think you're just going to get a job, work for a few years, have a family, and leave. . . . I didn't wear my wedding band and I made no mention that I was married and you're obviously not allowed to ask the question. And she felt like I deceived her, but she also had made it a point that she might not have hired me if she knew I was married because the woman [who] was my predecessor had left her.

So in addition to the double standards for competence that were explored in chapter 4, there were gender double standards in the effects of marriage on workers' credibility. For women, it negatively affected perceptions of their commitment, while it increased credibility for men.

Assumptions that workers should not have responsibilities outside work and should make their career their central life focus led managers in Wall Street firms to offer more opportunities to workers who did not have and *were not expected to acquire* obligations to family or anything else. Because of the cultural assumption, shared by both men and women, that women's primary life focus is childbearing and caregiving, women on Wall Street found that they were equated with work-family conflict even when they did not have children. This led managers and coworkers to view all women as less effective workers, leading to harsher scrutiny and worse performance evaluations even when their performance was actually similar. They also assumed that all women would have children, even if they were childless and showed no signs of starting a family. Maureen, who was single, childless, and thirty-nine years old at the time of the interview, described comments that coworkers had made to her.

> It's nothing I ever think about and certainly don't talk about. But people make comments. I've had someone say to me that of all the people they know at the firm, in their mind, it would not surprise them that I would have a child on my own and be a single mother. Where did that come from? I've never even talked about children, so it's very random.

While she had no desire to have children and had never expressed such a desire to others, at least some workers still viewed her as a potential mother. As this comment suggests, women were always under suspicion of desiring a family even if they were single and approaching the end of most women's childbearing years.

This suspicion could yield harsh treatment if women even suggested that they might eventually want more balance between work and personal life. Tracy's commitment to the workaholic ethic was tested after a business trip where her manager asked about her long-range plans. She told him that she was interested in moving into trading to reduce her need to travel, and then was suddenly transferred to a very undesirable part of the firm.

> I said, "In five years' time or three years' time, I don't see myself flying out here every week. It's wearing and tearing on me and . . . I'm getting married. I don't

> really feel like doing this. And I don't feel like I'm going to become a banker after this. I'd like to be something more markets related." People who got tired of capital markets [generally] became bankers. . . . Well, unbeknownst to me, [my firm] was about to do a restructuring so [my manager] went and took the opportunity to tell the woman who worked above him: "Tracy is interested in moving out of the group." Even though I had said it was my three- to five-year plan because that's what he asked about. So she called me and said, "I've got good news. I've got a good new job for you." I said, "Excuse me?" "You're going to go to high yield." Not trading. It was high-yield capital markets, which is M&A-related hours. Because you basically spend nights at the printers and crap like that and I knew that was what it was . . . and she said, "Well, between you and me, you should never tell anyone you want to have babies." . . . Who said anything about having babies?

Tracy viewed this as discrimination against her as a *potential* mother. She avoided the transfer to high yield and managed to find a trading position, but not without a fight.

Because of the view of all women as mothers or potential mothers, women's commitment to the workaholic standard was always suspect. After they had children, women often found that evaluations of their performance worsened and their bonuses declined because of the perception of them as less career committed. Todd had married another investment banker and described how she was treated after their first child was born: "I will say that my wife was penalized when she worked in investment banking. Her bonus was lower, and the perception of her changed. They perceived her as a mom rather than as a banker." In this and many other cases, mothers were automatically defined as uncommitted to their careers. On Wall Street, mothers who were career committed and fathers with desires for work-life balance did not fit the implicit model for family.

Discrimination against Pregnant Women and Mothers

Because of the implicit model of the breadwinner-homemaker family, mothers encountered discrimination on Wall Street. While the desire to spend time raising their children surely played a role in mothers' career decisions, leading 32 percent of the women to change jobs in an effort to attain work-life balance, this was far from the only influence on the gender-parenthood gap in opportunity and pay. A more important contributor was discrimination against pregnant women and mothers, and against all women as potential mothers. Cultural assumptions that women will drop back or drop out when they have children are widely held—by women, their husbands, their kin, their friends, and their communities, as well as their employers and managers. These choices reduced women's opportunities on Wall Street independent of so-called personal choices to work less and exhibited such a strong pattern of gender difference that they hardly seemed "personal."

Pregnancy and motherhood contributed to some of the most blatant gender discrimination in the 1990s. Discrimination on these bases negatively influenced evaluations of women's performance—sometimes even when they were not mothers. When asked about discrimination, Julie said,

> They were not actually comments directed at me, but it was interviewing a female, and then having a male ask me, "So, what did you think of her?" If I was feeling negative, like it was someone I did not want to hire, regardless, then they would make very gender specific comments to me. . . . You know. "She is getting married. She might want to have a kid." Things like that. If they are saying that to me about somebody else, then they are probably thinking that about me.

Julie was engaged to be married and was acutely aware of stereotyped beliefs about women's work commitment and long-term potential. These common stereotypes produced discrimination against all women as potential mothers, especially if they were married.

They produced skepticism about women's performance, negatively influenced their evaluations, and reduced their pay. These stereotypes also persisted even though only 7 percent of the women I interviewed, and 20 percent of the mothers, actually quit to be full-time mothers. As I illustrate below, these women were also pushed out by discrimination.

Discrimination on the basis of pregnancy was especially common. Thirty-six percent of women talked about pregnancy discrimination against themselves or other women. Renee described an instance of pregnancy discrimination that created a hostile work environment for her even though she was childless.

> I was at a meeting, for example, where the research analyst didn't show up because she was pregnant. Go figure. That is fine, but when the client caught on that everyone else had their research analyst except [my firm], the managing director said, "Damned women. Always getting pregnant." Of course, I was the only woman in the room when this happened. And I had worked the hardest on the presentation for this guy. All the eyes turned to me. I could see they felt bad for me, that my own firm was demeaning women like that. In fact, this client said to the senior MD, "Your behavior is offensive and we don't want to do business with you." So he got the message the hard way.

Renee was thankful that the client told her manager that his behavior was inappropriate and refused to work with him again. But her experience illustrates the blatant hostility that managers could have toward pregnant workers and how it created an inhospitable work environment for all women. Sometimes the hostility was less obvious, but women were concerned nonetheless about how they would be treated during pregnancy.

They had good reason to be concerned about how managers and coworkers would treat them when they were pregnant. Barbara worked as a trader during her first pregnancy.

> When I was pregnant, people I sat immediately with, they just did not think that I should come back to work. So they were mad at me if I did. One of my bosses and another MD would say, "Who's going to raise your children? Don't you think that you're the best person to raise your children?" They would give me lectures every day. "This is a serious thing. You're bringing someone into the world." On and on and on. "You never know. You don't know." Every time something came on the radio about a nanny, child abuse, or cigarette burns, they'd say, "Why would you subject your child to that?" I heard that kind of thing all the time. Also, toward the end of my pregnancy, one of the MDs did not want me to sit in his chair because he was afraid my water was going to break. So he absolutely forbade me from sitting in his chair. Sometimes I forgot, and I sat, and he said, "Get out of my chair! Get out of my chair! Don't you sit in my chair!" It was like a joke.

Women's efforts to combine career and family often failed to fit a mold for "family" that their male colleagues could fully understand. After her maternity leave, Barbara moved into a sales position at another firm so that she could escape this hostile environment.

Even if they did not experience obvious discrimination during their pregnancies, many women were treated differently after giving birth. Managers often expected that women would not return to work or would quit soon after their maternity leave. This made them skeptical about mothers' commitment, leading to more negative evaluations. Jessica described her manager's reaction to the birth of her daughter.

> The guy that I work for right now has a horrible reputation. He deserves it. The day after my daughter was born, he called me to ask me if I was coming back to work. Hello? I'm a banker; what answer would I ever give you but "Yes, I'm 100 percent committed" because

> I haven't been paid yet this year. (Laughter.) So even if [not coming back to work] was in my set of thought processes, you would never hear it out of my mouth. I think I actually didn't talk to him until a week later. He called the day after but I didn't talk to him for a week. But more so, he is a problem for me that I haven't figured out how to deal with yet. He has been a problem for many of the women.

Some managers' hostility toward mothers posed obstacles for women like Jessica who wanted to combine work and family. He questioned her commitment, but she returned to corporate finance after her maternity leave and was one of the most successful women. She also worked at a firm that was known to be family friendly, suggesting that the specific work group and manager were more important than formal policies.

In other cases, hostility and subtle forms of discrimination on the basis of pregnancy prodded women to leave the labor force. Recall from table 6.1 that three mothers actually had breadwinner-homemaker families. These women quit after their 1997 bonuses, thus permitting (or forcing) their husbands to increase their career commitment while reducing their own. In all three cases, their managers and coworkers evaluated their performance negatively relative to measurable results. In a particularly egregious case, Mia was fired during her second pregnancy.

> I think a lot of men were a bit jealous because they were a little more lenient on what I could do. And in a way, I didn't blame them for being jealous, but I was still performing as well as I had been in the past. I didn't think it was a detriment in my performance that was significant. . . . But this new research director, in November, he took me out for a dinner—he took certain analysts out alone for dinner to talk about their careers. And he had [small children], and he said, "Wow, my [kid is] one and a half. My wife

> quit work. Are you going to quit?" Things you're not supposed to ask. And so I hid this pregnancy from them, and then some people found out I was pregnant. . . . But I think part of it was just—it was definitely discriminatory. I think it was discrimination, and they paid. They settled with me, so they must have been a little bit nervous.

She was a research analyst with a coveted *II* ranking and lucrative offers from other firms. For eighteen months after her first child was born she worked long hours and traveled a lot, getting up at 5:30 every morning, working until 5:00, and then doing additional work at home after her child went to sleep. But her peers and managers still resented her and her firm fired her. This solidified her decision to leave the labor force.

For all three women who left Wall Street to be homemakers, biases against mothers were important catalysts for their career decisions. Two traders, Tracy and Fiona, became homemakers after they received disappointing bonuses and a lack of support for flexible work arrangements that were formally available. Fiona believed that her bonus was low in comparison to her performance after her maternity leave.

> I do feel that my bonus, even though it was in the top 10 percent, was not commensurate with my performance review and I think it had to do with the fact that I was on maternity leave when I got the bonus, because they may not have expected me to come back. . . . I got an amazing performance review like I had gotten in years past and I know for a fact that the firm had one of its best years in history, so I expected a significant amount—my bonus to exceed the previous year by a significant amount—and it only did by $35,000. And I think that they basically explained it to me that I had led the pack for so long and now everyone was just catching up. But I think that someone else with the

> other pieces of the puzzle would have gotten a more substantial increase given the year the firm had and given the performance on top of the prior year. . . . I think $35,000, although it's a lot of money, was too much leveling off to the prior year, given all the factors.

In her view, her bonus did not accurately reflect her P&L for the year. Difficulties arranging a job-sharing arrangement that the firm supposedly offered turned her coworkers' expectation that she would quit into a self-fulfilling prophecy.

Tracy, whose story was told in chapter 1, also received a lower-than-expected bonus after she worked out a flexible work arrangement.

> In [my product], you trade in the morning. It's very active. In the afternoon, there's not much activity at all. So I made a career decision to press to do something pretty innovative, which is flexible work time, where instead of working, say, a flexible work week where I only worked four days a week and therefore affecting my P&L and my contribution to the firm, I devised a way in which I would work five days a week but twice a week I would leave[in the afternoon], thereby reducing the amount of hours I worked by roughly 20 percent. It was actually just under 20 percent. And I took a 20 percent pay cut for that. . . . I had to fight actually to make it just salary. . . . My argument was that my bonus was reflective of my contribution to the firm, by definition.

After negotiating this arrangement using the logic of merit-based pay, her last bonus on Wall Street was low. Since her profit and loss margins were recorded, it was very clear that evaluations of her performance had unjustly turned negative. She said, "My last bonus was miserable. The one I left on. That was no incentive. If I was still trying to decide what I would do, that certainly pushed me over the edge, in terms of staying home." Pregnant again and married to a portfolio manager, staying home was attractive, especially compared to being undervalued at work.

These women attempted to use work-family policies but were penalized because they conflicted with the workaholic ethic of Wall Street culture. The women who became homemakers were further motivated by the fact that they were married to high-earning men, which gave them the financial option to stop working. So while they undoubtedly also wanted to spend more time raising their children, the decision to leave their careers was complex and at least partly fueled by a mismatch between performance and evaluations after they became mothers.

Conclusion

In Wall Street's male-dominated and workaholic culture, assumptions about the gender division of labor in the family led to beliefs that women would not live up to the demands of Wall Street careers and were less-than-ideal workers. Women's greater responsibilities for childcare may have affected their actual productivity and performance, but motherhood could also bias evaluations of performance over and above any actual changes in performance.[29] Based on the fact that mothers continued to work long hours but earned substantially less than their peers with identical hours and productivity-related characteristics, discrimination appears to play a large role in mothers' disadvantage. Meanwhile, men were viewed as more effective at work when they had children, even though they also worked fewer hours than did childless workers.

The broader cultural division of labor in the family had a disparate impact on women's careers and pay on Wall Street because all women were expected to quit when they had children—and all women were expected to have children. But women who quit were actually few in number. Four women quit to become homemakers, three of whom did not leave entirely voluntarily.[30] Contrary to stereotypes about women preferring the "mommy track" or "opting out" of careers, these women were pushed to leave by obstacles in the workplace. Of course, by leaving, they reinforced stereotypes that women want to cut back or stay home after they have babies. This perpetuated discrimination against women, while the workplace culture further reinforced the gender division of labor in the family.

Sometimes the influence of family responsibilities is portrayed as a supply-side influence on gender differences, meaning that it involves workers' characteristics or choices rather than "demand-side" aspects of the work environment like discrimination.[31] But the workaholic culture and demands for long hours cannot fairly be portrayed as worker preferences or choices. They are structural aspects of the work environment that, coupled with broader cultural injunctions, constrain women's success and produce systematic gender inequality. The combination of workplace culture and the broader culture surrounding family roles forced many women to view career and family as an either/or choice where men had a both/and option.

Of course, women's opportunities might have improved if the relentless time demands of Wall Street had lightened up and could better accommodate caregiving responsibilities. But Wall Street's workaholic culture defined careers and motherhood as incompatible, and the worker with a stay-at-home spouse was the norm as well as the ideal. Because of the spillover of the gender division of labor in the family into the workplace, this workaholic culture was highly gendered. As Martin has argued, Wall Street's work environment was *built out of* cultural beliefs about gender, including the breadwinner-homemaker family model.[32] These cultural beliefs were so widely held that they were invisible to many Wall Street workers, leading them to conclude that women's disadvantages were caused by their personal choices.

At the same time, securities jobs could have been managed differently while allowing workers with children to be effective employees.[33] In fact, Wall Street firms had formal work-family policies that permitted workers to do their jobs on a flexible schedule or flex-place as well as policies encouraging diversity and prohibiting discrimination. They also offered generous family leaves. In the next chapter, I will explore the effects and usage of these policies.

Chapter 7

WINDOW DRESSING

Workplace Policies and Wall Street Culture

While the discrimination described in the last three chapters was subtle and structural, workplace policies could have helped more women to succeed on Wall Street. Effective hiring initiatives, sexual harassment policies, and diversity programs could have improved women's odds, and legal settlements in high-profile discrimination cases allocated money to fund these types of initiatives. Flextime or flex-place policies could have eased work-family conflict and made better use of the skills and experience of women with children. Some work-family specialists and human resource managers have even argued that work-family policies make good business sense because they help employers recruit, retain, and motivate a committed workforce.[1] Given the investments that securities firms made in professional women's careers, work-family conflict and subtle gender discrimination were costly to these firms as well as to workers. But while these firms had policies to address these issues, they clashed with Wall Street's workaholic and macho culture.

Wall Street Policies

Wall Street firms received much fanfare in the late 1990s for family-friendly policies that went above and beyond the call of duty. Publications like the *Wall Street Journal*, the *New York Times*, *Business Week*, and *Working Mother Magazine* profiled the family leave, flextime, and telecommuting policies of major investment banks. These firms offered paid maternity leave, typically for twelve to fourteen weeks. This was often *in addition to* the unpaid leave mandated by the 1993 Family and Medical Leave Act (FMLA), allowing women up to six months of leave following the birth of a child. To put this in perspective, the FMLA guarantees twelve weeks of *unpaid* leave for dependent care in firms with fifty or more employees. Organizations in the United States are not legally required to provide *any* paid maternity leave, so Wall Street firms provided benefits that were beyond the requirements of the law and substantially more generous than the average U.S. organization.[2] They also formally offered part-time arrangements, job sharing, and/or telecommuting.

These firms also tried to comply with equal opportunity laws by hiring women whenever possible. Warren, who worked in corporate finance in a small investment bank, said, "Believe me, when we hire analysts, young kids out of college, we bust our ass to get women in here because diversity, I think, is important to us. . . . Because you see so many fewer women come and interview, I think we try to hire them." While these firms viewed themselves as meritocracies, they were aware of nondiscrimination laws and attempted to hire more women.

The implementation of equal employment opportunity guidelines and the effects of class action suits did not stop at hiring. All major Wall Street firms also had diversity initiatives, sexual harassment policies, and grievance procedures. Emma said,

> They try to do everything right. Have training programs. Have policies. Have committees. Have gender awareness. They really just try. We hire, I'm sure, a lot of consultants who help us formulate the right programs and do the right things. Wall Street has had some very high-profile discrimination cases and I just don't think any of these firms want to get their names

> splashed across the paper in that way. So I think they try to do the right thing.

Most workers said that their firms had diversity committees and sensitivity training. With these policies, Wall Street firms signaled to their employees that they were sensitive to work-family conflict and to difficulties integrating women into the previously all-male environment. But subtle discrimination and the disparate impact of work-family issues still reduced women's prospects despite written diversity, work-family, and sexual harassment policies. This occurred largely because formal policies and informal practices clashed, rendering formal policies ineffective.

Some research on organizations illuminates the tensions at work here. Institutional theories suggest that firms may adopt official policies without fully implementing them; they are symbolic and do not change organizational practices.[3] Scholars like Edelman argue that organizations respond to changes in the legal environment, like the enforcement of equal employment opportunity laws, by developing policies that signal legal compliance. Wall Street workers exhibited a high awareness of legal issues, suggesting that anxiety over legal vulnerability prompted Wall Street firms to create policies that would signal that they were committed to changing "business as usual." But once they were implemented, these policies were ambiguous and contested, serving an important symbolic function but having little impact on day-to-day activities and behavior.

Institutional theories predict that Wall Street firms developed paid maternity leave policies, sexual harassment procedures, and equal employment opportunity measures in response to discrimination lawsuits, rather than to assist and retain women employees. There is evidence that this is accurate since the stated intention of workplace policies conflicted with informal practices in the industry. It is clear that Wall Street's informal culture involved a workaholic ethic and a belief in the justice of competitive markets, and rewarded stereotypically masculine behavior (at least among men). Within this culture, workers who reported discrimination and sexual harassment, used work-family policies, or took parental leave often suffered negative career consequences.

Parental Leave

At the time of this study, some firms were moving toward making two weeks of their three-month leave a gender-neutral "parental leave," with the remaining two and a half months defined as "maternity leave." This was intended to acknowledge that men also have families, although it was generally women who used the leave. Most workers viewed these leave policies as very fair. Bonus pay structures meant that they usually reduced an employee's compensation for the year of the leave, regardless of whether or not the official firm policy guaranteed a "full" bonus. But most people accepted this because it reflected lower productivity due to absence and this fit with the logic of meritocracy.

Most Wall Street workers also believed that taking maternity leave had minimal impact on workers' careers but recognized that after maternity leave ended, Wall Street jobs did not accommodate caregiving responsibilities. When asked about the effects of taking maternity leave, Dylan said,

> It is much more of a meritocracy on Wall Street than in other places. I would say that [caregiving responsibilities] would affect a woman more if she's going to have to leave at a certain time to pick up her kids, or there is a certain environment that that person has created, and where their focus is. If they're not doing as good a job.

Many men and women believed that their firms accommodated child*bearing* in the short term but not necessarily intensive involvement in child *rearing*. Julie said,

> I think that in most cases [having children] doesn't affect [your work] that much. If you come back and pick up where you left off. Most people don't do that.

> I think that's probably the problem. The cases I have seen where women have tried to do a flexible schedule or work from home one day a week rarely work. I think it's those situations that have more of an effect. I don't think that it is leaving to have a baby and then coming back. I think it is trying to work around a child that's the problem. (Laughs.)

Of course, all parents who wanted to be involved with their children had to "work around a child," and this had a disparate impact by gender. After a maternity leave, women on Wall Street confronted the fact that they had responsibility for childcare that their male peers did not share. But there was also evidence that maternity leave itself was not entirely benign, since it did not fit with the ideal worker notion.

Some women felt pressure not to take a full maternity leave because of their managers' attitudes and behavior. Senior managers strongly influenced employees' use of work-family policies, and most senior managers in finance were men with stay-at-home wives.[4] This shaped expectations about workers' hours and level of devotion, leading some women to mimic male career patterns. Some senior women rejected parental leave policies, sending a powerful message to junior women that caused some of them to anticipate discrimination and make career changes accordingly. When she was pregnant, Valerie left her Wall Street firm and corporate finance to become a research analyst in a small firm. Regarding why she changed firms, she said,

> It was frowned upon at that firm for women to have babies while they were bankers. There weren't any good role models, and I didn't want to fight the fight. . . . The stress level here is much better. The people are more down-to-earth and nicer. There's a woman MD here who had two kids. She's my role model. At [my previous firm], a woman MD had a baby on Friday and was back on Monday. I would hate to be somewhere where that was an expectation.

Valerie was unwilling to maintain the workaholic patterns that senior women in her first firm exhibited. As she indicated, there were few senior women who provided good role models for balancing careers on Wall Street with involved parenting.

Securities workers rarely contested the definition of work as all-consuming, or of family as women's job. As a result, successful women in investment banking had to be remarkably stoic about life-changing family events in order to live up to the ideal worker notion. They did this by not taking the full maternity leave that their firms offered. Caitlin, who worked in public finance, also described a senior woman in her group who acted like childbearing should interfere as little as possible with work.

> There's another woman in my department who is every woman's worst role model. . . . Everything that is classic stereotyped bad stuff. She was back from maternity leave after two weeks, and made comments that the woman who took her full three months of maternity leave was "on vacation." She's not on vacation! She's on maternity leave. That woman definitely made derogatory comments about another woman. The most derogatory comments I've heard have come from another woman. . . . She just got promoted, too. What is this telling me?

The lack of work-life balance and the "superwoman syndrome" illustrated by these anecdotes suggested that some successful women wholeheartedly endorsed the workaholic culture. These women were probably successful because they accepted institutionalized cultural injunctions to prioritize work over everything else, but they discouraged other women's efforts to combine work and family in a more balanced way. And because managers influenced workers' ability to use work-life policies, their workaholic patterns intimated that no one should take parental leave if they wanted to get ahead.

This was even more the case for men, since the ideal worker notion was highly gendered. When it came to men's parental leaves, most fathers used vacation days for about a week after the birth of a child. Chris said, "Generally, guys whose wives have babies take a week off." Men did not fill out paperwork for a "paternity" or "parental" leave—they just took a small amount of time informally after the birth of their children and usually took it out of their vacation days. (Most Wall Street workers never used all of their vacation anyway.) But men also felt informal pressure not to take more time, and to take time through informal channels rather than using the formal leave policy. Ben had recently become a father and did not feel that he could take advantage of leave policies as a man, even in his administrative internal position.

> With the men I don't think it's paid. . . . I only know of one person who's ever done it so it's certainly not encouraged. And in fact, when the person did it, one of the senior people made a [sarcastic] comment [like] "Well, that's a career-enhancing move!" . . . If I'd asked for some time I'm sure they would have been great about it. But I definitely felt the pressure not to do that.

As Ben suggested, there were no good precedents for men, who felt that they could not use parental leave policies. The culture of Wall Street discouraged family responsibilities from interfering in the workplace and required men to exhibit stereotypical masculinity. This assumed a breadwinner-homemaker division of family labor and equated men with breadwinning and women with caregiving. Managers and coworkers assumed that work-family policies, including parental leave, were for women and indicated a lack of career commitment.

Not in My Job: Work-Family Policies in Practice

If maternity leave could harm Wall Street careers, then flextime and flex-place policies could be the kiss of death. The workaholic culture made face-time a marker of performance; anyone who did not seem to work enough hours received more negative evaluations. Caitlin talked about the emphasis on face-time in her job.

> About six months before I started, a memo had gone around stating that all analysts and associates were expected to be in their cubicles by 8:00 a.m. Which gets to more of the task-oriented job, as opposed to the output-oriented job. A lot of the analysts would come in at 8:00, buy the paper, go have breakfast, chat with people, start working by 9:00 or 9:30. Go to the gym, which they have here, in the early evening, come down and have dinner, and then leave at 8:00. That is the earliest that you can take a car home. It was just appalling. That kind of stuff still goes on.

Caitlin explicitly described how face-time did not necessarily correspond to productivity but was still emphasized. One of the consequences of this was that any work-family policies that reduced time in the office had negative effects on evaluations and bonuses. And that was assuming that the work group would accommodate using these policies in the first place.

Workers usually knew that flextime and flex-place policies existed, but few had attempted to use them and most did not think they were available to them. When asked whether their firms had work-family policies, most men and women gave a resounding cry of "Sure, but *not in my job*." Lisa, a research analyst, said, "They probably offer it in the company but not in my group." Melissa, who worked in public finance, said, "Not in this position." If these women, who worked in areas with more women, viewed family-friendly policies as inaccessible, then who was able to use these policies?

Those who knew of cases said that they were used primarily by administrative staff rather than professionals. Allison said, "It's usually the secretaries." Similarly, Ben, who worked in a support role, said of these policies,

> I think for administrative jobs, absolutely. Current investment banking jobs, it's very tough to do that. I'm

> only aware of one banker who works a shortened week and she's a very senior managing director.

In general, these arrangements seemed to apply only to positions that did not directly serve clients.

Many pointed to industry imperatives that made these options unavailable in their jobs. Elise said that flexible schedules were unfeasible for professionals in corporate finance because of client demands, regardless of the firm's official policies.

> For professionals there's no such thing as flextime or anything like that. And it's not so much the company's fault. It's just the industry. Clients expect to be able to get you twenty-four hours a day because they pay you a lot of money, so I don't know how the company can get around that. Maybe they can structure it so that you have [fewer] clients or something.

Renee also believed that investment bankers could not serve their clients properly on nontraditional schedules.

> Flextime, to be honest, in this job is impossible. Your clients will not understand if some stranger turns up. The relationship is with individuals. Flextime would not work in this job very well at all. My sense is, at [my firm] anyway, that there is a willingness, but that nobody really has a sense of what the policies really are.

Workaholic norms were so entrenched that investment bankers rarely even investigated the options that were formally available. Men and women on Wall Street believed that work in the securities industry could not be organized to make flexible arrangements feasible because the industry and its clients demanded too much dedication. Senior bankers and clients required Wall Street professionals to be at their beck and call at all times.

Informal attitudes within Wall Street firms toward those who used work-family policies revealed their lack of fit with the workaholic culture and its face-time demands. When asked how using these policies would affect a worker's career, Natalie said,

> I know that there are women in banking who have definitely felt that it would. Like, in talking about telecommuting, it was sort of jokingly referred to as "Mom's day off," which sort of defeats the purpose. It's like, "No, I am actually working when I am at home."

These types of informal attitudes reinforced gender inequality in the workplace and in the family because the firms' written policies were unable to change the notion of an ideal worker. As a result, workers in direct revenue positions who attempted to use work-family options met with resistance and received negative evaluations that did not match measurable performance indicators. Recall Tracy's story from chapter 1. When she pushed for a flextime arrangement that would minimally affect her revenues she encountered a lot of resistance.

> I went back to work and I was still nursing and my company provided a room for me to do that. To pump during the day. . . . And that was getting a lot of press simultaneously and [my firm]'s kind of in the forefront of this because they provided a room with a little refrigerator and had me do a number of interviews with CNN and ABC and I was in *Working Mother Magazine* and all this stuff. . . . Well, they asked me to do something—another interview—and I flatly declined. I said, "Look, here I am, you're saying how great it is to work here and sure it's great that you allow me to breastfeed, but I'm trying to negotiate a flexible work week and I don't think it's being negotiated fairly." Well, all of a sudden this was something that was done quite quickly. . . . One anecdote to that—I worked at primarily a male desk. There was only one other woman in the entire trading floor. I mean it's a male-dominated world and the men on the desk and even the

> women were quite jealous of the arrangement I made, even with the 20 percent pay cut. Their peer reviews of me were suddenly negative whereas before they had been quite positive.

Tracy took a 20 percent reduction in her salary, but using Wall Street's logic of meritocracy she argued that her bonus should reflect her profits and losses and should not be cut over and above any changes in her performance. Negotiating agreement from the firm on this point proved to be very difficult, despite its fit with the stated rationale of the pay system. So even though her firm was reputed to be among the most woman friendly and family friendly on Wall Street, she found that the reality did not match the reputation. After she changed her work schedule, her bonus was so low that it was her final push to leave the labor force.

As Tracy's story reveals, there was an inherent contradiction between work-family policies and the culture of this industry. Professionals who attempted to use these policies met resistance, suffered penalties, or found these arrangements simply unworkable. Barbara had arranged a four-day work week on paper, but found herself working five days in practice.

> I worked out, or thought I worked out anyway, a four-day work week at [my firm]. . . . I don't think that four-day work weeks, here anyway, with what I'm selling—it doesn't work for me. Because most of my customers are covered by someone who's there five days a week. I never really found good backup. I think a job share would work well. But if you're not there [for] a day, it's a market kind of thing where trades develop, are talked about, and are executed in an hour. . . . You can't always plan that the trade is not going to happen on Friday. Because it might, or you might need to talk about it on Friday. So it hasn't really worked that well. I always feel like I should come in, and I usually do come in. I definitely worked probably more than half of the Fridays.

After accepting a pay cut as part of her negotiation of a four-day week, most weeks she went to the office five days. As Barbara and Tracy discovered, the primary effect of using flextime and part-time options seemed to be a decline in pay and evaluations over and above actual changes in hours and revenue production.

Sexual Harassment and Diversity Policies

In addition to work-family policies, Wall Street firms also had diversity and sexual harassment policies that could have improved women's opportunities for success. But in this respect, Wall Street firms' culture of machismo and greater concern with their own legal protection than worker protection blunted their effectiveness. Diversity policies sometimes seemed out of place in the largely homogeneous workforce on Wall Street, and some workers viewed diversity policies as window dressing. Olivia, a Latin American woman who worked in emerging markets, said, "Supposedly yes, they have all that in place and we talk about it and diversity and blah, blah, blah. . . . Diversity overall, I think it's much more blah, blah, blah than what they really do. . . . It's a lot of sales pitch." Tracy also viewed her firm's diversity committee as ineffective, especially after they appointed the worst possible person to head it.

> They have diversity committees and things like that. And the ironic thing was one year the head of the diversity committee was the head of [a trading area] who was by far the biggest bigot as well as [a] sexist pig, as any woman within a five-mile radius could have told you. . . . When that news came out I remember turning to a female colleague [and saying], "This has got to be a joke. That is pathetic."

In her view, the selection of the head of the diversity committee signaled that its function was window dressing. Since the jurisdiction of diversity committees seemed relatively vague, her impression may have been accurate.

In fact, diversity committees had a vague mandate and few tangible effects. Sabrina, the only African American I interviewed, had firsthand experience with her firm's lack of real commitment to diversity. When she pursued a job on Wall Street, she was hired to fulfill equal employment opportunity requirements: "The two places I went, they had specific hiring goals that they wanted to fill. I fit the bill. But other than that, I couldn't see any real commitment to diversity." Sabrina never felt accepted and was derailed after she received no training or support. As her case suggests, diversity hiring initiatives and sensitivity training appeared to be designed to protect Wall Street firms from discrimination lawsuits rather than to foster a truly diverse workplace.

Legal protection was similarly the impetus for sexual harassment policies. Most workers believed that their firms were equipped to handle sexual harassment and took diversity issues seriously, but few of them had any experience with this.[5] Among the 36 percent of women who experienced sexual harassment, none of them used her firm's formal policies or grievance procedures to address the situation.

Some women observed that a specific firm's culture influenced whether its sexual harassment policies were effective; the culture influenced the work environment more than formal policies. Some firms just had an environment of sexual harassment. Barbara described her experiences at a major Wall Street firm where she was a summer associate during business school. There the sexually charged macho atmosphere led more than one more senior man to make repeated sexual advances toward her, even though they were married and they knew that she was married. She said, "The kind of sexual harassment that I experienced [as a summer associate] wasn't only illegal, it was a macho atmosphere." Barbara was thrilled when she received an offer elsewhere and did not have to consider returning to that firm after business school.

At least 45 percent of the women believed that sexual harassment policies were more window dressing than substance. When asked whether these policies were effective, Amanda said, "My sense is that if that happened they would try to cover it up before addressing it. They would view it more as trying to create trouble and not take it seriously." The experience of women who encountered sexual harassment largely confirmed her impression.

Fourteen percent of the women were harassed by clients. Claire worked in equity research and said that sexual harassment was rampant among clients.

> All the time clients. You just have to—especially when you go to Texas. I'm serious. It's terrible. . . . Your salesperson is usually a guy and he's like, "All right Claire, I'll protect you." Except for the ones that are like, "All right, we're going to Texas. Make sure you wear your halter top. We'll get lots of business." (Laughter.) . . . In some of the cases, when it really got out of hand, I've complained. I would complain to the salesman. I would say, "Look, I can't believe you let him get away with this. It's an unacceptable way to treat anyone, especially a woman coming down who wants to do business with him." One time I even complained to the director of research and complained to the head of sales. "This is an unacceptable situation here and I don't think you should have any other women analysts traveling down here because it's not good." And I think they said something to the salesperson to get him to control that client.

Women who encountered sexual harassment from clients usually talked to senior people informally and were generally satisfied with their handling of the issue, which ranged from closely supervising interactions with a client to reassigning the account or refusing to do business with the client.

But when sexual harassment occurred inside Wall Street firms rather than with clients, women on Wall Street believed that it would be more damaging to report it than to keep it quiet.[6] Eleven percent of women experienced harassment from coworkers in the form of a hostile work environment. Usually these women saw no benefit to filing complaints, and their typical response was to change jobs, which contributed to the sex segregation of Wall Street. In the case of one woman who did complain to her manager, he simply put her and her female colleague in a room with the offending man and told them to tell him the problem. Unsurprisingly, this only increased his hostility toward them.

Twenty-three percent of the women were harassed by managers, and none of them used formal channels to handle the situation. Elise described how she managed sexual overtures from a supervisor when she was an associate in corporate finance.

> I tried to be, unfortunately, as nice as I possibly could so I didn't make him mad and as complimentary as I possibly could, even though he made my skin crawl, and just nicely said that this was inappropriate. . . . I also have made sure that I never, ever put myself in a position where he and I are in one place alone, ever! . . . If I so chose to do something, the guy would be removed from the organization in probably twenty seconds. I have no doubt that the firm would respond appropriately. I just think there's no upside for me and so I won't do that. If I want to end my career, that's a great way to do it.

Like Elise, most women wanted to avoid making any waves when they were sexually harassed within their firms because they believed it would harm or destroy their careers. So they all handled sexual harassment by managers informally and individually. Following a common pattern, Elise changed jobs to escape this situation. She moved into another high-paying position and was one of the most successful women, but job changes to escape sexual harassment did not usually benefit women's careers. Daphne left her second job because of harassment from her boss.

> He would make rude comments and think it was funny to touch my butt and you name it. Inappropriate at all levels. . . . [But] you'd never say that to anybody in the industry. It's like ruining your career if you admit that.

> So, then again, it's one of those, it's not fair but just, I don't know. I feel like when I was in college, if anything was not fair I would really be more a rabble-rouser. Now I'm like, it's not fair, but move on. . . . And it was only after I left the company . . . that I talked to the managing director, the one who I told you was very good, and said, "Look, this was also what was going on." And he said to me, "Why didn't you tell me this ages ago?" Because as soon as you said anything to him about it, I would have been in trouble again, so what's the point? . . . He thought I should have talked to him and maybe I should have but like I said, if he said anything to the guy, I'd be in trouble for that, too. So when one of your direct bosses is the person who is doing it, you're going to be in trouble anyway so you might as well not say anything. It wasn't worth it.

Ultimately, women avoided using their firms' sexual harassment policies. The policies would perhaps protect Wall Street firms from liability in sexual harassment suits, but they were largely ineffective for women who actually experienced sexual harassment. Many workers, especially women, viewed sexual harassment policies as more lip service than substance. But some gradual shifts in the culture of Wall Street were occurring after the development of these policies, especially with respect to the sexually harassing environment.

A Kinder, Gentler Place

While investment banks' policies conflicted with Wall Street's culture, they also forced some changes in the macho nature of this culture. Some men and women viewed these changes as for the better. For example, when asked how his firm handled sexual harassment, Dylan said that the policies had toned down some of the more offensive aspects of Wall Street's culture and made it more hospitable for everyone. "I think that they've done a good job. It has helped the work environment. I was uncomfortable with a lot of the stuff that was said or how people were treated, so now it is much better." Dylan was a family-oriented research analyst with a high *II* ranking, a seat on the trading floor, and lots of experience on Wall Street. He felt that changes in the culture were beneficial and made it a more civilized place to work.

On the other hand, some men and women lamented a loss of humor and lightness in the work environment and were unsure that the increase in civility was worth the price. When asked about off-color humor in her work group, Caitlin said,

> There is no doubt that that stuff goes on. I'm not saying it's okay because everybody does it. In general, it's not a hostile environment for women at all, but given the backdrop of the sexual harassment issues in the last few years, and the fact that it is just a much more conservative department, people won't tell those jokes. I can get away with telling a dirtier joke than the men can. They won't tell a dirty joke in front me, and that kind of bums me out. I feel left out. It's just a much more "work is work" kind of department.

Similarly, when asked about topics of conversation on the trading floor, Penny also bemoaned the loss of freedom for sexual banter and smutty humor.

> That's changed. You used to be able to be a lot more open than you can now so I think the work environment on Wall Street has become a lot more cleaned up in the last few years or PC, whichever way you care to look at it. Which I think is a shame in a way, because working on a trading floor has always been one of the best opportunities to see men in their natural habitat. . . . They used to joke about sex a lot but they can't now. . . . One of the ways you can judge how much you trust somebody on Wall Street now is whether you can make a dirty joke with them or not.

From these women's perspectives, the underlying attitudes had not necessarily changed, but they had been driven underground in a way that made the work environment no more inclusive and decidedly less fun.

So the development of diversity policies, especially those related to sexual harassment, had somewhat changed the environment on Wall Street. It was perhaps producing a gradual shift away from the kinds of macho environments that Barbara described in her summer internship and that were made infamous in the "boom-boom room" case. There was a mixture of opinions about whether all of the change was good or bad, but the consensus was that it was gradually affecting the culture of Wall Street.

But while the culture of machismo and the fraternity-like atmosphere described in books like *Liar's Poker* and *The Bonfire of the Vanities* were slowly being toned down, subtle forms of discrimination continued to affect women's opportunities and were outside the jurisdiction of workplace policies.[7] Also, the globalization of financial markets meant that workaholic demands were actually increasing. So while there was a decline in outwardly hostile environments, women's difficulties managing work and family were likely increasing for those who had children. Existing work-family policies were not able to change this aspect of Wall Street's culture.

Conclusion

It might have been possible for diversity, sexual harassment, and work-family policies to provide women with better opportunities on Wall Street, but the appearance that equal employment opportunity had been achieved through formal policies while subtle discrimination still operated through the informal culture undermined the creation of a genuine meritocracy. It was hard for women to be judged on merit in an environment with little real commitment to diversity or integration. The fact that Wall Street was still dominated by white men bred the types of subtle gender discrimination that were discussed in chapters 4 and 5, affecting women's opportunities to perform and evaluations of their performance. Also, where sexual harassment was a feature of the work environment, women's opportunities were limited by the fact that others viewed them as sexual rather than professional, and by their decisions—often forced—to leave or change jobs.

In addition to the difficulties women had with the masculine culture, women who wanted to have families suffered disadvantages because extreme workaholism was a condition of work on Wall Street. Wall Street firms may have genuinely wanted to ease work-family conflicts for their workers, if they could accomplish this *without changing business as usual.* But ultimately the family-related policies of Wall Street firms were impotent because they conflicted with the logic of the industry, which assumed workers were available day and night, weekdays and weekends, by fax, beeper, and cellular phone, and without commitments to anything or anyone else. The informal culture on Wall Street further assumed that men would fit this mold and that women would not.

As a result, organizational policies designed to facilitate work-family balance were ineffective because professional employees did not believe that they were genuinely available in their jobs and believed that they would be penalized if they used them. Confirming this, perceptions of workers who actually used these policies were generally negative and influenced performance evaluations and bonuses. Efforts to develop more effective work-family policies would need to target attitudes about family as women's responsibility and implicit emphases on face-time.

Encounters with all of these difficulties and the ineffectiveness of firm policies derailed many women. But some women were highly successful in their first five to seven years on Wall Street in spite of this. Additional time in the industry (and the ensuing bear market) may have undermined some of them later in their careers, but their strategies for success are still instructive. In the next chapter, I explore the strategies and organizational arrangements that helped some women succeed on Wall Street.

Chapter 8

BEATING THE ODDS

The Most Successful Women

Earlier chapters have shown that women on Wall Street usually did worse than men because of subtle discrimination in account assignment and performance evaluations, a masculine culture, and family-related pressures. But 27 percent of the women were highly successful in their first five to seven years on Wall Street.[1] These women's 1997 compensation ranged from $415,000 to $750,000, with an average of $588,750.[2] Their cases challenge beliefs that gender is destiny and shed light on the prospects for gender equality in high-intensity jobs. Like many men, these highly successful women encountered expanding career opportunities in the 1990s bull market. The same processes affected both these women and their less successful counterparts, but they succeeded within Wall Street's existing culture and with existing policies despite manager and coworker preferences for others like themselves, double standards, stereotypes, and assumptions that they would have children and leave. How did these women succeed, and what can their experiences tell us about gender inequality in performance-based pay systems?

In general, professionals who succeed tend to look and think alike, so those who succeed despite looking different usually minimize the differences between themselves and the majority. Forbes described how he learned that he needed to lose his New York borough accent and assimilate to be successful in investment banking.

> One of the things that I very quickly clued in on is that people who sound like they're from Brooklyn or Queens stay in the back office and people who sound like they're from Connecticut end up in the front office. . . . That is a big implicit form of discrimination. . . . If you sound like you're from Queens you can't become an investment banker. Everybody tells me I sound like I'm from Ohio and I say "Thank you" when I hear that. You don't want to have an accent. . . . There's a certain amount of assimilation that takes place and either you decide you want to assimilate or you don't.

Like Forbes, who deliberately lost his accent, women who succeeded on Wall Street made themselves as similar to men as possible in their behavior and attitudes. They worked long hours, endorsed the myth of meritocracy, remained childless, and played golf. As long as they were feminine enough to avoid being labeled a "bitch" but otherwise resembled their male peers, they had a shot at success in this industry. Of course, it was not easy. The experiences of the highest-paid women illuminate strategies and organizational arrangements that allowed some women to beat the odds. Consider, for example, Elise.

Before she went to business school, Elise worked as an analyst in investment banking at one of Wall Street's most prestigious firms. She returned to the same firm after she completed her MBA, where she specialized in oil and gas industries. It was her intention to stay at that firm and become an MD, and she stayed on a linear path toward that goal. When I asked her about her expectations about hours when she returned as an associate, she said,

> I expected them to be very similar to the way they were when I was an analyst, so I expected them to be between seventy and a hundred hours. However, I think my first two years as an associate were a lot harder than as an analyst. More so because I think I put more pressure on myself to not just do the job but to do it really

> well because I felt I was going to be here for fifteen years versus two.

Elise was a vice president and still worked seventy hours per week.

She found it difficult to connect with the clients in oil and gas, but worked hard to fit in with her group and to demonstrate her competence and analytical skills. Working with these industries, she felt that being a woman was a disadvantage in the long run but she also gained valuable experience.

> I think it's important to work on big and important clients but I think it's a whole lot more important to be consistent with whatever you're working on. So I'm not so sure it's just the client base that matters. Like I'm not such a big believer that the high-profile deals get you promoted. I think working on a lot of stuff and doing well at pretty much everything is more beneficial.

Elise worked with oil and gas clients for two and a half years and then worked for one year as an internal consultant to the head of investment banking. At the end of that rotation she did not return to the oil and gas group because she did not think that she would have long-term success as a woman with clients in such a male-dominated industry. She said,

> I felt like the best way for me to get ahead as a woman in investment banking was maybe with the products. Because if you're an industry person, the CEO or the CFO is always going to understand the industry better than you because they live it. And the only talent you can really bring to that person is being able to be their confidante, meaning I know the top CEOs of the top three retail companies and the benefit for me is to tell CEO #1 something I learned from CEO #2 in an industry, because there's always product people who will tell the client about the product. I just realized that it's going to be extraordinarily hard for me to be that confidante to CEOs in any industry, especially [oil and gas industries],

> and I don't think that's bad or good—I just think that's a fact. So I figured from a product side I would always know more about the market and the product than the company, because that's not what they do for a living and I would have a lot more credibility out of the box.

Because she believed that credibility and expertise would be easier to establish in a product area, she moved into a group that specialized in high yield.

By the time she moved into this position, she had worked for the same firm for many years and was well connected with many senior people. Regarding the impact of changing areas within the firm a couple of times, she said, "Overall I think it's been helpful because I've met a whole lot more people. There's virtually no one that I don't know in the organization. I've worked in so many different places and I've been there so long. It doesn't hurt." Elise found that political alliances had been helpful and described herself as very satisfied with her career. She earned between $550,000 and $600,000 in 1997, which was above the $430,000 average for her graduating class.[3]

On a personal level, Elise had married another investment banker whom she met in business school. Unfortunately their relationship had soured, since he wanted a more traditional wife than she was willing to be. When asked if she thought the dissolution of her marriage was related to her career in any way, she said, "Only to the extent that he works at [another firm] and he wants Martha Stewart and that's not me. So I guess, in that way, yes. He didn't want an equal." She found that her career conflicted with her husband's ideas about the gender division of labor in the family, again illustrating a common assumption on Wall Street that women should support men's work rather than being committed to careers of their own. They did not have any children and were in the process of finalizing their divorce.

Elise's case is illustrative for a number of reasons. First and foremost, she strategically chose to leave a group where client relationships would be difficult for her to establish and to enter a product specialization where her expertise and credibility would be clear. She made this move after she had honed her skills and established a measure of competence in her first group, but before she was expected to originate client business. She also mobilized political support from senior people by staying in the same firm and working in multiple areas. Her rotation with the head of investment banking gave her exposure with many senior investment bankers. This increased her opportunities, gave her better access to resources, and helped her to compete effectively with the men at her firm. And because she did not have children, she deviated only slightly from the ideal worker notion, even while her personal situation further illustrates the entrenchment of the breadwinner-homemaker family model in Wall Street culture.

Like Elise, most highly successful women worked in male-dominated areas of the industry where they had to emulate male work patterns to survive. These were also the areas where women faced the toughest work environments, and 58 percent of the most successful women encountered hostility in the workplace. They only succeeded because they made particular sacrifices to get ahead. Renee described her early experiences working in corporate finance.

> I felt really odd, and I still do feel a little bit odd. My [first] year in particular was a real locker room year. Guys would come into my office and say, "Pull my finger." (Laugh.) It was bad. And I never stooped to that level. We were once on a boat trip—this was orientation week on the [harbor] cruise. We had a band going. It was just a really fun time for all the new people. Then all of the guys dropped their trousers. They just dropped their trousers and started dancing. I mean I was not about to drop my skirt. And it was like a social male macho mentality, like *Animal House*. That was my class in particular. So that really further alienated me. And I am, to this day, the only remaining female in my

> class. All three of the others left. I never dreamed I would be the only one left. I thought I would be the first to go, so it is a little ironic.

In this and other instances, a "thick skin" was required to survive in the most male-dominated areas of Wall Street. Some, like Renee, simply endured the culture of machismo, while 25 percent of the most successful women changed firms or areas when they encountered hostile work environments. They were still successful because they managed to move into equally high-paying areas of prestigious firms where there were opportunities for success. They represented 7 percent of all the women, compared to another 30 percent that moved into lower-paying areas in response to the same situation.

Sponsors and Strategies

How did these women succeed by Wall Street standards? As Kanter found thirty years earlier, sponsors were critical for nontraditional employees.[4] One-third of the most successful women had assistance from powerful male mentors. Caroline's mentor helped her to be promoted ahead of schedule and to gain extra credibility from her experience running a business.

> I had a terrific mentor, the head of the group at the time, and I think that when I first interviewed with the firm I thought that this person was very insightful, which is one of the reasons that I ultimately took the job. He said to me that most people on Wall Street, when they look at your résumé, will not give you credit for the business that you ran. . . . This person, who was head of my group, ultimately appreciated that fact. I worked my rear end off for the first year or year and a half, and he actually recommended to the firm that I be accelerated or pulled out of my class and move ahead a year. Which had only been done, I guess, in the history

> of the firm in investment banking, a couple of times. It was a pretty amazing thing for me.

A mentoring relationship with a powerful man in this and three other cases opened up avenues that were often closed for women. This suggests that organizations could improve their chances of retaining and promoting qualified women by actively fostering mentorship opportunities for them. Workers could also improve their probability of success by forming alliances with strong mentors. But these mentorship relationships were more difficult for women to establish because male managers often preferred to take junior employees who resembled them under their wing.

Given this disadvantage in finding mentors, some successful women improved their chances by establishing a specialized expertise. One-third of the most successful women had specialized knowledge and skills that made them indispensable to their firms. After she moved into sales, Barbara had more knowledge than other workers at her firm about the securities that she was selling.

> I was really lucky. I would have to say that I really felt that they were happy to have me. They were really happy to have someone who had worked in a top-three firm in mortgages. In a bulge-bracket. It was a very positive experience. There were reasons for it. There were things I knew that they didn't know, and we built on that.

Her experience as a trader at her first firm gave her valuable expertise with a type of securities that her second firm was only beginning to offer. Like Barbara, particular women could gain task-specific reputations that overrode negative beliefs about women's competence by covering a specific product or region that their firms valued, or by obtaining an *II* ranking in research.

Some women specialized in financial products rather than industries in order to insulate themselves from client biases. Like Elise, whom we met at the beginning of this chapter, these women avoided jobs that depended on building relationships that resemble friendships with male client executives. Instead they specialized in high-revenue products. Eleven percent of the women, and 42 percent of the most successful women, specialized in a product in order to establish their expertise, reduce their dependence on client relationships, and become less vulnerable to subjective evaluations of their competence. For example, Emma strategically chose to enter an extremely male-dominated specialty.

> I think the reason I wanted to go into a quantitative product and also an execution product is that I can say, "I did that deal." It's much more nebulous when you're in relationship management or something like that to say, "That's my relationship." Or things like that. But I can say, "I did that deal. I got this execution. I did this. I'm efficient." And it's very easy to point to. I would hate to be in relationship management where everything is a golf game and it is all about who did who go to school with. Those, I think, would be very difficult to have credibility in.

When she finished business school, she deliberately chose an area where she believed that her contribution to firm revenues would be visible so that her success would be more independent of the whims of clients.

Danielle chose a product area instead of an industry specialization for similar reasons.

> We had to deliver the goods so it wasn't just being nice to the clients. I think for women, being product people is a great thing because you get an expertise and you know something so that it is very easy to establish that you have something to offer. I just thought it was a much easier field for women to be successful [in]. It's objective.

Successful women chose jobs where their productivity would be harder to question. Since many women felt that client firms preferred to work with financial professionals who resembled their own executives, who were usually men, they were more likely to succeed in jobs where client preferences had less influence.

As this implies, the existence of tangible performance criteria was an important ingredient for women's success on Wall Street. Because workers' pay was dependent on how their managers, peers, and subordinates assessed their merits and subtle discrimination could affect these assessments, the less subjective the performance criteria the better for women. Forty-two percent of the most successful women worked in sales and trading or product-focused areas with clear criteria for evaluation. Barbara described how she had deliberately moved into sales because she expected to be rewarded for the revenue that she produced.

> When I was first working in sales and trading at [my first firm], I was trading mortgages. And I didn't really want to do that. I wanted to be in sales, because I knew that it would be more flexible in terms of if I produced. . . . Fortunately I was able to produce like I had expected and had hoped that I would. . . . One year I had more sales credits than anyone else at [my firm] in mortgages, in my department. And I think I was actually third on the whole floor. That was '95. So I put myself in the category of people that deserve more money. It was great. And what happens after that? Basically, the next year I produced even more. They gave me even more money.

Like Barbara, successful women selected areas of the industry where they would be evaluated more on production and less on subjective criteria. Emma described choosing to specialize in a quantitative product in corporate finance.

> I think some of the best advice I got was from a woman in that group. She was the only woman in that group and she said, "As a woman on Wall Street, go get the nerdiest job straight out of business school that you can get. Go get the quant job and then if you want to go be

> a generalist in corporate finance eventually, whatever, but at least you've established, 'I can handle this level of quantitative work.'" So I took the job at [my first Wall Street firm] in asset-backed securities just because that was the most quantitative job at the best firm that I would be able to get a job at.

Choosing a quantitative job insulated Emma from some biases in others' evaluations, since she had more concrete output than she would have had with client relationships. In this way, more objective measures of performance could be particularly helpful for women.

In contrast, women often fared poorly under subjective evaluation criteria because stereotypes or biases against women could enter into evaluations of their performance.[5] The most successful women knew this, and two-thirds of them worked in highly quantitative fields. One-third became specialists in a product where evaluations are more independent of relationships than in industry specializations. Seventeen percent of them worked in sales and trading, where their contribution to firm revenue was indicated clearly in a profit and loss book. In fact, 23 percent of the women I interviewed deliberately chose an area where their contribution to firm revenues would be clear. This did not make all of them successful, but it helped one-third of the most successful women and at least demystified the relationship between performance and pay for the rest. The more that criteria for performance were rational, objective, and transparent, the better women's chances were of overriding stereotypes of them as less competent.

Of course, most of the highly successful women did not have children at the time of the interview. The fact that women who succeeded by Wall Street standards tended to be childless suggests that women's success may be less threatening to the established order than making room for family life in Wall Street careers. This implies that gender equity might be achievable in highly demanding jobs if it were not for work-family issues that disproportionately affect women. Family responsibilities may threaten the status quo in jobs like these more than does incorporating women into the higher rungs of the workplace hierarchy. But these threats to the status quo are highly intertwined because the typical gender division of labor in the family makes work-family balance a de facto issue of gender inequality. As a result, the existence of successful women does not imply a clear recipe for equity. In fact, many of the same processes are working in these cases as in those of their less successful counterparts—these women have just made particular sacrifices to get ahead. But since the same processes operate for them, it is likely that their ranks thinned out further as additional time went on. One of the highest-earning women, Mia, had already left Wall Street to become a full-time mother since receiving her 1997 bonus.

Conclusion

The strategies of the most successful women suggest some ways to succeed within the existing system. As we have seen, these women avoided the jobs that were most dependent on relationships with male-dominated clients and with male managers and peers. Specializing in a financial product rather than an industry was one way to reduce dependence on buddy relationships with clients. Avoiding jobs that were team based could also be very important, since women's individual contributions could more easily be overlooked if they were part of a team than if they stood alone. This might have been one of the reasons why women have traditionally been more successful in equity research, where they work relatively independently.

Women who were highly successful were also unusual in a few ways. First, they typically had a powerful mentor who supported their careers, and this mentor was usually a man. As Kanter found over twenty years earlier, sponsorship is essential if higher proportions of women are to succeed in male-dominated professions.[6] Given that current management is highly male dominated, it is important for securities firms to raise workers' consciousness of preferences for others like themselves, and to develop incentives for managers to mentor workers who are different from them. These firms could develop stronger formal mentorship programs, including bonus incentives for senior workers who take nontraditional employees under their wing. In other words, they could augment the bonuses of those who mentor successful junior workers.

The most successful women were also career committed, determined to be successful, and strategic about managing their careers to maximize their success and longevity on Wall Street. Most of them were childless at the time of the interview and viewed motherhood as incompatible with their jobs. They also generally accepted the workaholic ethic of Wall Street culture. In the long run, work-family issues may be the most intractable obstacles to gender equality on Wall Street because most women want and eventually have children.

Finally, the most significant lesson of highly paid women involved their deliberate choice of jobs in areas with clear performance criteria. Women had better opportunities in areas where success depended less on the subjective evaluations of male managers and peers, or on buddy relationships with executives from male-dominated client companies. Given the bonus system, working in areas with more objective measures of production improved the odds that pay would reflect performance. This made meritocracy more real in these cases, and teaches an important lesson about how gender inequality is most likely to emerge. It may be that performance-based pay can be good for women, as long as criteria for performance are clearly measurable. On the other hand, performance criteria can never be completely objective. The more that subjectivity enters into evaluations, the more that subtle influences on evaluations turned meritocracy into a myth.

Chapter 9

THE MYTH OF MERITOCRACY

Gender and Performance-Based Pay

As chapter 8 revealed, some women succeeded on Wall Street despite the subtle discrimination and prevalent workaholism. Some might think that the existence of successful women supports the notion of a Wall Street meritocracy and therefore that less successful women deserved lower pay because they made personal choices that derailed their careers. But merit alone cannot explain the differences in men's and women's career trajectories.

The fact remains that women who were equal to their male counterparts as a group made less money. This is even more surprising given that Wall Street firms compete for the most talented individuals; this is, after all, the path to making the most money for both the firm and the client. The long bull market of the 1990s should have created more opportunity regardless of biases. With business booming, Wall Street firms should have tried to retain anyone who could skillfully manage the volume of work and contribute to their huge bottom lines, leading them to be gender blind. The performance-based pay system should have, theoretically, created equity by compensating workers on their worth rather than according to characteristics like gender. But men and women encountered different environments in this industry, and the bonus system encouraged unequal results independent of skill, effort, or other aspects of merit. The result is a larger-than-average gender gap in pay.

Gender and Career Trajectories

As the rest of *Selling Women Short* has demonstrated, gender shapes Wall Street careers right from the start. At the entry level, Wall Street firms made efforts to hire women, but women applied in smaller numbers than men. Women represented only 20 percent of incoming associates. Women also started in different areas of the securities industry, either because of their own preferences or because managers hired workers who resembled them or their clients. As a result, hiring practices had a disparate impact on women, who tended to be tokens and who were especially isolated in the highest-paying jobs, which had the highest proportion of men. As tokens, women were highly visible and vulnerable to performance pressures, stereotyping, and discrimination. They had to fight cultural assumptions that they were less competent than their male peers. Because of these assumptions, many of women's contributions to the productivity of their work groups were overlooked or devalued by their managers and colleagues, especially if indicators of performance were not clear-cut. Managers' and coworkers' preferences for coworkers similar to themselves gave further advantages to those in the majority. In most areas, these preferences favored men.

The processes that obstructed women's early careers meant that very few women made it into the senior ranks, and those who did had to overcome contradictory standards—those that applied to them as workers and those that applied to them as women. As one informant commented, most women who made it in finance had a "Stepford wife" quality to them; they were not necessarily strong role models or advocates for women in the junior ranks.[1] As a result, there were few real role models for new female hires, especially in the higher-paying areas. And the few pockets where there was greater diversity were usually job ghettos with lower pay.

Another significant barrier to many women's success was the intense time commitment that Wall Street required. This generated a culture of workaholism that precluded involvement in family life and defined the ideal worker as one with no extra-work responsibilities and preferably with a stay-at-home spouse. This definition of the ideal worker was based on the average life shared by the male majority and contradicted women's typical family situation, posing additional obstacles for women who did not want to, or could not, emulate male patterns.

Approximately one quarter of the women managed to succeed despite these obstacles. But women had a higher rate of attrition than men in the early part of their careers, were promoted at a lower rate, and often moved into lower-paying positions where there were more women. Given that fewer women continued to pursue their careers and were at higher levels, and those who remained continued to encounter obstacles to success, gender inequality on Wall Street probably worsened as their careers progressed further.

Markets and Meritocracy

Those who believe in the justice of competitive markets might argue that this type of inequality must be justified, otherwise firms that permit subtle discrimination would be at a disadvantage compared to those that do not.[2] That is, they would argue that discrimination must make firms more competitive or they would fail. But securities firms do not necessarily pay a high economic price for offering privileges to white men. They can distribute workers across work groups, or work within groups, in a variety of ways without changing the firm's profits. In some cases managers appeared to believe that distributing fewer good accounts to women was economically rational because they expected clients to prefer men or believed that investments in women's careers were a waste of resources because they would eventually leave the labor force. Firms also had substantial leeway when they allocated bonuses. Bonuses provided incentives for future performance, but pay that did not exactly match performance might have little impact on workers' motivation or subsequent performance, especially if performance was hard to measure and the fair bonus amount was unknown. Most of the influences on gender differences in access to accounts and performance evaluations were also subtle enough to be unconscious. Meanwhile, the ideology of market efficiency was used to justify inequalities that are incorporated into and perpetuated by the bonus system, defining them as meritocratic.[3]

A meritocracy is a system in which advancement is based on individual ability or achievement. While many touted Wall Street's compensation system as meritocratic, *Selling Women Short* shows how it is instead a self-reproducing system of structural inequality. Remember that the men and women I interviewed were similar, and yet a large gender gap remained after accounting for other influences. Wall Street's bonus system permits nonmerit influences to affect pay decisions, many of which have a disparate impact on women. While firm revenues and group revenues affected men and women alike, women were disproportionately funneled into groups with lower revenue potential. Perceptions of performance within teams of workers adversely affected women because of universal tendencies to prefer similar others and to view men as more competent than women. The lack of fit between Wall Street's workaholic culture and typical family arrangements had negative effects not only on women's performance but on how they were perceived and thus on evaluations of their performance, even in the face of contradictory information. Thus ends the myth of meritocracy.

If this kind of subtle discrimination can persist on Wall Street, which is supposedly driven only by money, then it's likely that similar processes operate in other settings with performance-based rewards. This isn't a "blame me first" polemic, rather the bonus system itself reproduces inequality by concealing information about criteria for determining bonus amounts and about others' pay and by holding women to higher standards than men. Recognizing this, 29 percent of the workers I interviewed viewed meritocracy on Wall Street as a myth.

Some of these workers disavowed meritocracy on Wall Street because bonuses seemed arbitrary. Large pay differences within work groups and disconnections between performance and pay made bonus amounts seem random. Vicki, who left Wall Street to work at a commercial bank, compared the pay at her current job with that of her first job in equity research.

> Working at [the Wall Street firm where I was an analyst], there were some people there who were making huge amounts of money, and there was a very large discrepancy between the highest-paid analyst and the lowest-paid analyst. One of the things that is just very obvious is that the pay scale where I am now is much more compressed. There is not nearly the same differentiation in compensation between people of a similar rank. That is just a lot better to be around. You're not making fifty thousand dollars, while somebody down the hall from you doesn't seem to be working as hard as you but is making five million.

From her perspective, pay on Wall Street did not correspond to effort or productivity. The lack of evidence that differences were merit based led her to view the bonus system as arbitrary and unfair.

For some workers, subjective evaluations even contradicted more objective measures of performance, leading to especially strong rejections of the myth of meritocracy. Tracy, the trader who left the industry after her flexible work arrangement led to a poor bonus, remarked,

> It's very subjective whereas you think in trading, "Okay, you made your P&L and you get X." But it's not. . . . The team review process, while it sounds good on paper, is difficult because it is very subjective and anyone can write a review on you. So if somebody doesn't like you because your trade affected them in some way . . . they can write a scathing review, unsolicited, on you and that can show up on your [evaluation form] or your comprehensive review that your manager puts together and suddenly you're faced with, "I don't like her because she wears really loud pink

> shoes." . . . Is it fair? I don't know. Because you can make your P&L and do your job and go to work every day but if you don't kiss everyone's butt or be everyone's little favorite you're not going to get your team review to be stellar.

Because she had profit and loss indicators to gauge whether or not her bonus accurately corresponded to her performance, she was particularly disturbed by subjective influences on her evaluations. When evaluations contradicted tangible evidence of performance, workers viewed meritocracy on Wall Street as a myth.

Women were much more likely than men to disbelieve the myth of meritocracy because, as this book has illustrated, women were more subject to nonmerit influences having a negative impact on their bonuses. Forty-three percent of women, compared to 9 percent of men, rejected the myth of meritocracy. Could Wall Street be a true meritocracy despite this? Theories and research on women's experiences in the workplace suggest that it is unlikely.

Theories about Stratification and Meritocracy

As chapters 4 and 5 discussed, theories in social psychology imply that a true meritocracy in a setting like Wall Street is improbable because of nearly universal preferences for others who resemble oneself and cultural tendencies to view men as more competent than women, even when men's performance is equal to or worse than that of women. Because men are the incumbents of Wall Street and have more status in general, women are at a disadvantage—it's as simple as that. This is common to many, if not most, occupations, but my findings reveal how they perpetuate gender inequalities in a performance-based system. When evaluations of performance are partly subjective, they will inevitably be swayed by attraction to and beliefs about others. Men's preference for other men and a cultural gender hierarchy that awards men higher status than women led to higher evaluations for men. In fact, most people, both male and female, unconsciously hold biases that favor men in this setting. That fact, coupled with the trend toward subjective performance reviews more generally, bodes ill for meritocracy anywhere.

Gender theories also predict that men will receive advantages on Wall Street even when their performance is identical to that of women because the industry is male dominated. Being in the minority can have detrimental effects beyond those created by the majority's attraction to similar others, as Kanter has pointed out.[4] Women's increased visibility as tokens forced them into stereotyped roles, heightening performance pressure on them and demanding that they represent all women while also meeting standards set by the male majority—a tall order for anyone. Even the most successful women, who sometimes believed that standing out from their peers had helped them, noted that they were held to different standards as women. For example, Julie noted,

> I actually think that being a woman has been an advantage. And I would be surprised if most of the women at my level didn't say that. I think that Wall Street desperately wants to hire and retain qualified women. And I think that if you are good, the senior management at these firms, especially the senior management at my last firm, they know who every single woman is at the VP level. They don't know every guy. To be able to get in the elevator and have them talk to me is an advantage. But if you are not performing well then it is probably going to hit you harder. I think that a weak woman stands out more than a weak man.

As this suggests, women who were exceptional could receive an advantage from their higher visibility, but mediocre men could pass through the ranks more easily than mediocre women. This type of double standard permeated the securities industry and prevented it from producing a true meritocracy.

Thirty-two percent of the women observed that women's performance was subject to different standards than men's, which affected their evaluations. Jacqueline, a research analyst, said that men held women to higher standards in their reviews.

> [The head of the group] who still runs research at [my first firm] probably had this deep-rooted belief that women belonged at home. And I think you could prove that women were not compensated at the same level men were for doing equal work. . . . We all had our year-end reviews and you get reviewed from all different constituencies. And there was one woman who was a great analyst. You couldn't possibly find fault with anything she did and she goes in there and he has something to say about her performance whereas the guys go in there and there's no big deal. Nothing. So I think he probably demonstrated some bias toward men in the performance reviews.

From her perspective, meritocracy must be a myth because subtle gender biases influenced the reviews on which compensation was based, leading to greater scrutiny of women with impeccable performance than of average-performing men.

Theories about gender and skill also suggest similar biases against women in performance evaluations because skill is an ideological category that is defined by the typical characteristics of workers who perform a particular task.[5] In other words, definitions of skill in a male-dominated setting like Wall Street are biased toward expertise and characteristics that are typically held by men, while those that most women possess are devalued—even if they might be readily applicable to the situation at hand. When pay is based on performance evaluations, cultural and job-specific definitions of skill and performance lead to systematic inequality rather than meritocracy. Illustrating this, Maureen said that performance evaluations rewarded men for stereotypical male behavior and devalued qualities more typical among women even if they improved performance.

> This woman is 5'10", played field hockey and lacrosse. She's not thin, she's not fat but she's not—she went to

> Harvard. She's not shy and timid. She can be really aggressive. She holds it back. She was told, like apparently every other analyst woman in her class, that she was very timid. She was like, "Oh my God! I've never in my life been called timid." I don't think she's timid. I think she has a manner about her which isn't—she doesn't shoot from the hip and make stuff up when she goes to a meeting, and she definitely kind of has a different style but women's style is categorized as "timid." . . . And guys who mouth off when they don't know what they're talking about, I find in the end, have been typically rewarded as opposed to being penalized and they . . . do huge damage.

In her view, men were rewarded for behaviors that negatively affected their performance, while women were penalized despite better performance. She added, "You're not out there beating your chest and doing this stuff, and you're not out there making noncredible threats, and so you get paid less because you're 'timid.'" From her point of view, compensation discrimination occurred partly because the value of women's contributions was not perceived, while stereotypically male behavior was idealized.

Along the same lines, Fletcher found that women engineering executives had relational skills that added value in the workplace but that remained invisible to their managers and colleagues—largely because they are acquired through gender socialization.[6] Similarly, Gutek's theory of sex-role spillover argued that as occupations become gender typed, the gender role becomes part of the work role.[7] Work in female-dominated jobs is then structured to take advantage of women's stereotyped traits while not rewarding them as skills, and male-dominated jobs incorporate men's stereotyped traits and define them as essential for performance—even when they actually detract from it, as Maureen observed. On Wall Street, the skills that were rewarded were those that fit with stereotypical masculinity, while women's contributions were discounted.

Accordingly, one-third of the women believed that the bonus

system perpetuated gender inequality by holding women to different and higher standards and by not rewarding them for attributes that contributed to their productivity. These women rejected the idea that Wall Street was a free market paradise, and their observations exposed the effects of entrenched cultural biases on the performance review system. But the "myth of meritocracy" still provides a potent interpretation of bonus pay for workers across pay levels. If you didn't get a good bonus, so the thinking goes, then you must just not be that good: it's not the system, it's you. Over two-thirds (71 percent) of Wall Street workers believed that the compensation system was a meritocracy, sometimes despite experiences that clearly contradicted the myth. They believed in it because they were high earners, they did not know how much others were paid, they compared their earnings only to others in the exact same job, and/or they had clear measures of performance that corresponded to their pay. In fact, a belief in meritocracy persisted, even among many workers at the bottom of the ladder.

A majority of Wall Street workers believed that the securities industry distributed pay fairly according to workers' merits. This is exactly what Wall Street firms have asserted when faced with sex discrimination cases, and none of these firms has accepted culpability in these cases even though they paid out large settlements. Many of those who rejected the myth of meritocracy responded by changing firms or leaving the industry rather than challenging its legitimacy. Thirty percent of the women, or 69 percent of those who challenged the myth of meritocracy, left Wall Street or sought a position at a different firm, and all of the men who regarded meritocracy as a myth did the same. Leaving their jobs after a disappointing bonus might have resolved their individual sense of injustice, but the system retained its legitimacy. In fact, the system maintained its legitimacy partly through the self-selection of dissenters out of the industry. The only ones left are those who closely hold to the myth and see it reinforced. At the end of the day, challenges to the myth of meritocracy produced higher attrition, but they did not destabilize Wall Street's claims to be a meritocracy. Yet, as this book has illustrated, the idea that the bonus system produces a meritocracy is false, since nonmerit influences affect the distribution of work, the evaluation of performance, and the allocation of pay.

Strategies and Solutions

Given the existence of systematic gender differences, what might have improved women's opportunities on Wall Street, leveling the playing field and making it better not only for the women but for the firms themselves? First, Wall Street firms could stop pretending that market forces lead to fair and unbiased outcomes. They don't. A variety of subtle social forces reinforce structural discrimination within the market. Continued fetishization of competitive markets, on Wall Street and in American society more generally, will perpetuate the kinds of subtle discrimination that I have uncovered in the securities industry.[8] But recognizing inherent cultural biases and how they operate in this setting and most others might encourage firms to raise their awareness of these biases to a conscious level, prompting managers and workers to take a second look at women's performance when they evaluate them. Senior managers could also make special efforts to scrutinize evaluations of men and women with widely different pay in the same job to determine whether gender bias entered into their relative bonus decisions. This could also make managers sit down and think about what skills are really in play in any given job and to evaluate how teams work together.

The most successful women also offered important lessons. One of their most fruitful strategies was to work in an area where performance was easier to measure, like quantitative underwriting products or sales and trading. Of course, truly objective performance criteria do not and cannot exist for some jobs, but there were areas where performance measures were clearer. Even in these areas, though, men were more likely to find mentors and account allocation was not always equitable, but Wall Street firms could work to establish more tangible criteria for performance in all areas. They could especially improve opportunities for women if they could develop more accurate measures of performance in investment banking and tie bonuses to those measures rather than relying on manager and coworker impressions. One strategy for doing this would be to tie bankers' pay more closely to the deals that they work on, paying them a fixed percentage, based on their rank, of the fees for the deals that they worked on. The remaining problem would be to develop more even-handed criteria for allocating work, which could be solved by developing an algorithm for allocating deals and accounts evenly across workers. These firms develop mathematical models for all sorts of other things, so why not for dividing work evenly across workers? This would produce greater equality in opportunities to perform. By doing this, women would not be passed over for the best accounts, and their contributions to the team could not be overlooked or discounted. These procedures would probably also benefit other disadvantaged workers like nonwhites and Hispanics.

But let me be clear that I am not suggesting that these firms need to spend more time or resources on performance reviews, which seem to already be out of hand. Tracy, who worked in trading, commented,

> [My firm] likes to pride itself on its touchy-feely peer evaluations and managerial evaluations that began in September or August in which case you had to solicit reviews from five to seven peers and then write reviews on your desk, your group, as well as anyone who asks you to write one on them. And it's something that from your standpoint as a nonmanagerial standpoint, takes a lot of time and there are deadlines. . . . And then it's a colossal time waste and from a managerial standpoint, they are just swimming in all this crap. They get three-page reviews on people and they've trimmed it down over the years because the place had been outrageous. I mean, it starts late August and it would be over in late October and a producing manager's time, a lot of it, would be spent doing these team reviews.

Firms that do comprehensive evaluations for sales and trading spend unnecessary time and effort soliciting reviews from their employees even though they already have ready access to profit and loss records that provide relatively objective criteria of performance. In fact, rather than increasing the time intensiveness of the review process, these firms might actually reduce it and improve the equity of its outcome by using existing measures of production and limiting the impact of coworker and manager impressions. Some firms already do this for sales and trading and for asset management. But in some cases they seem to fetishize performance reviews and the erroneous belief that these capture merit.

Another lesson of the most successful women was that women do best in jobs that are not relationship intensive. This contradicts stereotypes of women as "better at relationships" but follows from preferences among clients to work with those who resemble themselves. But not all women can enter high-paying jobs that are not relationship intensive because there are not enough jobs like that to go around—it is a relationship-intensive business. And even if a sufficient number of such jobs existed, if all women tried to enter those areas then they would soon become female job ghettos, and substantial evidence suggests that the pay would then go down.[9] Real equality also requires that women be able to succeed in the high-paying jobs that are dependent on relationships with clients or on teamwork. So what can securities firms do on this front?

Wall Street firms could reduce the impact of client preferences by prohibiting gender-stereotypical client entertaining activities. They could forbid workers of all ranks from taking clients to strip joints or on hunting expeditions. (To make it fair, they could also prohibit activities that are stereotypically feminine.) While some might view this as overly restrictive and politically correct, I suspect that these firms already prohibit their workers from taking clients to certain types of events. Imagine, for a moment, how management would react to a group of investment bankers taking a client to see Michael Moore or to a religious revival—it just would not happen. A similar logic could apply to events that are unfriendly to women. The firms could then solicit input from both men and women at all levels to establish a list of recommended alternatives for client entertainment. Since clients hire Wall Street firms to raise capital—not to arrange their social lives—they should not object to these changes, especially if firms can be creative about the alternatives.

To further reduce the impact of social psychological tendencies that disadvantage women workers, Wall Street firms could also encourage greater equality with a few very specific affirmative action and diversity initiatives. In the most male-dominated jobs, they could specifically try to retain and promote more women to create a better gender balance and to expand the pool of women available as mentors for junior women. The problem is not that there are no women in the senior ranks of investment banking, sales, and trading, but there definitely are not enough to reduce the impact of preferences for men or tokenism processes. Some affirmative action measures could help alleviate this in the short run. In the long run they could make it easier for women to find mentors who resemble them and for typically female work styles and relational skills to be appreciated and compensated, short-circuiting the structural discrimination.

Another issue, which I discussed at length in chapter 7, is the problem of work-family policies. Wall Street firms have already introduced these policies, but they cannot move beyond window dressing without some substantial reforms. These firms must assess the costs of losing women when they have children. If replacement and training costs are high, then there is a business case to reduce these costs by making the options that are available on paper more available in reality.[10] Some women believed that job shares could work well in sales and trading because they would not reduce the coverage on their accounts and clients could still maintain ongoing relationships with their salespeople or traders. But women who tried to work out these arrangements met resistance. Wall Street firms need to educate senior managers about the economic costs of attrition due to work-family conflict and the potential economic benefits of retaining highly trained and skilled workers by accommodating their family responsibilities. Making room for family life may present the biggest challenge to Wall Street's workaholic culture and its potential for gender equity, but it could help securities firms retain valuable female employees and improve the opportunities for women.

In terms of hours, the best individual strategy for women who wanted to have children while still being successful was to work in sales and trading. There they could work predictable market hours while being rewarded for measurable profits and losses. But these areas were among the most hostile environments for women, filled with male bravado, harassment, and discrimination. Discrimination against mothers, who are penalized over and above changes in their career commitment and performance, was especially common. These women should receive rewards proportional to their contributions, which could again be aided by closely connecting tangible measures of performance to bonuses. Without that, hostility and discrimination toward women, especially if they have children, will remain pervasive problems that lead some women to leave the labor force or change jobs after having children. The women who left were at least partly responding to dissatisfaction with their jobs or their treatment at work. Recognizing that women who leave their jobs often experience "pushes" from the workplace as well as "pulls" toward the home might encourage managers and human resource specialists to work harder to improve the satisfaction of skilled women with children and to provide win-win accommodations.

Selling Women Short has demonstrated that gender inequality coexisted with a compensation system that aimed to pay for performance. Men and women on Wall Street believed that the securities industry had mellowed since the era when blatant sex discrimination and sexual harassment were tolerated, as described in *Liar's Poker*, *The Bonfire of the Vanities*, and *Tales from the Boom-Boom Room*. But gender inequality remained, and many of the processes that maintained a boys' club in the higher echelons of Wall Street were subtle and operated through the performance review system. Economically irrational gender inequality persisted in Wall Street's highly rationalized compensation system because performance evaluations were vulnerable to gender double standards and subtle discrimination.

Wall Street workers reveal that organizations can maintain a myth of rationality, efficiency, and meritocracy while producing inequality that is not economically rational or based on merit. Gender stereotypes powerfully, if subtly, influenced evaluations of performance and this prevented Wall Street from being a genuine meritocracy. The fact that Wall Street created a gender hierarchy rather than a meritocracy should encourage other types of organizations, which are increasingly moving toward flat hierarchies and variable incentive structures like those of securities firms, to examine their own practices.

Many people find performance-based incentives appealing because they imply that people receive what they deserve based on their efforts. There are many longstanding performance-based reward systems, like the system of awarding grades based on academic merit. But any teacher can tell you that academic merit may not always be the only criterion for grades and that grading is not an exact science. There are, of course, better and worse methods for evaluating students' performance, and Wall Street might take lessons from the field of education—but first there must be recognition that no performance-based system produces perfectly just results. This challenges the entrenched assumption that performance-based pay structures produce a meritocracy. But because the system's winners support this ethos and the losers leave, the subjective influences that produce systematic inequality in opportunities and evaluations are often hidden.

What is encouraging is the fact that one quarter of the women succeeded within this system by its own standards. While their numbers in this cohort may have declined since the time of the original study, their experiences demonstrate that the glass ceiling is not impermeable. Women may eventually attain equity if firms can make the criteria for allocating work and evaluating performance more tangible and measurable. As organizations increasingly move toward variable pay and performance-based incentives, they should take this lesson to heart and work to develop clear and tangible measures of performance. Legal authorities vested with the protection of equal employment opportunity can also incorporate the findings of this study into their interpretations of discrimination cases involving workers who receive performance-based pay by scrutinizing performance evaluations carefully for bias and recognizing the effects of subtle and unconscious discrimination. Diversity committees in organizations should also tackle unconscious preferences and prejudices in an affirmative way, especially in the areas that have traditionally been the most male dominated or hostile to women entrants.

Appendix A

METHODOLOGY

This study began with three related questions. How does Wall Street's system of pay for performance allow gender inequality to persist? How do some women manage to become highly successful on Wall Street? And what can we learn from the Wall Street case about gender inequality more generally? At a general level, these are questions about the processes that lead to a well-known outcome: gender inequality in the workplace. At a more specific level, these questions hone in on the effects of a growing trend in advanced capitalism, which is the movement toward flat organizations that pay variable amounts based on performance evaluations.

These research questions called for an exploratory design that was intended to compare otherwise similar men and women and to generate theory. As it turned out, some well-developed social psychological theories provided insights that, coupled with an understanding of the variable pay system, suggested why performance-based pay systems can be bad for women. Removed from the laboratory, these processes interacted with social structures to produce uniquely determined outcomes. But these processes and the importance of the pay system for how they operated on Wall Street could not be uncovered using existing data or exclusively quantitative data. For this reason, I combined qualitative and quantitative approaches using a carefully designed sample.

I chose a "grounded theory" approach as the most appropriate research strategy. (See Glaser and Strauss 1967 or Strauss and Corbin 1998 for a description of this approach.) In-depth interviews with a carefully targeted group of men and women who started careers on Wall Street during the same period facilitated the process of discovery by enabling theoretical concerns to emerge and develop throughout the interview stage of the research. It was through this process of discovery that the performance-based bonus system and the degree of subjectivity in performance criteria emerged as pivotal influences on gender inequality in this setting.

Wall Street is an extreme case rather than a typical or representative one. The extreme nature of this case is useful for three reasons. First, the sharp contradiction between time demands in Wall Street's culture and the personal needs of workers calls attention to much-debated time-money trade-offs. These trade-offs are underlined in an industry that requires such intense time commitments from workers. Second, the extremely high pay of this setting offers Wall Street workers more choices than most other workers in terms of childcare and domestic arrangements and the outsourcing of personal and household care. As a result, their struggles with these work-life issues accentuate the constraints that these issues pose in contemporary workplaces. Third, and most important, the proportion of annual pay that takes the form of a variable bonus highlights the effects of a performance-based reward system on gender inequality. The importance of performance evaluations in this setting throws subjective and nonmerit influences into sharp relief. All of these phenomena may be found in other organizations in less extreme form, especially as greater numbers of them move toward variable pay and long hours. Understanding how gender inequality emerges among extremely similar men and women in this setting reveals the processes that reinforce inequality in a growing segment of the labor market.

Sampling

The study design required a sample that could compare men and women from a specific cohort of entrants to Wall Street who were similar in their credentials and background characteristics, the prestige of the firms where they started, and the market cycles that affected their careers. As a result, the sampling procedure had to locate a delimited group of financial professionals. Accomplishing this task required finding the population of interest and developing a strategy for sampling within it.

Traditional random sampling methods were unacceptable for obvious reasons. Attempting to draw a random sample within census tracts (the preferred method for securing an unbiased and representative sample) would have yielded too few Wall Street workers even in the New York City area, and any that did appear in the sample would be likely to have started at different times and to differ widely in their work experience and backgrounds. But abandoning the principle of randomness altogether and using a snowball sample, whereby initial respondents provide contact with others in their own networks, was also undesirable and involved unacceptable risks. The potential for self-selection and systematic bias would have compromised the findings. As a result, I rejected this type of sampling method as well.

The sampling strategy that I ultimately accepted was one that used placement reports and alumni information from graduate schools of business. Major Wall Street investment banks hire 75–85 percent of their incoming associates from the top four MBA programs in finance, with some associates coming from an additional two or three schools. Because the firms of interest hire the majority of their incoming associates from the top MBA programs, I drew my sample from the placement reports and alumni directories of five elite graduate programs in finance for the years 1991–93. Most members of these cohorts were in their early to mid-thirties at the time of the interview, a prime time in the life cycle for family formation.

These years were also chosen because these graduates would have passed their first promotion and would have been in the position of vice president or higher at the time of the interview if they had remained in the industry. While there would be advantages to examining professionals who are more advanced in their careers, especially in terms of differences in compensation, locating a cohort that had passed two or more promotional levels would have been difficult because women have higher rates of attrition and are harder to locate, making it even more difficult to obtain a suitable comparison sample of more senior women that did not include only the most successful. This would probably also have negatively affected the response rate and created greater selection bias. Since the early years of an investment banker's career are the most likely to result in attrition, and reaching the VP level is a substantial accomplishment in itself, this sampling design was optimal for addressing the primary research questions of this study.

In MBA programs, women represented approximately 25–30 percent of all graduates in the 1990s. Employees in major investment banking firms claimed that approximately 15–20 percent of incoming associates in an average year were women. Confirming this, among the names obtained through the five graduate schools of business, women were 19.8 percent of the graduates who entered investment banks upon graduating. This suggests that my sampling strategy obtained a reasonable approximation of the population of interest.

From the cohort of graduates, I compiled a list of those who obtained jobs as associates in the major investment banks to provide the sample population.[1] These organizations are primary underwriters of initial public offerings and mergers and acquisitions. They developed as distinct from commercial banks because of the separation of securities from depository banking activities in the Glass-Steagall provisions of the 1933 Banking Act.[2]

For the purposes of this study, I used Eccles and Crane's original framework and accounted for mergers by including employees and former employees at Morgan Stanley, Goldman Sachs, Merrill Lynch, Lehman Brothers, Salomon Brothers, Smith Barney, Credit Suisse First Boston, J. P. Morgan (a commercial bank that expanded into investment banking in the 1980s), Bear Stearns, and DLJ. Because it was important to delimit the scope of the study and traditional investment banks maintained a higher level of prestige than commercial banks, I selected only workers who began their careers at the above ten firms. An MBA graduate who started in any of these firms was eligible for selection.

The five graduate schools of business contained 621 graduates for the three years included in the sample. To obtain comparable samples of men and women from the lists of MBA graduates, I separated all eligible respondents' names by gender to create lists of 498 men and 123 women.[3] I then selected samples of men and women using a random numbers table. I attempted to locate and contact as many potential respondents as possible. I sought those who had left the companies where they started investment banking careers using telephone directories, Internet searches, and alumni directories. Women were more difficult to locate because many had married and changed their surnames since business school and many did not have a telephone number listed in their name. In another strategy to locate more potential respondents, at the end of each interview I asked respondents if they knew the whereabouts of their classmates or individuals who were in their incoming class of associates.[4] Among those selected for an interview, 29 were impossible to find (17 women and 12 men), and 10 refused to participate (5 women and 5 men). So the response rate is 66 percent and the cooperation rate is 88 percent. This compares favorably with many other studies, especially of professionals.

The final sample contained 44 women and 32 men. The initial target of equal size samples of each gender was abandoned due to the greater interest in women's experiences in a historically male-dominated field, as well as women's greater willingness to be interviewed. The sample included those who remained in major investment banks, those who moved into other financial organizations, and those who left finance careers entirely.

This sampling strategy proved to be very effective and provided a number of advantages. First, these men and women were very similar in their background characteristics, education, skills, and qualifications. Because they graduated from elite MBA programs, all of them shared the most important educational credential for a career on Wall Street. These MBA programs also tend to admit students who are similar in their class background, previous educational and work experience, and their performance on the GMAT. This group of individuals entered a small set of organizations with comparable prestige within a single industry during a short period of time; they faced similar market conditions and their initial employers had similar organizational prestige. As a result, this study can assess gender differences among very comparable men and women. Also, I was able to study these individuals without the involvement of the firms. It would have been extremely difficult to gain the cooperation of even one of these highly secretive organizations. Even if they had provided access, a firm-generated sample would likely have contained less variation in areas of financial services, and respondents might have been less candid if they believed that their employer could have access to the data.

The Interview

In 1998 and 1999, I conducted interviews that combined fixed-choice (quantitative) and open-ended (qualitative) questions. Responses to fixed-choice questions were used to construct the measures used in the statistical analyses, while open-ended qualitative responses revealed the processes underlying the quantitative results. Interviews lasted an average of one hour and were partially structured to elicit respondents' career histories from the time they completed their bachelor's degrees until the time of the interview, their responses to events, their motivations for making career decisions, and their total compensation for 1997. By collecting quantitative and qualitative data, I was able to analyze both outcomes (the degree of gender inequality in pay) and processes (the mechanisms that produced this inequality) for men and women who were highly similar in their background characteristics, educational and work qualifications, and the organizations and market cycles in which they began their careers.

The interview schedule was developed over a period of months, during which eleven pretests helped to refine and reorder a complete career history questionnaire. (See appendix C.) This structured interview format was necessary to guide respondents' stories and to facilitate recall. The interview assumed the form of a career history from before the MBA until the time of the interview. The final interview schedule was structured to ensure comparability across respondents while remaining open-ended enough to permit probing and discovery, and to accommodate new insights as they occurred. I made only a few minor changes after the interviewing began, largely to make the career histories easier for respondents to recall and to accommodate emerging insights about the subjectivity or objectivity of performance criteria.

I approached respondents by telephone, usually with an initial voice-mail message indicating the purpose of the call. In some cases, home addresses were available through telephone directories, and respondents received letters in advance indicating the nature of the study. The initial contact described the purpose of the study, confidentiality of responses, and the nature of participation—a one-time interview lasting approximately forty-five minutes. Because the gender component of the research question might be expected to intrigue female respondents, I told women that I was particularly interested in women's experiences, including how they balance work and family life. For men, I also mentioned an interest in work and family life, but focused more on job changes and career paths. I did not inform men that I was studying gender differences. This small degree of deception was necessary in order to reduce rejections from potential male respondents.

The interviews took place at a time and location of each respondent's choice. I conducted all interviews myself, and they lasted between forty minutes and one hour and fifteen minutes. Some people allotted me a very short time slot, in which case I had to selectively ask the most important questions and omit some probes. I tape recorded most interviews,[5] which were later transcribed verbatim and analyzed. Fixed-choice questions were fully structured, while open-ended questions were semi-structured but also flexible to allow for probes into transition points, motivations for career decisions, and choices concerning work-life balance and other aspects of their experiences.

Because of the time-intensive single-interviewer design, the sample size is smaller than might be desirable for quantitative analysis. But the in-depth interview offers some unique advantages over a large-scale survey with exclusively fixed-choice answer categories. Most important, it captures the processes involved in professionals' careers as they developed over time rather than providing a snapshot of the outcomes (as in a purely quantitative survey). Admittedly, there may be problems with memory recall, and respondents may subjectively reinterpret their pasts. But the in-depth interview offered insights into the meaning of people's lives as they experienced them. Responses to open-ended questions revealed how social psychological processes interacted with the compensation system to heighten a pattern of gender inequality. The insights from the open-ended responses complemented the quantitative analyses using the same sample to present an overall picture of young financial professionals, the culture of finance, and gender differences on Wall Street.

Appendix B

QUANTITATIVE MEASURES AND MODELS

The fixed-choice questions yielded data that were amenable to statistical analysis. In these questions, I collected information about background characteristics, work-related characteristics, rank in the industry, area of finance, and whether the respondent still worked for one of the original nine Wall Street firms at the time of the 1997 bonus payment. The variables and how they were coded are listed in table B.1.

Compensation

The outcome of interest was total compensation in 1997. While some bemoaned the emphasis on money, all Wall Street professionals had a strong sense that their pay was an indicator of their success and their value as professionals. This orientation suggests that earnings are an appropriate proxy measure for success in the industry.

I asked respondents to check the appropriate box on an income scale for their total compensation in 1997. (See the questionnaire in appendix C for the scale.) I asked them to indicate a range rather than detailed earnings information in order to maximize the likelihood that they would answer the question. Income in dollars was coded as the midpoint of the range, except for eight respondents who

Table B.1
Variables and Measures

Variable	*Coding*
Background Characteristics	
Gender	0 = male, 1 = female
Race	0 = white, 1 = nonwhite
Marital status	0 = not married, 1 = married
Parental status	0 = has no children, 1 = has children
Economics major	0 = other major; 1 = economics, business, or finance undergraduate
Math major	0 = other major, 1 = mathematics or engineering undergraduate
GPA	Undergraduate grade point average (0.0–4.0)
GMAT score	Score on GMAT (0–800)
Job-related Characteristics	
Previous experience	0 = no previous experience, 1 = previous experience as financial analyst, summer associate, or sales assistant
Below VP rank	1 = below VP
VP rank	1 = VP
Above VP rank	1 = above VP
Hours per week	Natural logarithm (ln) of estimated hours per week
Area of the Industry in 1997	
Corporate finance	1 = corporate finance
Sales and trading	1 = sales and trading
Public finance	1 = public finance
Research	1 = research
Asset management	1 = asset management
Support	1 = corporate support area
Firm tier in 1997	0 = outside top 9 firms, 1 = works in top 9 firms
Dependent variable	
Compensation	Natural logarithm (ln) of total compensation

gave detailed income figures. Those who earned over $1,000,000 were coded as $1,100,000 because the categories immediately below it were $100,000 apart. Only three respondents earned over $1 million in 1997, and this coding produced very similar results to a tobit model that treated the top category as open-ended. Because ordinary least squares (OLS) models are more easily interpretable, I used OLS regression for the models in tables B.2 and B.3.

In these models, I omitted five respondents (three women and two men) who refused to disclose their compensation. I also excluded three men who left Wall Street for entrepreneurial opportunities prior to receiving a 1997 bonus, because they were not paid on Wall Street during the year in which pay was measured.

Hours per Week

The regression models accounted for the natural logarithm of estimated hours per week. Using the raw number for estimated hours would tell us the percent change in earnings for each additional hour per week, under the assumption that the dollar increment for each additional hour is the same at all levels of time. But in this demanding profession one would expect that returns to hours might increase at higher levels. By logging the hours per week, the coefficient indicates the percent change in earnings for each additional 1 percent increase in hours per week. This assumes that the dollar increment for additional hours may change at higher levels of hours. A value of 1 would indicate that earnings increase in proportion to hours, while a coefficient larger than 1 implies increasing returns to hours worked.

While some might argue that productivity actually declines when work hours exceed some threshold, such that each additional hour worked would produce smaller gains in productivity, evidence that face-time influences perceptions of performance implies higher returns for longer hours. At the same time, models using hours worked instead of the natural logarithm of hours worked produced similar results.

The Interaction of Gender and Parental Status

Because previous research has revealed differential consequences of parenthood for men and women, I tested for interactions between gender and parental status in multivariate models as well as the main effects of both marriage and parenthood. They were not statistically significant in any models, which was puzzling given the well-known relationship between motherhood and lower wages for women. I attempted to further investigate the effects of children on earnings. First I explored the possibility that the model was overspecified due to the inclusion of married, children, and gender*children, since only one parent, a divorced mother, was unmarried at the time of the interview. But removing the variable for marriage did not change the results: the main effects of children and the interaction term for gender*children were not statistically significant. This was unexpected given that all but one of the parents in the sample started their families after beginning their careers on Wall Street and had preschool children. This is the family stage when parenthood should have its largest impact on earnings.

In another effort to ascertain differential effects of parenthood for male and female securities professionals, I re-ran all models separately for female and male respondents. In neither case was parenthood statistically significant nor of substantial magnitude. These results were identical regardless of whether being married was included in the models.

Since it was also possible that differences in hours explained pay differences by gender and parental status, I assessed the impact of gender and parental status on self-reported hours. A comparison of means using an ANOVA model revealed statistically significant differences in self-reported hours, as I discussed in chapter 6. A regression model testing the effects of mother/childless woman and father/childless man on hours per week found significant and negative results for the mother variable with $p < .01$. The father variable was not statistically significant. This suggests some impact of motherhood on women's hours, although this only explained 7 percent of the variance in hours and was not detectable in models controlling for other variables. This implies that differences in hours might explain a small portion of differences between mothers and childless women. But, given that hours dropped out of the full model controlling for area and rank in table B.3, the importance of this variable should not be overestimated.

The Statistical Models

The zero-order correlation of gender and compensation reveals that gender alone explains approximately 18 percent of the variance in income ($r = -.43$). But to understand whether other variables explained part of the gender gap in pay among otherwise similar men and women on Wall Street, I ran OLS multiple regression models that controlled for other relevant influences on pay. I excluded consistently nonsignificant variables from these models. The results were similar with or without these variables, and they did not affect the magnitude or significance of other coefficients.

To further test the accuracy of the OLS models, I used bootstrap techniques. Bootstrap techniques test for inaccuracies in standard errors that may occur in small samples. If there were outliers or small skews in the sample that affected the results, the bootstrapping procedure would indicate wide divergence in the standard error terms.[1] But I found that bootstrap coefficients and standard errors were almost identical to the OLS models.

The regression model presented in table B.2 explained 23 percent more of the variance than gender alone. I used the formula $100^*g = 100^*\{\exp(c) - 1\}$ to calculate the percentage difference, where c is the unstandardized regression coefficient, and g is the relative effect on Y of the presence of the factor represented by the dummy variable, in this case, the effect of being female on pay.[2] This revealed that accounting for gender explained 12 percent more than work-related characteristics and background alone.

To calculate the percent change in the gender coefficient, I used the formula $(b1 - b2)/b1$, where b1 is the unstandardized coefficient for gender in a bivariate regression and b2 is the unstandardized

TABLE B.2
Effects of Background and Human Capital Characteristics on Total Compensation

Variable	*Regression Coefficients*	*Difference in Pay*
Background Characteristics		
Gender	–.5**	39%
	(.15)	
Married	.31	—
	(.18)	
Children	–.09	—
	(.18)	
Credentials		
Economics major	.44*	55%
	(.17)	
Math major	.32	—
	(.21)	
Previous experience	.23	—
	(.14)	
Work Effort		
Ln (hours)	1.17*	5.3% per hour
	(.45)	
Constant	7.71**	
	(1.83)	
R^2	.41	
N	68	

Note: Numbers in parentheses are standard errors. All numbers are rounded to two decimal places.

Two-tailed significance: $^{*}p < .05$ $^{**}p < .001$

coefficient for gender in table B.2. This represents the percentage change in b1.[3] The inclusion of background and work-related characteristics in the model reduced the effect of gender by only 2.3 percent. The 95 percent confidence interval for this coefficient is –.79 to –.21, suggesting that gender produces a penalty for women of 21

TABLE B.3
Effects of Job-Related Characteristics on Total Compensation

Variable	*Regression Coefficients*	*Difference in Pay*
Background characteristics		
Gender	–.34*	29%
	(.15)	
Married	.22	—
	(.17)	
Children	–.08	—
	(.18)	
Credentials		
Economics major	.27	—
	(.14)	
Work effort		
Ln(Hours)	.90	—
	(.48)	
Area of Finance		
Corporate finance	.55*	173%
	(.24)	
Sales and trading	.74**	210%
	(.26)	
Public Finance	.21	—
	(.34)	
Research	.54	—
	(.28)	
Asset management	.36	—
	(.26)	
Job-related Characteristics		
VP	.36*	43%
	(.15)	
Above VP	.61*	84%
	(.25)	
Top firm 1997	.41*	51%
	(.20)	
Constant	7.94***	
	(1.96)	
R^2	.54	
N	68	

Note: Numbers in parentheses are standard errors. All numbers are rounded to two decimal places.

Two-tailed significance: *$p < .05$ **$p < .01$ ***$p < .001$

percent to 55 percent within this population. This again attests to an important independent effect of gender on compensation in this industry. It is worth noting that the models in tables B.2 and B.3 both have sufficient statistical power to detect an effect of this magnitude. In fact, one could argue that the presence of a gender coefficient of this magnitude and statistical significance in a small sample actually attests to the strength of this effect in the population from which the sample was drawn.[4]

The full model in table B.3 improved upon table B.2 by 20 percent. The gender coefficient suggests that the effect of gender is reduced by 17 percent with the addition of job-related characteristics, as compared to the model in table B.2. The gender coefficient of –.44 has a 95 percent confidence interval of –.72 to –.16, implying that the actual penalty of being female, controlling for other variables in the model, is likely to lie between 14 percent and 51 percent.

Appendix C

INTERVIEW SCHEDULE

I. Background Information

I'd like to begin by asking some general background questions.

A. Ascribed Characteristics

1. What year were you born?
2. Are you male or female?
   - □ 0. male
   - □ 1. female
3. How would you describe your racial identity?
   - □ 0. white
   - □ 1. black
   - □ 2. Asian
   - □ 3. other (please explain)
4. What is your religious affiliation?
   - □ 1. Catholic
   - □ 2. Protestant (specify)
   - □ 3. Jewish (Reform, Conservative, Orthodox, Hasidic, nonreligious)
   - □ 4. none
   - □ 5. other (please explain)

5a. What country were you born in?
   - □ 0. United States
   - □ 1. other

5b. What country did you grow up in?
- ☐ 0. United States
- ☐ 1. other

6. Did you grow up in an urban, suburban, or rural area?
- ☐ 1. urban
- ☐ 2. suburban
- ☐ 3. rural
- ☐ 4. other (please explain)

7. What region did you grow up in? (Northeast, South, Southwest, Midwest, etc.)
- ☐ 1. Northeast
- ☐ 2. Midwest
- ☐ 3. South(east)
- ☐ 4. Southwest
- ☐ 5. Pacific

B. Social Capital

1. What is the highest level of education your mother attained?
- ☐ 1. less than high school
- ☐ 2. high school
- ☐ 3. some college
- ☐ 4. bachelor's degree
- ☐ 5. graduate degree

2. What is your mother's occupation?
Probe: Did this change over time?

3. What is the highest level of education your father attained?
- ☐ 1. less than high school
- ☐ 2. high school
- ☐ 3. some college
- ☐ 4. bachelor's degree
- ☐ 5. graduate degree

4. What is your father's occupation?
   Probe: Did this change over time?
5. When you were growing up, did you live with both parents?
   - □ 0. no
   - □ 1. yes

   Probe: Did that change at any time while you were growing up? Please explain.
6. When you were growing up, did your family belong to any social clubs or associations, such as political parties, country clubs, or sports organizations?
   - □ 0. no
   - □ 1. yes

   Probe: Which ones? Who belonged?
7. When you were growing up, did your parents belong to any professional clubs or associations, for example, the American Bar Foundation, the Association of Professional Women, the American Dental Association, etc.?
   - □ 0. no
   - □ 1. yes

   Probe: Which ones? Who belonged?

C. Family Variables

Now I'd like to ask you some questions about your current relationship and family situation.

1. Are you married?
   - □ 0. no
   - □ 1. yes (complete 2–7, then skip to 10)
2. Have you ever been married before?
   - □ no (skip to 7)
   - □ yes (answer 3–7, then skip to D)
3. When were you married? (month, year)

4. When did your marriage end? (month, year)
5. What did your wife/husband do for a living?
6. Did it end in divorce?
   - □ 0. no (please explain)
   - □ 1. yes

   Probe: What do see as the primary reasons why it ended this way? Do you see this as being related to your career in any way? Do you think the divorce was related to your expectations about having a family, or about who should be responsible for breadwinning or child rearing? How?
7. Do you have a domestic partner (someone you live with)?
   - □ 0. no
   - □ 1. yes
8. Do you expect or hope to marry in the future?
   - □ 0. no
   - □ 1. yes
9. How do you expect your expectations about marriage in the future to affect your career?
10. When did you get married? (month, year)
11. What is your husband's/wife's highest level of education?
    - □ 1. less than high school
    - □ 2. high school
    - □ 3. some college
    - □ 4. bachelor's degree
    - □ 5. graduate degree
12. What is your husband's/wife's occupation?

    Probe: Has this changed since you met?
13. Do you and your husband/wife come from similar social backgrounds?
    - □ 0. no
    - □ 1. yes

Probe: In what way are they similar or different?

14. Before you married, how did you think that marriage would affect your career?
15. Have your ideas about that changed? How?
16. Who do you consider the breadwinner in your family?
    - □ 1. self
    - □ 2. spouse
    - □ 3. both equally
    - □ 4. other

    Probe: Why do you think about it that way?
17. Do you have any children or stepchildren?
    - □ no
    - □ yes (skip to 19)
18. Do you expect or want to have children in the future?
    - □ 0. no

    Probe: Why? How do you expect the decision not to have children to affect your career?
    - □ 1. yes

    Probe: How many? When? How do you think becoming a parent will affect your career? How do you expect to manage childcare?
19. How many children (stepchildren) do you have?
20. When was your first child (or stepchild) born? (month, year)
21. How did you think that becoming a parent would affect your career before you had children?
22. Have your ideas about that changed? How?

    Probe: How do you manage childcare?

Before we move on to talk about your work history, I'd like to know about your career aspirations at this point in time.

What would you like to be doing with your career in five years?

D. Human Capital

Now, I'd like to ask you some questions about your educational and work history prior to starting your MBA. Let's start with education.

1. When did you receive your bachelor's degree? (month, year)
2. From what institution did you receive your bachelor's degree?
3. What was your undergraduate major?
4. What was your undergraduate GPA?
5. What was your score on the GMAT?
6. During the period between receiving your bachelor's degree and starting your MBA, what were you doing?
   - □ 0. working
   - □ 1. traveling (skip to 11)
   - □ 2. other (please explain) (skip to 11)
7. How many jobs did you have between completing your BA/BS and starting your MBA?
8. Were any in finance?
   - □ 0. no (skip to 10)
   - □ 1. yes (answer 9; skip to 11)
9. What type of firm?
   Probe: What group were you in? (What products and companies did you specialize in?)
10. During that period, did you have any work experience that helped to prepare you for your career in investment banking?
    - □ 0. no
    - □ 1. yes

    Probe: What position was that? What did you learn?
11. When you studied for your MBA, were you a full-time or a part-time student?

- □ full-time
- □ part-time
- □ other/change over time (please explain)

12. Did you have any part-time jobs during the academic year while you studied for your MBA?
    - □ 0. no
    - □ 1. yes (How many?)
13. Were any in finance?
    - □ 0. no (skip to 15)
    - □ 1. yes
14. What type of firm?

    Probe: What group were you in? (What products and companies did you specialize in?)
15. Did you have any summer jobs while you studied for your MBA?
    - □ 0. no
    - □ 1. yes (How many?)
16. Were any in finance?
    - □ 0. no (skip to 18)
    - □ 1. yes
17. What type of firm?

    Probe: What group were you in? (What products and companies did you specialize in?)
18. During the period while you were in business school, did you have any work experience that helped prepare you for your career in investment banking?
    - □ 0. no
    - □ 1. yes

    Probe: What position was that? What did you learn?
19. When did you graduate with your MBA? (month, year)
20. What was your main reason for pursuing an MBA degree?

II. Work History

Now I'd like to know about your jobs in investment banking after finishing business school. I begin with the first job in an investment bank, then I ask about the progression from there, and finally about your current position.

A. First Job

To begin, think of the first job you had after your MBA.

1. On what date did you first work in investment banking? (month, year)
2. Why were you interested in working in finance when you graduated from business school?
3. What was the title of your first job in investment banking?
4. What group or division did you work in when you first started as an associate? (M&A, chemicals, technology, etc.)
5. Approximately how many employees were in your group/division when you started?
6. What were your most important duties?
7. How did you first find a job in an investment bank?
   - □ 0. just asked if they were hiring
   - □ 1. campus placement office
   - □ 2. friends
   - □ 3. relatives
   - □ 4. headhunter
   - □ 5. other (please specify)

B. Interests and Expectations

Now I have some questions about your expectations about working in investment banking.

1. What were your expectations when you entered your first job in terms of:
   a. hours
   Probe: How did your early experiences compare to your expectations?
   b. pay
   Probe: How did your early experiences compare to your expectations?
   c. required skills
   Probe: Did you have any surprises in terms of what you were expected to know?
2. How many supervisors did you have?
3. Is there anyone you considered a mentor in that first job?
   □ 0. no (skip to 6)
   □ 1. yes (answer 4a, 4b, 5)

4a. Was that person a man or a woman?
   □ 0. man
   □ 1. woman

4b. What was his/her position in your group?

5. What kinds of things did that person do to help you when you were in your first job?
   Probe: What was s/he like in terms of managerial style and personality?
6. Were most of your peers male or female, or were they evenly mixed?
   □ 0. male
   □ 1. female
   □ 2. 50/50
7. How did you feel about the social environment in that first job? Did you feel that you fit in, and in what ways?
   Probe: Did you feel that your peers were similar to or different from you?
   □ 0. similar
   □ 1. different (please explain)

8. What was the racial and ethnic composition of the group?
   - □ 0. all white
   - □ 1. mostly white, with just a few others
   - □ 2. racially mixed (Probe: What was the mix?)
   - □ 3. other (please explain)
9. How many of the people you worked with as an associate (or other title) are you still in touch with?

   Probe: Would you consider these people "friends"? Why or why not? Did you know any of them before you started working together (from college, business school, etc.)?
10. Did you usually have an analyst working for you when you were a starting associate?
    - □ 0. no
    - □ 1. yes

    Probe: When did you start to receive analyst support?
11. What was your managerial style like at first?

    Probe: Did it change over time?
12. Did you have any contact with clients when you started as an associate?
    - □ 0. no (skip to 15)
    - □ 1. yes
13. How much contact did you have with clients? (Was it telephone contact, at meetings, or also social?)
14. If also social, what kinds of social activities did you engage in with clients during your first job in investment banking?

    Probe: Can you give me some examples?
15. On what date did you leave your first job in an investment bank, either because you were promoted, you wanted to leave the firm, or you wanted to leave the industry? (month, year)

C. Mobility within Investment Banking

1. Do you currently work in a "Wall Street" financial institution?
   - □ no (answer 2–6)
   - □ yes (skip to 7)
2. When did you leave the investment banking industry? (month, year)
3. After your first job, were you promoted?
   - □ no (skip to 9)
   - □ yes
4. How many times were you promoted before leaving the industry?
5. What was your title after your last promotion in investment banking?
6. When were you promoted to that position? (month, year)
7. Have you ever thought of leaving?
   - □ no
   - □ yes

   Probe: Why did you consider leaving?
8. Do you ever talk to headhunters?
   - □ no (Why not?)
   - □ yes (Probe: What kinds of things have they offered you? What would it take for you to leave?)
9. Did you, at any time while in investment banking, change firms?
   - □ 0. no (skip to 18)
   - □ 1. yes
10. How many times did you change firms?
11. When did you change firms? (month, year)
12. How did you find the position in the firm you moved into?
13. What was (were) your reason(s) for changing firms?

14. Did you enter a similar or different department and position in the new firm?
    Probe: If different, how?
15. How did the new firm compare to the old one in terms of prestige, market share, and diversity of products?
16. How did people react to you at the new firm?
    Probe: Did it require a large social adjustment?
17. How did your move between firms affect your client relationships? (Did clients move over to the new firm with you, or did you need to establish new client relationships?)
18. Have you ever changed departments or divisions within an investment banking firm?
    - □ no (skip to 24)
    - □ yes
19. How many times did you change departments?
20. What department(s) did you change to? From?
21. When did you change divisions or departments? (month, year)
22. What was your reason for changing divisions or departments within the firm?
23. What effect did the change have on your career? (Prospects, prestige? Was it a lateral, upward, or downward move?)
24. On what date did you start working at your present job/last job in an investment bank (including date of promotion into that job)? (month, year)
25. What is the title of your present/last job?
26. What group or division do you work in now/did you work in in your last job in investment banking? (M&A, chemicals, technology, etc.)
27. Approximately how many employees are/were in your group?
28. On average, how many hours a week do/did you work? (if no longer in investment banking, skip to 33)

29. What is your typical daily work schedule on weekdays? What about weekends?
30. How important are/were the deals that your group brought into the firm for the group's position in the firm?
    - □ 3. very important
    - □ 2. somewhat important
    - □ 1. a little bit important
    - □ 0. not very important
31. What makes a particular deal important in comparison to others? (How do you define a "big deal" or an "important deal"?)
32. Have you been (were you) assigned to the most important deals your group works on during your career in investment banking?
    - □ 0. no
    - □ 1. yes

    Probe: Why do you think that is? Do you bring in any of your own deals?
33. How do you think that the deals that you've worked on have affected your bonus ranking?
34. How do/did you perceive your bonus as ranked in comparison to others at your level?
    - □ 3. top 10%
    - □ 2. top 25%
    - □ 1. top 50%
    - □ 0. bottom 50%

    Probe: Why do you think that you are ranked this way?
35. Do you expect to be promoted to a higher-level job in this company? If so, when?
    - □ 0. I do not expect to be promoted.
    - □ 1. I expect to be promoted within ___ years.
    - □ 2. I expect to be promoted within ___ months.

    Probe: Why do you expect to be promoted? (Or why do you expect not to be promoted?)

36. If you expect to be promoted, what is the title of the next job you expect to be promoted to?
37. How long do you see yourself staying in this business?
38. Do/did you work for one or more supervisors?
    □ 0. no
    □ 1. yes (How many? Do you have one person you work for most of the time?)
39. Is/was your supervisor a man or a woman? (Or, are your supervisors mostly men or mostly women?)
    □ 0. man
    □ 1. woman
40. Can you describe some of the personalities and managerial styles? (If only one, describe that person's personality and managerial style.)
    Probe: How do/did you get along with the person/people you work for?
41. Do/did you usually have subordinates (analysts and associates) working for you in your current/last job?
    □ 0. no (skip to 43)
    □ 1. yes
42. What kind of a manager are you now/were you in your last job?
    Probe: Are there many people who want to work for you? Why or why not? How do you feel about that?
43. How do/did you establish relationships with most of your clients? (How do/did you meet them, are/were you referred to them, do/did you acquire clients by reputation or through supervisors, etc.?)
44. How important are relationships in getting and keeping clients? Would you say that relationship management is a large part of the job, or

that you are mostly involved in producing an analytic product or service?

- ☐ 2. relationships most important
- ☐ 1. relationships and analytical work equally important
- ☐ 0. more analytical work, less relationship management in my job

45. Are/were most of your peers at your level male or female, or are/were they evenly mixed?
    - ☐ 0. male
    - ☐ 1. female
    - ☐ 2. 50/50
46. What is/was the racial/ethnic composition of the group?
    - ☐ 0. all white
    - ☐ 1. mostly white, with a few others
    - ☐ 2. racially mixed (please specify mix)
    - ☐ 3. other (please explain)
47. How do/did you feel about the social environment in your current/most recent job? Did you feel that you fit in, and in what ways?
    Probe: In what ways do/did you feel that your peers are similar to or different from yourself?
48. Would you describe any of your peers (or former peers) to be "friends"?
    - ☐ 0. no
    - ☐ 1. yes

    Probe: How many?
49. Do/did you engage in any social activities with coworkers outside of the work setting?
    - ☐ 0. no (skip to 52)
    - ☐ 1. yes
50. Which coworkers do/did you tend to socialize with (peers, higher-ups, subordinates, etc.)?
51. What kinds of activities do/did you engage in together?

Probe: How much time do/did you spend with coworkers outside of work? How does that compare with the time you spend/spent with other friends (at that time)? With family? How do you feel about the time you spend/spent with coworkers outside work?

52. When people are not talking about work itself, what are/were the major topics of conversation around the office (on a social level)?
53. Are there a lot of sports analogies in the work environment? (For example, if someone completes a big deal or trade, do they call it a "slam dunk"?)

    Probe: Can you give me some examples? How do you feel about the use of sports analogies?
54. Do people joke around when they're working?
    - □ 0. no
    - □ 1. yes

    Probe: What are the jokes usually about? Why do you think that is?
55. If there is off-color humor, what is it usually about?
    - □ 0. women
    - □ 1. sex
    - □ 2. racial/ethnic groups
    - □ 3. homosexuals
    - □ 4. celebrities
    - □ 5. other
56. Have you ever dated anyone you work with? (By "work with" I mean not just in same firm, but someone you have contact with in your job.)
    - □ no (skip to 60)
    - □ yes (How many?)
57. How long did it last?

58. What did you perceive to be the potential for that relationship? (How long did you expect it to last?)
59. What was the outcome of that experience?
    Probe: Did that experience have any impact on your career prospects in the company? On the other person's?
60. Do you know of coworkers who have had affairs with others in the firm?
    - □ no
    - □ yes

    Probe: How many? What was (were) the outcome(s)? How do office affairs affect the careers of the people involved?

D. *Current Job Outside Investment Banking*

Now I'd like to know about your current job, and how you left investment banking to enter that position.

1. What were your reasons for leaving investment banking as a career?
    - □ 1. hours
    - □ 2. stress
    - □ 3. family responsibilities
    - □ 4. sexual harassment
    - □ 5. discrimination
    - □ 6. coworker networks
    - □ 7. organizational culture
    - □ 8. better opportunities elsewhere
    - □ 9. other
2. How did you find your present job?
    - □ 0. just asked if they were hiring
    - □ 1. campus placement office
    - □ 2. friends
    - □ 3. relatives

- ☐ 4. headhunter
- ☐ 5. other (please specify)

3. What did you find appealing about this job, in comparison to the financial firm you were working for before?
4. On what date did you start working at your present job? (month, year)
5. What is the title of your present job?
6. What kind of organization do you work for?
7. What department are you in?
8. On average, how many hours a week do you work?
9. What is your typical daily work schedule on weekdays? What about weekends?
10. Do you expect to be promoted to a higher-level job in this company? If so, when?
    - ☐ 0. I do not expect to be promoted.
    - ☐ 1. I expect to be promoted within ___ years.
    - ☐ 2. I expect to be promoted within ___ months.

    Probe: Why do you expect to be promoted? (Or why do you expect not to be promoted?)
11. If you expect to be promoted, what is the title of the next job you expect to be promoted to?
12. How do you feel about your decision to pursue this career path?
13. Where do you see your career five years from now?
14. Please check the one answer that shows how much you earned *last year* before taxes from your current job (including bonus, if any).
    - ☐ under $50,000
    - ☐ $50,000–74,999
    - ☐ $75,000–99,999
    - ☐ $100,000–124,999

- ☐ $125,000–149,999
- ☐ $150,000–174,999
- ☐ $175,000–199,999
- ☐ $200,000–249,999
- ☐ $250,000–299,999
- ☐ $300,000–349,999
- ☐ $350,000–399,999
- ☐ $400,000–449,999
- ☐ $450,000–499,999
- ☐ $500,000–549,999
- ☐ $550,000–599,999
- ☐ $600,000–699,999
- ☐ $700,000–799,999
- ☐ $800,000–899,999
- ☐ $900,000–999,999
- ☐ over $1,000,000

E. Experiences with Diversity Issues

Now I want to talk about any experiences you may have had with diversity issues at any time while you were working in an investment bank.

1. Do you feel that you have ever experienced discrimination for any reason in your career in investment banking? (By "discrimination," I mean treatment that was biased against you and based on some factor other than your work ability or qualifications.)
   - ☐ no
   - ☐ yes

   Probe: How were you discriminated against?
   Who discriminated against you?
   - ☐ 1. supervisor(s)
   - ☐ 2. coworker(s)
   - ☐ 3. client(s)

Probe: Why did you feel that your experiences were discriminatory? Can you describe some specific instances of discrimination?

2. Have you ever experienced an incident you would describe as sexual harassment in your career in investment banking?
   - ☐ 0. no (skip to 6)
   - ☐ 1. yes
3. How many incidents of sexual harassment did you experience (that you can specifically recall)?
4. Did you feel that you were sexually harassed by:
   - ☐ 1. supervisor(s)
   - ☐ 2. coworker(s)
   - ☐ 3. client(s)
5. Can you describe your experiences of sexual harassment?

   Probe: How did you respond to your experiences of sexual harassment? How, if at all, did the firm respond?
6. What does the firm you work for do to combat sexual harassment?
   - ☐ policies
   - ☐ grievance procedures
   - ☐ educational seminars (if so, then for whom?)
7. In your opinion, is the firm equipped to deal with sexual harassment effectively?
   - ☐ 0. no
   - ☐ 1. yes

   Probe: What policies, persons, or departments can you attribute this to?

F. Work-Life Balance Policies

Now, I'd like to know if you ever took time off from your career in investment banking.

1. Did you ever take a leave of absence for any reason (including maternity leave) during your career in investment banking, and then return?
   - □ 0. no (answer 2–3, 9–16)
   - □ 1. yes (skip to 4)
2. Can you think of anyone you know who took leave?
   - □ 0. no
   - □ 1. yes

   Probe: What happened to him or her? Is s/he still in the business?
3. How do you feel about people who do take leave?

   Probe: What does it say about their attitudes toward their career?
4. How long a leave did you take? (weeks/months)
5. When did that leave begin? (month, year)
6. What was the title of your position at that time?
7. What was your reason for taking a leave?
8. How did your supervisors and coworkers respond to your taking leave?
9. How much parental/maternity leave is provided at the company where you work now? (months/weeks)
10. How much is paid? (months/weeks)
11. Do both men and women receive the same parental leave options where you work now?
    - □ 0. no
    - □ 1. yes
12. How do you think taking parental/maternity leave affects an employee's career?

    Probe: Why? Does that affect your feelings about this firm or career?
13. Does the company you work for now offer options that accommodate employees' family

obligations (such as flex-time, job sharing, on-site day care centers)?

☐ 0. no (skip to G)

☐ 1. yes

14. What options do they offer?
15. Who generally takes advantage of these options? (Clarify level and position in the firm, gender, age, marital status.)
16. Do you think that using these options affects employees' careers?

☐ 0. no

☐ 1. yes

Probe: What effect does it have?

G. Job Satisfaction

The next questions concern how you feel about your current or last job in investment banking.

1. Do you feel satisfied with your career in investment banking?
   Probe: What aspects of your career do you find satisfying? Are there any particular aspects of the job you feel detract from your overall satisfaction with your career?
2. What sacrifices have you had to make to do your job?
3. How important is your career to your happiness?
   Probe: Are there other activities that are more important?

H. Compensation

My last question is about compensation. Once again, I assure you that this is completely confidential, and I do not have your social security number.

1. Please check the one answer that shows your most recent total annual compensation (*salary and bonus*) from a job in an investment bank.
   - ☐ under $50,000
   - ☐ $50,000–74,999
   - ☐ $75,000–99,999
   - ☐ $100,000–124,999
   - ☐ $125,000–149,999
   - ☐ $150,000–174,999
   - ☐ $175,000–199,999
   - ☐ $200,000–249,999
   - ☐ $250,000–299,999
   - ☐ $300,000–349,999
   - ☐ $350,000–399,999
   - ☐ $400,000–449,999
   - ☐ $450,000–499,999
   - ☐ $500,000–549,999
   - ☐ $550,000–599,999
   - ☐ $600,000–699,999
   - ☐ $700,000–799,999
   - ☐ $800,000–899,999
   - ☐ $900,000–999,999
   - ☐ over $1,000,000

Notes

Introduction

1. McGeehan 2004.

2. Ackman 2004b; Gibson 2004; Martinez 2004; McGeehan 2004.

3. *New York Times*, June 6, 2000; *Wall Street Journal*, July 29, 1999, July 30, 1999, September 24, 1999.

4. A. Fisher 1989; Herera 1997.

5. A. Fisher 1989.

6. Edelman (1990, 1992) has argued that organizations adopt equal employment and affirmative action policies to signal compliance to legal authorities, without much substance to those policies. In other words, the policies and procedures may be more symbolic than substantive.

7. Antilla 2002; *New York Times*, February 27, 1999; *Wall Street Journal*, June 22, 1999.

8. *New York Times*, February 27, 1999, C14.

9. *New York Times*, February 27, 1999; Antilla 2002.

10. *New York Post*, August 31, 1999.

11. *Wall Street Journal*, July 29, 1999, July 30, 1999, September 24, 1999; *New York Times*, August 3, 1999, June 6, 2000.

12. Ackman 2004b; Gibson 2004; Martinez 2004; McGeehan 2004.

13. McGeehan 2004.

14. Title VII protects both women and men from discrimination on the basis of sex. It does not protect against discrimination on the basis of sexual orientation or gender expression.

15. While sex may be a bona fide occupational qualification (BFOQ) for jobs that use specific reproductive capacities (e.g., gestational surrogate or sperm donor), this loophole has also been historically used in other occupations where its legitimacy is questionable (e.g., prison guard or flight attendant). In other words, gender stereotypes have been used to provide exemptions from EEOC sanctions under the BFOQ provision. Similar stereotypes do not provide legally permissible exemptions in cases of racial discrimination.

16. *Griggs v. Duke Power Company* 401 U.S. 424 (1971). The courts were largely favorable to employees during the 1970s, but reverted to favoring employers during the 1980s. In the *Griggs* decision, the court protected employees by interpreting disparate impact broadly. But the disparate impact doctrine began to crumble

with decisions in *Watson v. Fort Worth Bank & Trust* (*487 U.S. 977 [*1988*]*) and *Wards Cove Packing Co. v. Antonio* (*490 U.S. 642 [*1989*]*). In *Watson*, the Supreme Court ruled that plaintiffs must demonstrate specific, isolated employment practices that caused the disparity, rather than placing the burden of proof on employers (as in the earlier *Griggs* decision). In *Wards Cove*, the Court ruled that employers need only produce sufficient evidence that their practices have some legitimate justification, and not that the practices producing disparate impacts were "essential" or "indispensable" to their business interests. In 1991 Congress overturned the precedent set by the Court in *Wards Cove*, with amendments to the Civil Rights Act. It codified the doctrine of disparate impact based on the earlier *Griggs* decision and placed the burden of proof firmly on the employer to demonstrate that the challenged practice is "job-related" and a "business necessity." See Archer 2000; Hoff 1991.

17. *Barron's* 1997.

18. Antilla 2002.

19. EEOC Guidelines on Discrimination because of Sex, 29 C.F.R., Section 1604.11 (a)(3).

20. Barr 1993; Fain and Anderton 1987; Glass 1988.

21. Goldstein 1988; Hoff 1991; MacKinnon 1989.

22. Eisenstein 1988; Finley 1993; Guthrie and Roth 1999a; Krieger and Cooney 1993; Magid 2001; W. Williams 1993. In 1978, Congress amended Title VII to prohibit discrimination because of pregnancy. Employers may not legally consider an employee's pregnancy in making employment decisions, and they must treat pregnancy-related disabilities in a similar fashion to other disabilities that similarly affect an employee's ability or inability to work.

23. Gruber 1992; Roth 1999.

24. Fletcher 1999; Foschi 1996; 2000; Reskin 2000; Ridgeway 1997; Ridgeway and Correll 2004.

25. Becker 1991; Hakim 2001; Mincer and Polachek 1980. For comprehensive reviews of human capital theories and other supply-side explanations for women's lower earnings, see Blau and Ferber 1992; England 1992; Marini 1989.

26. Ryder 1965.

27. For more detail about the sample and methodology, see appendix A.

Chapter 1. The Playing Field: Wall Street in the 1990s

1. Ackman 2004a.

2. For example, see Becker 1971, 1991.

3. *Wall Street Journal*, May 9, 1999. The index dipped below 8,000 in the recession that began in 2000.

4. SIA Research Department 1998. NYSE broker-dealers account for about half of worldwide revenue and profits. The data presented are based on these firms be-

cause of data availability and because they reflects the core business of U.S. brokerage activity.

5. The ranking of investment banks was drawn from Eccles and Crane 1988.

6. SIA Research Department 1998.

7. *Investment Dealers' Digest* 1998a.

8. *Investment Dealers' Digest* 1998b.

9. SIA Research Department 1998.

10. *Investment Dealers' Digest* 1997.

11. *Wall Street Journal*, October 21, 1998.

12. An informant in the industry estimated the recruitment rate at 15–20 percent. Confirming this estimate, the sampling frame for this research contained just less than 20 percent women (19.8 percent).

13. *New York Times*, February 24, 1998; *Wall Street Journal*, September 18, 1998, October 9, 1998, October 14, 1998, October 19, 1998, December 16, 1998.

14. SIA Research Department 1998.

15. *Investment Dealers' Digest* 1998c.

16. *Investment Dealers' Digest* 1998a.

17. I define "success" as working in corporate finance, research, sales, trading, or asset management and earning at or above the median in corporate finance for their graduating class (as defined by a survey of executive recruiters in *Investment Dealers' Digest* 1998b), earning at or above the average estimated by *Investment Dealers' Digest* (1998c) for equity research, or earning more than the sample median in sales and trading or asset management. I define those who worked in these areas but earned less than average as less successful. I also define those who worked in lower-paying areas like public finance or support functions, who left a higher-paying area for a lower-paying one, or who moved from a top Wall Street firm to a lower-tier financial firm or out of the industry as less successful.

18. I use the term "derailed" to describe workers who made choices that, deliberately or not, moved them off the fast track to success on Wall Street. Some derailments had more serious long-term effects than others. Some derailed professionals entered other positions where they might regain access to a path to success, although they would be behind schedule. But Wall Street contains a regular timetable for promotion and the pay that goes with it. From this perspective, derailment is an appropriate metaphor for the setbacks that some workers faced.

19. To protect the confidentiality of respondents, all names are pseudonyms. This includes not only respondent names but also names used in quotes and some place-names.

20. *Investment Dealers' Digest* 1998b.

21. See Jacobs and Gerson 2004 for more detail on the frequency with which both men and women desire to effectively combine paid work and family life, and the desire of many workers to work fewer hours—especially those who work over fifty hours per week.

22. According to *Investment Dealers' Digest* 1998b, the average in corporate finance for her graduating class in 1997 was $430,000, with most corporate finance workers earning between $300,000 and $600,000.

23. Note that these were relatively light hours for Wall Street but much higher than the average for the labor force as a whole. (See Jacobs and Gerson 2004.) The median among the Wall Street professionals interviewed in this study was sixty hours per week.

24. Because the men and women I interviewed, and Wall Street, were predominantly white, this book cannot offer a systematic analysis of race. The effects of race may be similar in some ways to the effects of gender, but how they are similar and how they are different cannot be explained using the experiences of seven nonwhite cases, especially given that these cases involved people of various races. I will mention race where it is relevant, but I am unable to systematically analyze it.

Chapter 2. Pay for Performance: Wall Street's Bonus System

1. Eccles and Crane 1988.

2. A. Fisher 1989, 32; emphasis in original.

3. Chen and DiTomaso 1996; Smith et al. 2001.

4. These averages are the arithmetic mean rather than the median.

5. Blume, Siegal, and Rottenberg 1993; Kessler 2003; Lechner 1980; Matthews 1994. Until May 1, 1975, commissions for sales and trading were fixed at $0.26 per share. This dropped to $0.12 per share by the end of 1977, and the importance of commission revenue for securities firms continued to gradually decline.

6. A. Fisher 1989, 56.

7. It is worth noting that Wall Street workers viewed executive recruiters as useful sources of information on compensation amounts, especially given that Wall Street firms are very secretive about bonus pay.

8. U.S. Bureau of the Census 1998.

9. *Investment Dealers' Digest* 1998b.

10. Blume, Siegal, and Rottenberg 1993; Hoisington 1976; Lechner 1980; Matthews 1994. Commission revenue constituted 61 percent of the revenues in major Wall Street securities firms in 1965, but was reduced to 50 percent in 1975, and to 17 percent by 1991 (Matthews 1994).

11. Blume, Siegal, and Rottenberg 1993; Jensen 1976; Kessler 2003; Matthews 1994.

12. Previous research has documented men's greater tendency to ask for or demand resources and rewards, as well as the greater likelihood that they will receive what they ask for. See Babcock and Laschever 2003.

13. Kessler 2003, 122–23.

14. *Investment Dealers' Digest* 1998c.

15. Some research analysts moved out of top Wall Street firms, usually to buy-side research positions. These workers were not included in the averages that

I compare to *Investment Dealers' Digest* (1998c) estimates. Including them, the range of earnings was $112,500 to $425,000, with a median of $193,750.

16. Since the market crash of 1987, markets are frozen after a certain volume of trades has been exceeded in a day in order to prevent trading frenzies caused by sudden fluctuations in the stock market.

17. In one case, after four years there were too many associates remaining in the group for all to become vice presidents. The firm's response to this glut of employees was to lay off approximately half of the associates rather than hold them back from promotion. So these firms adhered quite diligently to the lockstep promotion schedule. There were a few cases where people were held back from promotion by one year, often because they had moved to a new area where they had limited experience.

18. In some firms, this title is director or principal.

19. Baron and Bielby 1980; Bird 1996; Blau and Ferber 1992; Dixon and Seron 1995; England and Farkas 1986; England 1992; Marini 1989; Jacobs 1989; Reskin and Roos 1990; Reskin 1993; Reskin, McBrier, and Kmec 1999.

Chapter 3. A Woman's Worth: Gender Differences in Comparison

1. Only those who worked in the securities industry in 1997 were included, eliminating from the compensation data three men who had moved into other industries. Some of the men and women I interviewed left the industry after December 1997 but before the time of the interview. Because they were paid in the securities industry in 1997, I included them in compensation data and statistical analyses of compensation.

2. U.S. Census Bureau, 1998.

3. Becker 1971, 1991; Mincer and Polachek 1980.

4. See Hakim 2001.

5. Blau and Ferber 1992; Kilbourne et al. 1994; Marini 1989. Some have argued that this can occur as a consequence of "statistical discrimination," whereby employers decide not to hire certain types of workers based on the average characteristics of the group to which they belong (Mincer and Polachek 1980). For example, if a majority of women prioritize family over paid employment and will interrupt their labor force participation for childbearing and child rearing, then employers may statistically discriminate against all female workers including the minority that is more work-committed than family-committed.

6. The model is an ordinary least squares (OLS) multiple regression model, which assumes that the background characteristics included in the model have a linear effect on total compensation. For more detail on quantitative measures and models, see appendix B. Undergraduate GPA and GMAT had no significant effects in any statistical models and are not presented in table B.2.

7. I asked each professional approximately how many hours he or she worked per week. Self-reported hours are expected to be inaccurate and somewhat inflated,

although I expect that men and women inflated their weekly hours in similar ways. (See Jacobs and Gerson 2004 for evidence for this assumption.) In fact, one might think that there could be gender differences in the accuracy of self-reported hours, with women more likely to underreport hours because of the social stigma attached to excessive hours among women, especially those with children. But this potential difference in reporting would only widen the gender gap in earnings between men and women who work the same actual hours per week.

8. England 1992; Guthrie and Roth 1999a; Kilbourne et al. 1994; Petersen and Morgan 1995; Reskin 1993; Reskin and Roos 1990.

9. Baron and Bielby 1980; Bielby and Baron 1984; Dixon and Seron 1995; Guthrie and Roth 1999a; Halaby 1979; Reskin and Roos 1990.

10. Blau and Ferber 1992; England 1992; Epstein et al. 1999; Jacobs 1989; Kilbourne et al. 1994; Marini 1989. Using the metaphor of "revolving doors," Jacobs argues that women experience a high degree of mobility over the life course among female-dominated, sex-neutral, and male-dominated occupations, and that this mobility ultimately reproduces patterns of sex segregation. So women may enter high-paying, male-dominated occupations, but many of them abandon these positions or move into part-time or lower-prestige work as they encounter glass ceilings and hostile environments. In highly male-dominated jobs, women may experience pressure as "tokens," whereby they are highly visible and differences between them and the dominant group become exaggerated (Kanter 1977). Token women in male-dominated jobs may be highly constrained in their behavior and experience limitations to their further advancement or to increases in pay. Jacobs attributes the revolving door phenomenon to social control processes within workplaces, which can take obvious or subtle forms. Jacobs also suggests that discrimination by employers, harassment by supervisors and coworkers, and less access to informal organizational support contribute to a revolving door pattern for women.

11. Erickson, Albanese, and Drakulic 2000; Foschi 2000; Martin 2001; Pierce 1995; Reskin 2000; Ridgeway 1997.

12. Petersen and Morgan 1995; Treiman and Hartmann 1981. Treiman and Hartmann found that occupational segregation accounted for 35–40 percent of gender inequality when they controlled for 479 occupational categories. In a study of 16 occupations, Petersen and Morgan found that occupation-establishment segregation explained an average of 89 percent of within-occupation wage differences.

13. Budig and England 2001.

14. England 1992; Kilbourne et al. 1994.

15. Nelson and Bridges 1999. Also, see chapter 2 for criteria that influence bonuses on Wall Street and are not merit related.

16. England 1992; Reskin 1993; Reskin, McBrier, and Kmec 1999; Tomaskovic-Devey 1995.

17. This suggests that women may be more likely to be held back from promotion, although the reasons for that are unclear. The few cases where workers were held back from promotion usually involved a move into a new area where they had to learn new skills. But women were only slightly more likely to have this experience than men (one man and three women).

18. *New York Times*, February 27, 1999.

19. A. Fisher 1989; Herera 1997.

20. Rank affects earnings, although promotions to higher ranks on Wall Street are lockstep. Table 3.2 reveals that women were less likely to have attained the rank of vice president, while men were more likely to be above the vice presidential level. Because this would have influenced pay, I accounted for it in the statistical model in table B.3. Because the effects of having an undergraduate major in mathematics or engineering, previous experience on Wall Street, undergraduate GPA, and GMAT score were nonsignificant in all statistical models, they were not included in this regression analysis.

21. As table 3.1 illustrates, women on Wall Street were also slightly less likely than men to have spouses or children. At least at the time of the interview, many of these women did not have the kinds of family responsibilities that would make such trade-offs rational.

22. I put the average for all other characteristics into the regression equation and then computed the expected pay at 40, 50, 60, 70, 80, 90, and 100 hours for men and for women to form the two lines in the graph.

23. Nelson and Bridges 1999.

24. Acker 1990; Martin 2001.

25. Babcock and Laschever 2003.

Chapter 4. Making the Team: Managers, Peers, and Subordinates

1. An "opportunity context" is the environment that influences the opportunities that are available. This context enables or constrains individuals, leading to positive or negative economic outcomes. The opportunity context on Wall Street plays an important role in the career consequences of an individual's credentials, family background, and work experience.

2. Acker 1990; Ferree, Lorber, and Hess 1999; Lorber 1994; Ridgeway 1997; Ridgeway and Correll 2004; Risman 1998.

3. Martin 2001; Reskin 2000, 2003.

4. In Kanter's (1977) classic analysis, the proportion of a group within a work environment affects how its members are treated. When women are less than 15 percent of the group, they are isolated tokens and viewed as special for their group. At the same time, they are expected to represent their group. Sabrina fit this description as the only African American. But Kanter argues that as a minority increases to 20–30 percent, the majority feels more threatened and engages in more

overt boundary-heightening activities. So when women reach 20–30 percent on Wall Street, men are likely to view them as a greater threat and engage in more boundary work to guard the industry as their territory. Women in Sabrina's group represented 20 percent, which was similar to the proportion of women in Wall Street firms at the entry level.

5. *Investment Dealers' Digest* 1998c. The average for research analysts without *II* rankings was $200,000–$350,000.

6. Twenty-eight men (88 percent) and 28 women (64 percent) said that their work groups were mostly male. Thirty men (94 percent) and 35 women (80 percent) said that their work groups were all white or mostly white.

7. Ridgeway 1997; Reskin 2000.

8. Martin 2001; McIntosh 1993. Subtle forms of discrimination might be best understood from the perspective of the dominant group, but dominant group members are often unaware of their privileges. Privileges usually operate in ways that are invisible to those they privilege, such that men think that sexism does not affect them because they are men, or whites believe that racism does not affect them because they are white (McIntosh 1993). On the other hand, women have a unique standpoint on how men's interactions with each other in organizations unconsciously support and encourage men's careers because those interactions have a visible impact on women's experiences (Martin 2001).

9. Berscheid and Hatfield 1978; Fiske, Lin, and Neuberg 1999; Foschi, Lai, and Sigerson 1994; McPherson, Smith-Lovin, and Cook 2001; Reskin 2003; Ridgeway 1997; Ridgeway and Walker 1995; Smith-Lovin and McPherson 1993; Webster and Foschi 1988.

10. Erickson, Albanese, and Drakulic 2000; C. Fisher 1982; Ibarra 1997; Kanter 1977; Marsden 1987; Tsui and O'Reilly 1989.

11. Sexuality, especially the assumption of heterosexuality, is also infused in this phenomenon. Acker (1990) discusses how organizations not only are gendered but also contain assumptions about sexuality. The assumption of heterosexuality in Wall Street firms implies that mixed-sex interactions are always open to being interpreted as sexual while same-sex friendships tend not to be subject to this interpretation. The greater level of comfort with same-sex peers and subordinates is then also connected to assumptions about heterosexuality on Wall Street.

12. See table 2.1.

13. In comparison, 66 percent of men indicated that they had a mentor. Ninety percent of their mentors were men.

14. Martin 2001.

15. Budig 2002; Fairhurst and Snavely 1983; C. Williams 1992, 1995; Yoder 1991, 1994.

16. Berger et al. 1977; Ridgeway and Walker 1995; Webster and Foschi 1988. Gender effects are a specific case of the general tendency to give the benefit of the doubt to higher-status individuals while holding lower-status individuals to a

higher standard. In this specific case, gender is a status characteristic, and men are accorded higher status than women.

17. Foschi, Lai, and Sigerson 1994; Foschi 1996, 2000.

18. Analysts in investment banking are the lowest-ranking employees. They are usually young college graduates who work for two years to gain some experience before going to graduate business school, and should not be confused with research analysts. In research, "analyst" is the general title of professional employees, who usually completed an MBA. In investment banking, analysts perform the most menial tasks for senior bankers who bring in client business.

19. Babcock and Laschever 2003; Bybee, Glick, and Zigler 1990; Clancy and Dollinger 1993; Cross and Madson 1997; McCrae and Costa 1988; McGuire and McGuire 1982.

Chapter 5. Bringing Clients Back In: The Impact of Client Relationships

1. Internal clients are investment bankers, salespeople, and traders. Research analysts often advise these other areas, providing recommendations of prospective investment banking clients in their industries and recommending buy, sell, or hold on companies' stocks.

2. Consumer preferences are important for any industry that delivers a service. A substantial body of research in economics has examined consumer-driven discrimination (Andersen and La Croix 1991; Arrow 1972; Becker 1971; Caplow 1954; Crofton 2003; Holzer and Ihlanfeldt 1998; Kahn 1992; Kahn and Sherer 1988; Nardinelli and Simon 1990; Neumark, Bank, and Van Nort 1996). Like research on employer discrimination, this work usually emphasizes deliberate discrimination rather than subtle preferences that privilege some workers.

3. Strong relationships were also advantageous from the client's perspective, since a stronger relationship offers a greater ability to trust the service provider and reduces the risks of opportunism in the course of a transaction (Baker 1990; Portes and Sensenbrenner 1993). Compared to shopping for the best price among competing financial institutions, trust provides advantages that offset any additional costs of services from a firm with an existing relationship.

4. I was unable to interview clients, so I rely on finance professionals' interpretations of their client interactions. Since relationships are interactive, each party's interpretations affect the character of the relationship itself. Given that information from the perspective of clients was not available, I must use workers' interpretations to analyze the importance of client relationships, which is an important piece of the story of gender inequality on Wall Street.

5. Erickson, Albanese, and Drakulic 2000; Tsui and O'Reilly 1989.

6. The exception to this in Maureen's remark was children. But discussing children could have very different career implications for women than for men. Children may be a form of positive social capital for men, defining them as serious and

stable workers. For women, on the other hand, talking about their children could give clients the impression that they were not focused on their careers and were unprofessional. I discuss the effects of children for men and women in detail in the next chapter.

7. Bernstein 2001; Erickson and Tewksbury 2000.

8. Acker 1990; Martin 2001; Threadgold and Cranny-Francis 1990. Some might argue that clients could get an extra sexual thrill from attending strip clubs with female bankers, but this would be counterproductive to their image as knowledgeable professional experts. Clients might sexualize women who wanted to go to strip clubs, but they probably would not view them as more competent or trustworthy.

9. Average pay in public finance was $260,000. For a comparison with other areas, see figure 2.1.

10. Reskin and Roos 1990.

11. I would argue that employers hire men first for traditionally "male jobs," and women first for traditionally "female jobs," rather than always expressing a preference for men. But all jobs on Wall Street are historically male jobs; thus, men are at the top of the industry's labor queue.

12. This informant was a personal contact, not a respondent.

13. Trentham and Larwood 1998.

14. This assumption is historically false, as there has been substantial conflict between Asian cultures that continues today.

Chapter 6. Having It All? Workplace Culture and Work-Family Culture

1. E.g., Budig and England 2001; Waldfogel 1997.

2. To construct this figure, I ran multiple regression models that calculated the effects of background characteristics (marital status, undergraduate major, and previous experience on Wall Street), average hours per week, rank (below or above vice president), and firm prestige on total compensation in 1997 for each parental status. I then computed the estimated pay by entering the group mean for each characteristic into the regression equation. The numbers presented in figure 6.1 reflect group differences when the effects of these variables are accounted for. I did not include area of the firm largely for empirical reasons. The number within each parental status group was too low to account for all of these influences simultaneously. Also, mothers often changed areas because of work-family conflict or discrimination on the basis of pregnancy or motherhood, so that area appeared to often be a consequence of the processes that I explore in this chapter rather than a cause. Raw averages for each group exhibit a similar pattern, as shown in table 6.2. In an analysis of variance, the difference in raw means across groups was statistically significant.

3. Hochschild 1997; Schor 1991. Hochschild's analysis emphasizes workers' incentives to spend more time at work and disincentives to spend time at home. Schor is more ambivalent about workers' preferences to work, viewing managers as the more important force in the trend toward long hours. She argues that employers pay a premium to overwork employees, which most workers accept even if many might prefer to work less.

4. Clarkberg and Moen 2001; Harrison and Bluestone 1988; Jacobs and Gerson 2004. These scholars argue that jobs have increasingly been divided between high-paying jobs that require long hours and low-paying jobs that do not provide full-time work. As a result, workers at the top of the labor market, like Wall Street professionals, are overworked while many at the bottom are underemployed.

5. Bailyn 1993; Blair-Loy 2003; Blair-Loy and Wharton 2004; Jacobs and Gerson 2004.

6. Bernard 1981; Gerson 1985; Skolnick 1991; J. Williams 2000. This gendered division of labor fails to fit the reality of most contemporary families in the United States, in which women are in the labor force. Single-parent homes make up approximately one-third of families with children under eighteen.

7. DiMaggio and Powell 1991; Friedland and Alford 1991; Jepperson 1991.

8. Blair-Loy 2003; Clarkberg and Moen 2001; Moen 1992.

9. Clarkberg and Moen 2001. Preferences for one or both partners to work part-time were very common in their study of couples.

10. Clarkberg and Moen 2001, 1133.

11. Blair-Loy and Wharton 2004. Blair-Loy (2003) defines the "devotion to work schema" as an ideal that is shared by workplace organizations and many workers, in which work requires an intense commitment that precludes much involvement in other pursuits such as caregiving.

12. Blair-Loy 2003; Hays 1999. Blair-Loy called this the "family-devotion schema."

13. This reflects another cultural ideology that is dominant in the United States: individualism. According to this ideology, individuals have control over their destiny through the choices they make, and many social structural forces that affect people's outcomes are denied, ignored, and rendered invisible.

14. Nick's experience fits well with Hochschild's (1997) argument that workers prefer to spend time at work than at home. Hochschild claims that this preference is common because contemporary workplaces "value the internal customer" and provide rewards, encouragement, and a warm social environment. At the same time, she claims that as family life has become increasingly complex and homemakers are less common, the home requires work and involves emotional stress that many people prefer to avoid.

15. Nine of the seventeen fathers were extremely devoted to their careers and made large sacrifices in their personal lives. They all had homemaker wives, as did

five other men who worked fewer hours and made time with their families a higher priority.

16. Wall Street workers were unusual in two noteworthy ways. First, only one of the workers I interviewed was a single parent–one mother was divorced. Second, the breadwinner-homemaker family has declined to approximately 10 percent of families within American society, largely due to economic necessity. But because Wall Street workers earned enough to support their families without a second income, the breadwinner-homemaker family was common in this industry. Men on Wall Street all married women who earned less than they did, and most married women who worked in low-paying occupations (e.g., teacher, flight attendant, social worker). Three men married another professional, but their wives ended their careers to become homemakers.

17. U.S. Bureau of the Census 2002. Among women aged 15–44, 44 percent of are childless. Among American women aged 25–34 with postgraduate degrees, the group most likely to be childless or delay childbearing, 42 percent were childless.

18. Gerson 1985; Hays 1999; Hertz 1997; Risman 1998; J. Williams 2000.

19. Same-sex relationships and same-sex mating markets might destabilize this process, but only one woman had a same-sex partner and this couple did not have children. Her partner had a similar job in the securities industry, so her situation resembled that of many of the women in relationships with professional men. Without more cases, I cannot determine if same-sex couples on Wall Street would have different dynamics vis-à-vis parenting roles.

20. This represents eleven of the twenty-six women with partners. According to Wall Street standards (see chapter 1, note 17), twelve women (27 percent) were highly successful. Among them, four were married to men who earned even more than they did.

21. For simplicity I use the word "men" here because all of the mothers were heterosexual.

22. Hays 1999; Hertz 1997.

23. This figure and table 6.2 use raw averages for pay and hours for each gender and parental status, rather than the estimated pay figures presented in figure 6.1. The estimated pay in figure 6.1 already accounts for differences in hours.

24. Childless men were much more likely to arrange a group dinner in the office or to horse around while they worked. This time was likely included in their estimations of their hours because it constituted face-time even though it was not productive time.

25. Recall from chapter 3 that hours were not significantly related to pay after accounting for all background characteristics, area, rank, and firm.

26. Gutek 1985.

27. Regarding litigators, see Pierce 1995.

28. Acker 1990; Martin 2001.

29. Budig and England 2001. After assessing a number of other theories for the wage gap, including explanations based on education, training and work experience (or "human capital"), and sex segregation, Budig and England argued that the residual wage difference between mothers and nonmothers could be a result of productivity differences, employer discrimination, or some combination of both.

30. In the remaining case, Kim left the industry after she got married but before she had children. Her primary reason for leaving was to relocate for her husband's job. She also expected have children soon and to be a full-time mother for at least a few years.

31. Becker 1971; England 1992; Marini 1989. "Supply side" generally refers to characteristics that workers bring to the labor force and the choices that workers make. "Demand side" refers to employers' preferences, tastes, or requirements, which affect the jobs available to workers and the terms of those jobs.

32. Martin 2001.

33. In fact, it could be argued that workers with a better work-life balance are likely to be healthier and happier, and therefore more effective when they are at work.

Chapter 7. Window Dressing: Workplace Policies and Wall Street Culture

1. Blair-Loy and Wharton 2004; E. Kelly 1999. Kelly refers to this as the "business case" for work-family policies.

2. Guthrie and Roth 1999b.

3. See Dobbin et al. 1993; Edelman 1990, 1992; Guthrie and Roth 1999b; Sutton et al. 1994; Sutton and Dobbin 1996.

4. Blair-Loy and Wharton 2004.

5. Fifty-three percent of workers (40) said that their firms were equipped to manage sexual harassment effectively, including 56 percent of men (18) and 50 percent of women (22).

6. The belief that reporting sexual harassment can produce retaliation and greater difficulties in the workplace is common and there is evidence to support it. See Fain and Anderton 1987; Fiske and Glick 1995; Livingston 1982; Roth 1999; Tangri, Burt, and Johnson 1982.

7. Lewis 1989; Wolfe 1987.

Chapter 8. Beating the Odds: The Most Successful Women

1. As success is defined in chapter 1, note 17.

2. The median was between $580,000 and $625,000, or $602,500.

3. *Investment Dealers' Digest* 1998b.

4. Kanter 1977.

5. Chen and DiTomaso 1996; Kanter 1977; Reskin 2003.
6. Kanter 1977.

Chapter 9. The Myth of Meritocracy: Gender and Performance-Based Pay

1. This person was an informant who contacted me because she had heard about my research, not someone I interviewed.
2. See Becker 1971 for the most influential statement of this point.
3. Nelson and Bridges 1999. See also Frank 2004 on the elevation of free market ideology in American cultural rhetoric.
4. Kanter 1977.
5. Collins 2002; England 1992; Nelson and Bridges 1999; Phillips and Taylor 1980; Steinberg 1990.
6. Fletcher 1999.
7. Gutek 1985.
8. See Nelson and Bridges 1999 for further arguments on the fetishizing of market processes in American organizations and law, and Frank 2004 on the same process in American culture and politics.
9. England 1992; Reskin, McBrier, and Kmec 1999; Tomaskovic-Devey 1995. There is substantial evidence that jobs become devalued when they feminize. The causal direction for this relationship is debatable. Jobs may feminize because they are becoming less attractive to men, or the influx of women itself may lead to a decline in pay and prestige.
10. Blair-Loy and Wharton 2004; Kelly 1999.

Appendix A. Methodology

1. Eccles and Crane 1988. Eccles and Crane wrote a comprehensive study of investment banking organizations in the 1980s. I used their rankings to determine the pool of top firms that I would include in this study.
2. E. J. Kelly 1985; Walter 1985.
3. I attempted to contact anyone with a gender-ambiguous first name in order to ascertain which sampling frame to put them in.
4. They were presented with a list of specific names of classmates who had been selected. This proved to be a useful strategy for locating respondents.
5. Three respondents refused to permit tape recording. In those cases, I took detailed notes during the interview and transcribed it as soon as possible after the interview's completion.

Appendix B. Quantitative Measures and Models

1. Bollen and Stine 1990. I also used correlation coefficients and collinearity diagnostics to test for multicollinearity. The variance inflation factors and condition

index for the OLS models suggested that multicollinearity was not a problem. Regression diagnostics also revealed no outliers that would have skewed the results of the models.

2. Halvorsen and Palmquist 1980.

3. The same formula was used to calculate the change in the coefficient from the model in table B.2 to the full model in table B.3.

4. Cohen 1988.

References

Acker, Joan. 1990. "Hierarchies, Jobs, Bodies: A Theory of Gendered Organizations." *Gender & Society* 4, 2 (June): 139–58.

Ackman, Dan. 2004a. "Morgan Stanley and the Women." *Forbes*, July 7.

———. 2004b. "Morgan Stanley: Big Bucks for Bias." *Forbes*, July 13.

Andersen, Torben, and Sumner J. La Croix. 1991. "Customer Racial Discrimination in Major League Baseball." *Economic Inquiry* 29, 4 (October): 665–77.

Antilla, Susan. 2002. *Tales from the Boom-Boom Room: Women vs. Wall Street*. Princeton, NJ: Bloomberg Press.

Archer, Miles F. 2000. "Case Note: Mullin v. Raytheon Company: The Threatened Vitality of Disparate Impact under the ADEA." *Maine Law Review* 52:149.

Arrow, Kenneth J. 1972. "Models of Job Discrimination." Pp. 83–102 in *Racial Discrimination in Economic Life*, ed. Anthony H. Pascal. Lexington, MA: Lexington Books.

Babcock, Linda, and Sarah Laschever. 2003. *Women Don't Ask: Negotiation and the Gender Divide*. Princeton: Princeton University Press.

Bailyn, Lotte. 1993. *Breaking the Mold: Women, Men and Their Time in the New Corporate World*. New York: Free Press.

Baker, Wayne E. 1990. "Market Networks and Corporate Behavior." *American Journal of Sociology* 96, 3 (November): 589–625.

Baron, James N., and William T. Bielby. 1980. "Bringing Firms Back In: Stratification, Segmentation, and the Organization of Work." *American Sociological Review* 45 (October): 737–65.

Barr, Paula A. 1993. "Perceptions of Sexual Harassment." *Sociological Inquiry* 63:460–70.

Barron's: The Dow Jones Business and Financial Weekly. 1997. "The New Glass Ceiling: How Women Are Held Back by Sexism at Work and Child-rearing Duties at Home," by Gene Epstein. December 1, pp. 35–39.

Becker, Gary M. 1971. *The Economics of Discrimination*. Chicago: University of Chicago Press.

———. 1991. *A Treatise on the Family*. Cambridge, MA: Harvard University Press.

Berger, Joseph, M. Hamit Fiske, Robert Z. Norman, and Morris Zelditch Jr. 1977. *Status Characteristics and Social Interaction: An Expectations-States Approach*. New York: Elsevier.

Bernard, Jessie. 1981. "The Good Provider Role: Its Rise and Fall." *American Psychologist* 36:1–12.

Bernstein, Elizabeth. 2001. "The Meaning of Purchase: Desire, Demand, and the Commerce of Sex." *Ethnography* 2, 3 (September): 389–420.

Berscheid, Ellen, and Elaine Hatfield. 1978. *Interpersonal Attraction*. 2nd ed. New York: Random House.

Bielby, William T., and James N. Baron. 1984. "A Woman's Place Is with Other Women: Sex Segregation within Organizations." Pp. 27–55 in *Sex Segregation in the Workplace: Trends, Explanations, Remedies*, ed. Barbara F. Reskin. Washington, DC: National Academy Press.

Bird, Chloe E. 1996. "An Analysis of Gender Differences in Income among Dentists, Physicians, and Veterinarians in 1987." *Research in the Sociology of Health Care* 13 (Part A): 31–61.

Blair-Loy, Mary F. 2003. *Competing Devotions: Career and Family among Women Executives*. Cambridge, MA: Harvard University Press.

Blair-Loy, Mary F., and Amy S. Wharton. 2004. "Organizational Commitment and Constraints on Work-Family Policy Use: Corporate Flexibility Policies in a Global Firm." *Sociological Perspectives* 47, 3 (Fall): 243–68.

Blau, Francine D., and Marianne A. Ferber. 1992. *The Economics of Women, Men and Work*. 2nd ed. Englewood Cliffs, NJ: Prentice-Hall.

Blume, Marshall E., Jeremy J. Siegel, and Dan Rottenberg. 1993. *Revolution on Wall Street: The Rise and Decline of the New York Stock Exchange*. New York: W. W. Norton.

Bollen, Kenneth A., and Robert Stine. 1990. "Direct and Indirect Effects: Classical and Bootstrap Estimates of Variability." *Sociological Methodology* 20:115–40.

Budig, Michelle J. 2002. "Male Advantage and the Gender Composition of Jobs: Who Rides the Glass Escalator?" *Social Problems* 49, 2: 258–77.

Budig, Michelle J., and Paula England. 2001. "The Wage Penalty for Motherhood." *American Sociological Review* 66, 2 (April): 204–25.

Bybee, Jane, Marion Glick, and Edward Zigler. 1990. "Differences across Gender, Grade Level, and Academic Track in the Content of the Ideal Self-Image." *Sex Roles* 22, 5–6 (March): 349–58.

Caplow, Theodore. 1954. *The Sociology of Work*. Minneapolis: University of Minnesota Press.

Chen, Chao C., and Nancy DiTomaso. 1996. "Performance Appraisal and Demographic Diversity: Issues Regarding Appraisals, Appraisers, and Appraising." Pp. 138–63 in *Human Resource Strategies for Managing Diversity*, ed. Ellen E. Kossek and Sharon A. Lobel. Oxford: Blackwell.

Clancy, S. M., and S. J. Dollinger. 1993. "Photographic Depictions of the Self: Gender and Age Differences in Social Connectedness." *Sex Roles* 29, 7–8: 477–95.

Clarkberg, Marin, and Phyllis Moen. 2001. "Understanding the Time Squeeze: Married Couples' Preferred and Actual Work-Hour Strategies." *American Behavioral Scientist* 44, 7: 1115–35.

Cohen, Jacob. 1988. *Statistical Power Analysis for the Behavioral Sciences*. 2nd ed. Hillsdale, NJ: Erlbaum.

Collins, Jane L. 2002. "Mapping a Global Labor Market: Gender and Skill in the Globalizing Garment Industry." *Gender & Society* 16, 6 (December): 921–40.

Crofton, Stephanie O. 2003. "An Extension on the Traditional Theory of Customer Discrimination: Customers versus Customers." *American Journal of Economics and Sociology* 62, 2 (April): 319–43.

Cross, Susan E., and Laura Madson. 1997. "Models of the Self: Self-Construals and Gender." *Psychological Bulletin* 122, 1 (July): 5–37.

DiMaggio, Paul, and Walter Powell. 1983. "Introduction." Pp. 1–38 in *The New Institutionalism in Organizational Analysis*, ed. Walter W. Powell and Paul J. DiMaggio. Chicago: University of Chicago Press.

Dixon, Jo, and Carroll Seron. 1995. "Stratification in the Legal Profession: Sex, Sector, and Salary." *Law and Society Review* 29, 3: 381–412.

Dobbin, Frank, John R. Sutton, John W. Meyer, and W. Richard Scott. 1993. "Equal Opportunity Law and the Construction of Internal Labor Markets." *American Journal of Sociology* 99:396–427.

Eccles, Robert G. and Dwight B. Crane. 1988. *Doing Deals: Investment Banks at Work*. Boston: Harvard Business School Press.

Edelman, Lauren B. 1990. "Legal Environments and Organizational Governance: The Expansion of Due Process in the American Workplace." *American Journal of Sociology* 95, 6 (May): 1401–40.

———. 1992. "Legal Ambiguity and Symbolic Structures: Organizational Mediation of Civil Rights Law." *American Journal of Sociology* 97: 1531–76.

Eisenstein, Zillah R. 1988. *The Female Body and the Law*. Berkeley: University of California Press.

England, Paula. 1992. *Comparable Worth: Theories and Evidence*. New York: Aldine de Gruyter.

England, Paula, and George Farkas. 1986. *Households, Employment and Gender: A Social, Economic and Demographic View*. New York: Aldine Publishing Company.

Epstein, Cynthia Fuchs, Caroll Seron, Bonnie Oglensky, and Robert Sauté. 1999. *The Part-Time Paradox*. New York: Routledge.

Erickson, Bonnie, Patricia Albanese, and Slobodan Drakulic. 2000. "Gender on a Jagged Edge: The Security Industry, Its Clients, and the Reproduction and Revision of Gender." *Work and Occupations* 27, 3 (August): 294–318.

Erickson, David John, and Richard Tewksbury. 2000. "The 'Gentlemen' in the Club: A Typology of Strip Club Patrons." *Deviant Behavior* 21, 3 (May–June): 271–93.

Fain, Terri C., and Douglas L. Anderton. 1987. "Sexual Harassment: Organizational Context and Diffuse Status." *Sex Roles* 17:291–311.

Fairhurst, Gail, and B. Kay Snavely. 1983. "A Test of the Social Isolation of Male Tokens." *Academy of Management Journal* 26:353–61.

Ferree, Myra Marx, Judith Lorber, and Beth Hess. 1999. *Revisioning Gender*. Thousand Oaks, CA: Sage.

Finley, Lucinda M. 1993. "Transcending Equality Theory: A Way Out of the Maternity and the Workplace Debate." Pp. 190–207 in *Feminist Legal Theory Foundations*, ed. D. Kelly Weisberg. Philadelphia: Temple University Press.

Fisher, Anne B. 1989. *Wall Street Women: Women in Power on Wall Street Today*. New York: Alfred P. Knopf.

Fisher, Claude S. 1982. *To Dwell among Friends*. Chicago: University of Chicago Press.

Fiske, Susan T., and Peter Glick. 1995. "Ambivalence and Stereotypes Cause Sexual Harassment: A Theory with Implications for Organizational Change." *Journal of Social Issues* 51:97–115.

Fiske, Susan T., Monica Lin, and Steven L. Neuberg. 1999. "The Continuum Model: Ten Years Later." Pp. 231–54 in *Dual Process Theories in Social Psychology*, ed. Shelly Chaiken and Yaacov Trope. New York: Guilford Press.

Fletcher, Joyce K. 1999. *Disappearing Acts: Gender, Power, and Relational Practices at Work*. Cambridge, MA: MIT Press.

Foschi, Martha. 1996. "Double Standards in the Evaluation of Men and Women." *Social Psychology Quarterly* 59, 3 (September): 237–54.

———. 2000. "Double Standards for Competence: Theory and Research." *Annual Review of Sociology* 26:21–42.

Foschi, Martha, Larissa Lai, and Kirsten Sigerson. 1994. "Gender and Double Standards in the Assessment of Job Applicants." *Social Psychology Quarterly* 57, 4 (December): 326–39.

Frank, Thomas. 2004. *What's the Matter with Kansas? How Conservatives Won the Heart of America*. New York: Metropolitan Books.

Friedland, Roger, and Robert R. Alford. 1991. "Bringing Society Back In: Symbols, Practices, and Institutional Contradictions." Pp. 232–63 in *The New Institutionalism in Organizational Analysis*, ed. Walter W. Powell and Paul J. DiMaggio. Chicago: University of Chicago Press.

Gerson, Kathleen. 1985. *Hard Choices: How Women Decide about Work, Career, and Motherhood*. Berkeley: University of California Press.

Gibson, Gail. 2004. "2 Wins for Working Women." *Baltimore Sun*, July 19.

Glaser, Barney G., and Anselm L. Strauss. 1967. *The Discovery of Grounded Theory: Strategies for Qualitative Research*. Chicago: Aldine Publishing Company.

Glass, Becky L. 1988. "Workplace Harassment and the Victimization of Women." *Women's Studies International Forum* 11:55–67.

Goldstein, Leslie Friedman. 1988. *The Constitutional Rights of Women*. Madison: University of Wisconsin Press.

Gruber, James E. 1992. "A Typology of Personal and Environmental Sexual Harassment: Research and Policy Implications for the 1990s." *Sex Roles* 26:447–64.

Gutek, Barbara A. 1985. *Sex and the Workplace*. San Francisco: Jossey-Bass Publishers.

Guthrie, Douglas, and Louise Marie Roth. 1999a. "The State, Courts, and Equal Opportunities for Female CEOs in U.S. Organizations: Specifying Institutional Mechanisms." *Social Forces* 78, 2 (December): 511–42.

———. 1999b. "The State, Courts, and Maternity Policies in U.S. Organizations: Specifying Institutional Mechanisms." *American Sociological Review* 64 (February): 41–63.

Hakim, Catherine. 2001. *Work-Lifestyle Choices in the 21st Century*. New York: Oxford University Press.

Halaby, Charles N. 1979. "Job-Specific Sex Differences in Organizational Reward Attainment: Wage Discrimination vs. Rank Segregation." *Social Forces* 58, 1 (September): 108–27.

Halvorsen, Robert, and Raymond Palmquist. 1980. "The Interpretation of Dummy Variables in Semilogarithmic Equations." *American Economic Review* 70, 3 (June): 474–75.

Harrison, Bennett, and Barry Bluestone. 1988. *The Great U-turn: Corporate Restructuring and the Polarizing of America*. New York: Basic Books.

Hays, Sharon. 1999. *The Cultural Contradictions of Motherhood*. New Haven: Yale University Press.

Herera, Sue. 1997. *Women of the Street: Making It on Wall Street–The World's Toughest Business*. New York: John Wiley.

Hertz, Rosanna. 1997. "A Typology of Approaches to Child Care." *Journal of Family Issues* 18, 4 (July): 355–85.

Hochschild, Arlie Russell. 1997. *The Time Bind: When Work Becomes Home and Home Becomes Work*. New York: Metropolitan Books.

Hoff, Joan. 1991. *Law, Gender, and Injustice: A Legal History of U.S. Women*. New York: New York University Press.

Hoisington, Harland W., Sr. 1976. *Reforms: Wall Street, 1790–1974*. New York: Vantage Press.

Holzer, Harry J., and Keith R. Ihlanfeldt. 1998. "Customer Discrimination and Employment Outcomes for Minority Workers." *Quarterly Journal of Economics* 113, 3 (August): 835–67.

Ibarra, Herminia. 1997. "Paving an Alternate Route: Gender Differences in Managerial Networks." *Social Psychology Quarterly* 60, 1 (March): 91–102.

Investment Dealers' Digest. 1997. "A Market on Fire." By Brian Garrity. October 13, pp. 26–33.

———. 1998a. "In Search of Fees." By Adam Reinebach and Brian Garrity. January 26, pp. 16–21.

———. 1998b. "Putting on the Brakes." By Jed Horowitz and Erica Copulsky. May 11, pp. 20–27.

———. 1998c. "Skyrocketing Pay Makes Research Analysts the Envy of Wall Street." By Erica Copulsky. May 11, p. 28.

Jacobs, Jerry A. 1989. *Revolving Doors: Sex Segregation and Women's Careers*. Stanford: Stanford University Press.

Jacobs, Jerry A., and Kathleen Gerson. 2004. *The Time Divide: Work, Family and Gender Inequality*. Cambridge, MA: Harvard University Press.

Jensen, Michael C. 1976. *The Financiers: The World of the Great Wall Street Investment Banking Houses*. New York: Weybright and Talley.

Jepperson, Ronald L. 1991. "Institutions, Institutional Effects, and Institutionalism." Pp. 143–63 in *The New Institutionalism in Organizational*

Analysis, ed. Walter W. Powell and Paul J. DiMaggio. Chicago: University of Chicago Press.

Kahn, Lawrence M. 1992. "The Effects of Race on Professional Football Players' Compensation." *Industrial and Labor Relations Review* 45, 2 (January): 295–310.

Kahn, Lawrence M., and Peter D. Sherer. 1988. "Racial Differences in Professional Basketball Players' Compensation." *Journal of Labor Economics* 6, 1 (January): 40–61.

Kanter, Rosabeth Moss. 1977. *Men and Women of the Corporation*. New York: Basic Books.

Kelly, Edward J., III. 1985. "Legislative History of the Glass-Steagall Act." Pp. 41–65 in *Deregulating Wall Street: Commercial Bank Penetration of the Corporate Securities Market*, ed. Ingo Walter. New York: John Wiley.

Kelly, Erin. 1999. "Theorizing Corporate Family Policies: How Advocates Built the 'Business Case' for 'Family-Friendly' Programs." *Research in the Sociology of Work* 7:1169–1202.

Kessler, Andy. 2003. *Wall Street Meat: Jack Grubman, Frank Quattrone, Mary Meeker, Henry Blodget and Me*. Atherton, CA: Escape Velocity Press.

Kilbourne, Barbara, Paula England, George Farkas, Kurt Beron, and Dorothea Weir. 1994. "Returns to Skill, Compensating Differentials, and Gender Bias: Effects of Occupational Characteristics on the Wages of White Women and Men." *American Journal of Sociology* 100:689–719.

Krieger, Linda J., and Patricia N. Cooney. 1993. "The Miller-Wohl Controversy: Equal Treatment, Positive Action and the Meaning of Women's Equality." Pp. 156–79 in *Feminist Legal Theory Foundations*, ed. D. Kelly Weisberg. Philadelphia: Temple University Press.

Lechner, Alan. 1980. *Street Games: Inside Stories of the Wall Street Hustle*. New York: Harper and Row.

Lewis, Michael. 1989. *Liar's Poker: Rising through the Wreckage of Wall Street*. New York: W. W. Norton.

Livingston, Joy A. 1982. "Responses to Sexual Harassment on the Job: Legal, Individual, and Organizational Actions." *Journal of Social Issues* 38, 4: 5–22.

Lorber, Judith. 1994. *Paradoxes of Gender*. New Haven: Yale University Press.

MacKinnon, Catharine. 1989. *Toward a Feminist Theory of the State*. Cambridge, MA: Harvard University Press.

Magid, Julie Manning. 2001. "Pregnant with Possibility: Reexamining the Pregnancy Discrimination Act." *American Business Law Journal* 38: 819.

Marini, Margaret Mooney. 1989. "Sex Differences in Earnings in the United States." *Annual Review of Sociology* 15:343–80.

Marsden, Peter V. 1987. "Core Discussion Networks of Americans." *American Sociological Review* 52, 1 (February): 122–31.

Martin, Patricia Yancey. 2001. " 'Mobilizing Masculinities': Women's Experiences of Men at Work." *Organization*, 8, 4: 587–618.

Martinez, Jose. 2004. "The Woman Who Won $12M Settlement from Morgan Stanley." *New York Daily News*, July 14.

Matthews, John O. 1994. *Struggle and Survival on Wall Street: The Economics of Competition among Securities Firms*. New York: Oxford University Press.

McCrae, R. R., and P. T. Costa, Jr. 1988. "Age, Personality, and the Spontaneous Self-Concept." *Journal of Gerontology: Social Sciences* 43: S177–85.

McGeehan, Patrick. 2004. "Merrill Lynch Ordered to Pay for Sexual Bias." *New York Times*, April 21.

McGuire, W. J., and C. V. McGuire. 1982. "Significant Others in Self-Space: Sex Differences and Developmental Trends in the Social Self." Pp. 71–96 in *Psychological Perspectives on the Self*, ed. J. Suls. Vol. 1. Hillsdale, NJ: Erlbaum.

McIntosh, Peggy. 1993. "White Privilege and Male Privilege." Pp. 30–38 in *Gender Basics*, ed. Anne Minas. Belmont, CA: Wadsworth.

McPherson, Miller, Lynn Smith-Lovin, and James M. Cook. 2001. "Birds of a Feather: Homophily in Social Networks." *Annual Review of Sociology* 27:415–44.

Mincer, Jacob, and Solomon Polachek. 1980. "Family Investments in Human Capital: Earnings of Women." Pp. 169–204 in *The Economics of Women and Work*, ed. Alice Amsden. New York: St. Martin's Press.

Moen, Phyllis. 1992. *Women's Two Roles: A Contemporary Dilemma*. New York: Auburn House.

Nardinelli, Clark, and Curtis J. Simon. 1990. "Customer Racial Discrimination in the Market for Memorabilia: The Case of Baseball." *Quarterly Journal of Economics* 105, 3 (August): 575–96.

Nelson, Robert L., and William P. Bridges. 1999. *Legalizing Gender Inequality: Courts, Markets, and Unequal Pay for Women in America*. New York: Cambridge University Press.

Neumark, David, Roy J. Bank, and Kyle D. Van Nort. 1996. "Sex Discrimination in Restaurant Hiring: An Audit Study." *Quarterly Journal of Economics* 111, 3 (August): 915–41.

New York Post. "Suit Charges Sex Bias at J. P. Morgan." August 31, 1999: p. 18.

New York Times. "J. P. Morgan Weighs Merger and Cuts Jobs." February 24, 1998, pp. D1, D10.

———. "Bias at the Bull: Merrill Lynch's Class-Action Settlement Draws a Crowd." February 27, 1999, pp. C1, C14.

———. "If Wall Street Is a Dead End, Do Women Stay to Fight or Go Quietly?" August 3, 1999, pp. D1, D6.

———. "Morgan Stanley Is Cited for Discrimination against Women." June 6, 2000, pp. C1, C2.

Petersen, Trond, and Laurie A. Morgan. 1995. "Separate and Unequal: Occupation-Establishment Sex Segregation and the Gender Wage Gap." *American Journal of Sociology* 101, 2: 329–65.

Phillips, Anne, and Barbara Taylor. 1980. "Sex and Skill: Notes towards a Feminist Economics." *Feminist Review* 6 (Winter): 79–88.

Pierce, Jennifer. 1995. *Gender Trials: Emotional Lives in Contemporary Law Firms*. Berkeley: University of California Press.

Portes, Alejandro, and Julia Sensenbrenner. 1993. "Embeddedness and Immigration: Notes on the Social Determinants of Economic Action." *American Journal of Sociology* 98, 6 (May): 1320–50.

Reskin, Barbara. 1993. "Sex Segregation in the Workplace." *Annual Review of Sociology* 19:241–70.

———. 2000. "The Proximate Causes of Employment Discrimination." *Contemporary Sociology* 29, 2 (March): 319–28.

———. 2003. "2002 Presidential Address: Including Mechanisms in Our Models of Ascriptive Inequality." *American Sociological Review* 68, 1 (February): 1–21.

Reskin, Barbara F., and Patricia A. Roos. 1990. *Job Queues, Gender Queues: Explaining Women's Inroads into Male Occupations*. Philadelphia: Temple University Press.

Reskin, Barbara F., Debra B. McBrier, and Julie A. Kmec. 1999. "The Determinants and Consequences of Workplace Sex and Race Composition." *Annual Review of Sociology* 25:335–61.

Ridgeway, Cecilia L., and Henry A. Walker. 1995. "Status Structures." Pp. 281–309 in *Sociological Perspectives on Social Psychology*, ed. Karen S. Cook, Gary Alan Fine, and James S. House. Boston: Allyn and Bacon.

Ridgeway, Cecelia. 1997. "Interaction and the Conservation of Gender Inequality." *American Sociological Review* 62, 2 (April): 218–35.

Ridgeway, Cecelia, and Shelley Correll. 2004. "Unpacking the Gender System: A Theoretical Perspective on Gender Beliefs and Social Relations." *Gender & Society* 18, 4 (August): 510–31.

Risman, Barbara. 1998. *Gender Vertigo: American Families in Transition.* New Haven: Yale University Press.

Roth, Louise Marie. 1999. "The Right to Privacy Is Political: Power, the Boundary between Public and Private, and Sexual Harassment." *Law and Social Inquiry* 24, 1 (Winter): 45–71.

Ryder, Norman B. 1965. "The Cohort as a Concept in the Study of Social Change." *American Sociological Review* 30, 6 (December): 843–61.

Schor, Juliet. 1991. *The Overworked American: The Unexpected Decline of Leisure.* New York: Basic Books.

Securities Industry Association (SIA) Research Department. 1998. *1998 Securities Industry Factbook.* Ed. Grace Toto and George Monahan. New York: Securities Industry Association.

Skolnick, Arlene. 1991. *Embattled Paradise: The American Family in an Age of Uncertainty.* New York: Basic Books.

Smith, D. Randall, Nancy DiTomaso, George F. Farris, and Rene Cordero. 2001. "Favoritism, Bias, and Error in Performance Ratings of Scientists and Engineers: The Effects of Power, Status, and Numbers." *Sex Roles* 45, 5–6 (September): 337–58.

Smith-Lovin, Lynn, and J. Miller McPherson. 1993. "You Are Who You Know: A Network Approach to Gender." Pp. 223–54 in *Theory on Gender/Feminism on Theory*, ed. Paula England. Hawthorne, NY: Aldine de Gruyter.

Strauss, Anselm, and Julia Corbin. 1998. *Basics of Qualitative Research: Grounded Theory Procedures and Techniques.* Thousand Oaks, CA: Sage.

Steinberg, Ronnie J. 1990. "Social Construction of Skill: Gender, Power, and Comparable Worth." *Work and Occupations* 17, 4 (November): 449–82.

Sutton, John R., and Frank Dobbin. 1996. "The Two Faces of Governance: Responses to Legal Uncertainty in U.S. Firms, 1955–1985." *American Sociological Review* 61:794–811.

Sutton, John R., Frank Dobbin, John W. Meyer, and W. Richard Scott. 1994. "The Legalization of the Workplace." *American Journal of Sociology* 99:944–71.

Tangri, Sandra S., Martha R. Burt, and Leanor B. Johnson. 1982. "Sexual Harassment at Work: Three Explanatory Models." *Journal of Social Issues* 38 (Winter): 33–54.

Threadgold, Terry, and Anne Cranny-Francis. 1990. *Feminine, Masculine and Representation*. London: Allen and Unwin.

Tomaskovic-Devey, Donald. 1995. "Sex Composition and Gendered Earnings Inequality: A Comparison of Job and Occupational Models." Pp. 23–56 in *Gender Inequality at Work*, ed. Jerry A. Jacobs. Thousand Oaks, CA: Sage.

Treiman, Donald, and Heidi Hartmann. 1981. *Women, Work, and Wages: Equal Pay for Jobs of Equal Value*. Washington, DC: National Academy Press.

Trentham, Susan, and Laurie Larwood. 1998. "Gender Discrimination and the Workplace: An Examination of Rational Bias Theory." *Sex Roles* 38, 1–2: 1–28.

Tsui, Anne S., and Charles A. O'Reilly. 1989. "Beyond Simple Demographic Effects: The Importance of Relational Demography in Superior-Subordinate Dyads." *Academy of Management Journal* 32, 2: 402–23.

U.S. Bureau of the Census. 1998. "Historical Income Tables–People." *March Current Population Survey*. Washington, DC: GPO.

———. 2002. "Fertility of American Women." *June Current Population Survey*. Washington, DC: GPO.

Waldfogel, Jane. 1997. "The Effect of Children on Women's Wages." *American Sociological Review* 62, 2 (April): 209–17.

Wall Street Journal. "Citigroup Expecting to Chop 8,000 Jobs: Cuts Amount to 5% of Total but Turmoil in Markets May Lead to More in '99." September 18, 1998, pp. A3, A4.

———. "Wall Streeters Are Preparing for Layoffs." October 9, 1998, pp. C1, C13.

———. "Merrill Cuts 3,400 Jobs, Reports Loss." October 14, 1998, pp. C1, C19.

———. "Canadian Imperial Bank to Cut 5% of Global Investment-Banking Staff." October 19, 1998, p. A12.

———. "Goldman Picks Cohen, Others to Be Partners." October 21, 1998, pp. C1, C10.

———. "Bull Market Now May Be the Longest." December 16, 1998, pp. C1, C25.

———. "Dow Industrials Shatter the 11,000 Mark." May 9, 1999, pp. C1, C13.

———. "About 2,200 Women Seek to File Claims in Salomon Bias Suit." June 22, 1999, p. C17.

———. "Morgan Stanley Executive Files Charges with the EEOC Alleging Gender Bias." July 29, 1999.

———. "Morgan Stanley Agrees to Discuss Policies on Hiring with EEOC." July 30, 1999, p. B8.

———. "Morgan Stanley Is Told by Judge to Produce All Sex Complaints." September 24, 1999, p. C12.

Walter, Ingo. 1985. *Deregulating Wall Street: Commercial Bank Penetration of the Corporate Securities Market*. New York: John Wiley.

Webster, Murray, Jr., and Martha Foschi. 1988. *Status Generalization: New Theory and Research*. Stanford: Stanford University Press.

Williams, Christine. 1992. "The Glass Escalator: Hidden Advantages for Men in the 'Female' Professions." *Social Problems* 39, 3 (August): 253–67.

———. 1995. *Still a Man's World: Men Who Do "Women's Work."* Berkeley: University of California Press.

Williams, Joan. 2000. *Unbending Gender: Why Family and Work Conflict and What to Do about It*. New York: Oxford University Press.

Williams, Wendy W. 1993. "Equality's Riddle: Pregnancy and the Equal Treatment/Special Treatment Debate." Pp. 128–55 of *Feminist Legal Theory Foundations*, ed. D. Kelly Weisberg. Philadelphia: Temple University Press.

Wolfe, Tom. 1987. *The Bonfire of the Vanities*. New York: Bantam Books.

Yoder, Janice. 1991. "Rethinking Tokenism: Looking beyond Numbers." *Gender and Society* 5, 2 (June): 178–92.

———. 1994. "Looking beyond Numbers: The Effects of Gender Status, Job Prestige, and Occupational Gender-Typing on Tokenism Processes." *Social Psychology Quarterly* 57, 2 (June): 150–59.

Index